THE HOPE OF
THE POOR

PHILOSOPHY, RELIGION AND
ECONOMIC DEVELOPMENT

Gordon Graham

imprint-academic.com

Published in the UK by
Imprint Academic, PO Box 200, Exeter EX5 5YX, UK

Distributed in the USA by
Ingram Book Company,
One Ingram Blvd., La Vergne, TN 37086, USA

ISBN 9781788361019 Paperback

A CIP catalogue record for this book is available from the
British Library and US Library of Congress

Contents

Preface

I have been interested in the rather disparate topics of this book for many years, and addressed several of the issues touched upon here at greater length in previous publications, notably *Living the Good Life* (Paragon Press, 1990), *Ethics and International Relations* (Blackwell, 1997), *Evil and Christian Ethics* (Cambridge UP, 2001), *The Re-Enchantment of the World* (Oxford UP, 2007), and *Wittgenstein and Natural Religion* (Oxford UP, 2015). The occasion to try and organize my thoughts about all these topics into an integrated whole came with the opportunity to teach a course on 'Moral Philosophy and Aspects of Poverty' at Princeton Theological Seminary. The course ran several times and I owe a great debt to the students who enrolled in it. The challenging questions they raised in class, and the highly informed and insightful projects and papers that many of them completed, provided me with constant intellectual stimulus. In preparing for the course, and then working on this book, I was led to read extensively in development economics and social anthropology. Though the book is still primarily philosophical, it has been significantly enriched by these other disciplines. I am especially grateful to Professor Sir Angus Deaton who visited the class, and then generously commented on, and corrected, the material in Chapters Three and Four. I am also grateful to my daughter Kirsty for assembling the bibliography, and to my daughter Lindsay for compiling the index. A part of the material on John Macmurray in Chapter 6 was first published in *Scottish Philosophy After the Enlightenment* (Edinburgh UP, 2022).

Some truly excellent anthropological studies, among them Matthew Desmond's *Evicted* (2016) and John McManus's *Inside Qatar* (2022), have made me especially conscious of the intense pressures that poor people can experience in a variety of contexts, and how remotely my arguments about poverty touch on their existence. The book, of course, is *about* the poor, not *for* the poor. Nevertheless, I hope that I have succeeded in resonating sympathetically with difficulties that I myself have never been forced to confront.

This book is dedicated to *The Soko Fund*.

Gordon Graham
September 2022

Chapter One

Philosophical Preliminaries

The American *Book of Common Prayer* includes a daily petition: 'Let not the needy be forgotten, O Lord, or the hope of the poor be taken away.' This prayer raises a question. Just what is it that God is being asked not to take away? What *is* the hope of the poor? A common view — held by national governments, international organizations such as the World Bank and the International Monetary Fund, and global charitable agencies like Oxfam and the Gates Foundation — is that the best hope for the world's poor lies in 'development', an essential element of which is economic growth. Interpreted in this way, the hope of the poor rests on empirically complex, but essentially instrumental and technical issues.

The petition, however, admits of quite different interpretations. It might be thought to refer to what *as a matter of fact* poor people do hope for, or to what poor people *have reason to* hope for. A further possibility is that the phrase refers chiefly to a *sense* of hopefulness, saying in effect, 'do not let the poor sink into despair.' All these interpretations raise further questions. Just who are 'the poor'? What exactly makes their poverty problematic? Why, and how, should third parties be involved in addressing the problem?

This book aims to address these questions. It is impossible to discuss them adequately without attention to substantial empirical matters, and so recurrent topics in ethics have to be explored alongside contemporary issues in anthropology, international relations, and development economics, with debates about 'aid' being especially important. Ultimately, though, the book is an exercise in moral philosophy — an exploration of what it means to be human, how we should try to live our lives, and the relevance of material poverty to the answers we arrive at. Moral philosophy as I understand it seeks to answer these enduring questions as comprehensively as possible, while observing the strictest requirements of conceptual clarity, analytic precision, logical rigour, and truth to the facts.

The argument that follows advances a number of connected claims. First, the foundation of human equality is rational agency. Second, hoping, properly so called, is an exercise of practical reason in search of wisdom about how to live. Third, thinking hopefully about poverty requires the investigation of philosophical as well as empirical questions. Fourth, since religion is a notable feature of life in poor places, it must be given a role in the exercise of rational agency. The articulation, criticism, and defence of these contentions will surface at many different places throughout the book — often in dialogue with the philosophical ideas of Aristotle, Hume, Reid, Kant, Marx, Nietzsche, and Mill. The purpose of this opening chapter is to explore them in a way that sets the stage for the chapters that follow.

I. Our Common Humanity

In *The Anti-Christ*, Nietzsche fiercely attacks the idea that human beings have souls, because he thinks this means, 'everybody is equal to everybody else... that little bigots and three-quarters madmen are permitted to imagine that for their sakes the laws of nature are continually being broken — such a raising of every sort of egoism to infinity, to impudence, cannot be branded with sufficient contempt. And yet it is to this pitiable flattery of personal vanity that Christianity owes its victory — it is with this that it has persuaded over to its side — all the dross and refuse of mankind'(*The Anti-Christ* §43). Nietzsche is underlining the *factual* inequality of human beings. Some are 'little bigots', others are broad minded and humane. Some have amazing talents, most do not. These are observable facts whose moral relevance the ancient world would have taken for granted. Modern thought, in sharp contrast, insists that there is some fundamental perspective from which all human beings are equal. But from what perspective can we meaningfully declare 'little bigots' to be the equal of saints and heroes, or the most accomplished artists, scientists, and athletes to be the equal of philistines, ignoramuses, and slobs?

It is key to Nietzsche's point that, as a matter of observable fact, human beings are very obviously *unequal*, not only in terms of social goods like wealth, power, and education, but also in natural endowments like strength, agility, health, and physical beauty. It was these natural differences that made the inequality of human beings seem evident to the ancient world, and while progress has to some degree reduced social inequalities, they remain so evident that the modern world cannot plausibly deny them. So the explanation of human equality has to be normative rather than empirical. A familiar way of expressing this point is to say that while human beings are not naturally equal, they are nonetheless of 'equal moral worth'. *Moral* equality transcends *natural* inequality; human beings *ought* to be treated equally, *regardless* of social possessions and natural endowments.

Apart from a few latter-day Nietzscheans, almost everyone will now agree with this. But exactly what is the rational basis for their agreement? The history of philosophy is surprisingly muted and/or discordant on this point. While the equal moral worth of human beings is widely *affirmed*, there is considerable uncertainty about the grounds for its affirmation. The American *Declaration of Independence* famously states the equality of all men to be 'self-evident', thus implying that the belief in human equality does not need any basis. But then it goes on to assert the existence of 'unalienable Rights' endowed by the Creator, thereby implying that human equality does have a basis in theologically grounded natural rights. Other declarations (France in 1789, the United Nations in 1948) say much the same, though using the expression human rights and making no appeal to God. Stripped of this appeal, however, no concept of natural or human rights has won universal acceptance as the basis of human equality. Indeed, Jeremy Bentham famously dismissed natural rights as 'nonsense on stilts' and offered a Utilitarian principle instead. In promoting human happiness, he says, 'each is to count as one and no one more than one.' This principle has also found followers. But what is *its* basis?

The difficulty of formulating a convincing norm of human equality in the face of observed inequality opens the door to Nietzsche's scathing attack on 'the Socialist rabble' who, he says, happily get rid of God, without realizing that this puts paid to both natural rights and utilitarianism. It seems that empirical differences between individuals are enduring and ineliminable. This enables him to reformulate the perfectionist ethics of the ancient world, the belief that judgements of worth must always be relativized. There is no such thing as 'good' and 'bad' *simpliciter*, only better or worse *for* and *at* something—better for health or business, say, better at sport or music. Nietzsche is not alone in this reversion from modernity to perfectionism. Alasdair MacIntyre's highly influential book *After Virtue,* though it expressly departs from Nietzsche, argues in a similar spirit. According to MacIntyre, morality has lost its moorings in our communal life. A major consequence is that the widely endorsed concepts of rights and utility are 'a matching pair of incommensurable fictions'. They can offer no adequate account of equal moral worth. At best, he holds, they 'provide a semblance of rationality for the modern political process, but not its reality' (*After Virtue* p.68).

Even if we were to discount Nietzsche, and reject MacIntyre's historical analysis, there is a further serious problem about the application of the concepts of rights and utility. Their boundaries are too flexible to produce definitive judgements. Which beings have rights, and whose utility should be taken into account? The founding fathers confidently asserted the evident equality of 'all men' while at the same time giving constitutional protection to slavery. Their Creator, it seems, endowed inalienable rights on only *some* human beings. Conversely, environmentalists have stretched the concept of 'right bearer' to apply to animals, trees and landscapes, and even the natural world as a whole. This places 'respect for nature' alongside, and even on a par with, 'respect for persons', in which case natural right casts no special light on our common humanity.

So too with the Utilitarian alternative. Are human beings equal because they all pursue happiness and are all susceptible to pain? If so, this does not differentiate them from other sentient beings. Bentham, in fact, expressly included animals in the calculation of 'pleasure and pain' because he thought, correctly, that the only relevant issue is the ability to cause and relieve suffering. This criterion will exclude trees and landscapes, but it cannot privilege human beings over other animals. Once again, it seems, despite ubiquitous appeals to rights and utility, an explanatory basis for the affirmation of the equal moral status of all human beings eludes us.

If we cannot base the equal moral worth of human beings on natural rights that they possess, or on their sensibility to pleasure and pain, where else can it lie? Immanuel Kant advances a different basis – the human capacity for rational freedom. Human beings are free to reason for themselves about how to live, and their moral equality lies in the obligation each one has to respect the rational freedom of everyone else. Initially it may seem that the same doubts arise about this suggestion as about the preceding ones. Is rational freedom characteristic of all and only human beings? Some animals seem to move about freely and act intelligently. Their intelligence is of a decidedly lower order than that of human beings certainly, but even if a greater capacity for reason marks off people from animals in general, this could not be the basis of their common humanity. Rational ability varies between people just as greatly as physical strength. People who can reason well for the purposes of everyday life may nevertheless be quite unable to follow mathematical proofs, philosophical arguments, or scientific theories. If physical strength cannot constitute a basis for equality, neither can intellectual prowess, since it differs between human beings no less markedly.

However, this is true only if we think of intellectual theorizing, mathematical calculation, and the like as the quintessential exercise of reason. In fact, reason takes many forms. Technical facility, artistic creativity, business acumen, sports coaching, etc. constitute exercises in reason no less than the intellectual enterprises of science, mathematics, and philosophy because they also involve observation, thought, reflection, and judgement. Furthermore, since they all require deliberation about good and bad, right and wrong, wise and foolish, better and worse, *practical* reason is fundamental to them. Good decisions and wise choices are key to human conduct of every kind. Politicians, painters, musicians, builders, mechanics, teachers, doctors, parents, and so on all have to think about what to do and how best to do it. Precisely the same is true of scientists, mathematicians, and philosophers, who must decide which experiments are worth conducting, which mathematical problems are worth tackling, and which ideas are most promising. Whatever task we undertake, and however simple or complex it may be, going the right way about it, doing it well, and learning from experience are rational requirements. Whether the task in hand is making a machine, singing a song, conducting a criminal inquiry or developing a philosophical argument, our actions involve the self-conscious deliberation called 'practical reason'.

Accordingly, provided we do not confine reason to strictly intellectual activity, the Kantian contention that human beings are rational agents does give us a basis for equality since it is fundamental to *all* human agency. Infancy, incapacity, and senility mean that some human beings at some points in their lives cannot exercise rational agency. Limitation in this respect will be discussed in a later chapter. For the moment enough has been said to support the general proposition that practical rationality is the distinguishing mark of human beings. As homemakers, scientists, musicians, athletes, parents, politicians, cooks, farmers, soldiers, teachers, friends and enemies, we are able to think out better ways of performing the tasks we set ourselves. This does not imply that human beings do things equally well. All it means is that they are equally able to make choices, reflect on them retrospectively, and project them into the future.

Rational agency, then, distinguishes people from primates and other highly developed animals. To affirm this, we need not deny that the behaviour of some animals is very sophisticated and sometimes displays a high degree of effective intelligence. This has impressed some observers when they have found animals using and even fashioning tools. Yet, however intelligent animals may be, their motivation is still confined to needs, feelings, and instincts. Human beings, like other animals, also have needs and feelings. What makes them rational *agents*, however, is their ability to respond to these in considered ways. This rational faculty, let it be noted, is no guarantee of practical success. Kant observes at one point that from the perspective of satisfying basic needs such as food and shelter, instinct might serve us better than reason, as it does other animals. Indeed, our rational faculty opens us up to a wider range of possible mistakes and failures. From this he concludes, however, that the ultimate value of rationality cannot lie in outcomes, but in the exercise of reason itself.

II. Agency

Rational agency, then, is the foundation of our common humanity. It also enables us to think beyond the immediate present and relate to the future, not merely by wishing and predicting, but by hoping and planning. To wish for something I only have to imagine myself in possession of it, and acts of imagination do not need to be constrained by realities. Wholly fanciful wishes can be just as pleasing as wishes more likely to be granted. Hoping, properly so called, on the other hand, requires reflection and assessment. That is why unrealistic hopes, however heartfelt, are no better than wishful thinking. When we hope for something, practical rationality requires us to take proper account of reality in a way that mere wishing does not.

Within limits, it is possible for human beings to let themselves be directed entirely by felt needs and instinctive desires without ever asking this reflective question: 'What do I want out of life?' When they do ask this question, it is possible to limit deliberation to the calculation of means to ends. Limiting deliberation in this way, however, leaves a no less relevant but higher order *normative* question unanswered. What I *want* is a matter of psychology. What I *ought to want* is a matter of rationality, and it is the possibility of asking *this* question that sets human beings apart. All animals respond to felt needs, and intelligent animals can devise better means of satisfying their desires. It is only human beings who can pose this normative question. Furthermore, 'what ought I to want?' is a question that *any and every* human being is able to pose — if they choose to do so. Practical rationality at this higher level thus transforms human beings from their status as sophisticated biological organisms to responsible agents. The transformation takes place over the course of life. As organisms, human neonates are no less sophisticated than adults; they become responsible rational agents as they move from infancy to adulthood.

Responsible agency does not merely *aid* human existence. It shapes it. Organisms live and die. In the period from birth to death they may flourish or they may struggle, depending on external events and circumstances. Since human beings are organisms, they too move from birth to death, and practical rationality plays a part in determining whether they flourish and how much they struggle. Their rational agency does more than this, however. It enables them to *lead* a life, that is to say, to have a life-story. The powers of reflective memory and prediction give human lives a narrative structure, a 'before' and 'after' any given moment. This makes it possible for organic struggling and flourishing to take on meaning and significance. Since other animals lack reflective memory and prediction, they simply live well or badly for varying periods of time. Insofar as a pet, for instance, can be said to have a life-story, it is one constructed and recounted by a human being. As 'part of the family' pets can play meaningful roles in human lives. But humans are not meaningful parts of their pets' lives; they are simply sources of care and attention.

Plants struggle for life under some conditions, and flourish under others. It is plausible to interpret 'struggle' on the part of a rational agent as an attempt to secure what is hoped for, and, correspondingly, to see 'flourishing' as hope realized. Construed in this way, hoping is an *essentially* practical matter. That is to say, I need to do more than simply embrace an imaginative vision of how my life might be. Serious hope requires me to set my sights on it and take practical steps, however small or faltering, to realize it.

It is common to think of action as the realization of previously formulated beliefs, a conception of practical reason that is conveniently labelled 'intellectualism'. Plato articulates and defends this kind of intellectualism in a number of dialogues, most famously the *Republic*. If human conduct is to be fully rational, Socrates contends, it requires a knowledge of 'the Good', something that only philosophical thought at the highest level can secure. While Platonic intellectualism has proved to have considerable appeal, in reality the degree to which reflective self-consciousness can be theoretically informed is rather limited. Time, circumstance, and opportunity all influence the extent to which any 'philosophy', however theoretically coherent, can actually be lived. More importantly for present purposes, this intellectualist conception of practical reason, as Plato fully recognized, is deeply anti-egalitarian. Only *some* people are capable of abstract philosophical reasoning. By Plato's account, the person who has undergone the rigours of intellectual training that knowledge of the good necessitates is a 'philosopher-king', and as such, someone whose superior knowledge properly entitles them to direct the actions of others for the good of all. A well-ordered society, consequently, is organized on a hierarchical basis similar to the organization of an army or a hospital. People with superior intellectual ability determine what is best, and in the light of that knowledge exercise authority over people who cannot obtain this knowledge for themselves.

The concept of a 'philosopher-king', and the hierarchical thinking that comes with it, may seem too far removed from modern ways of thinking to warrant much attention. Yet it remains as obvious to us as it was to Plato that the intellectual ability of human beings varies greatly. Some people are good at formulating, investigating, understanding, and debating fundamental questions about right and wrong. Others are not. Modern versions of intellectualism, however, have striven to avoid the implications Plato drew from intellectual inequalities by means of a two-step revision. First, philosophy is replaced by science and thus 'philosopher-kings' replaced by 'experts' in the natural and social sciences. Such 'experts' now have a prominent role in a large number of areas relevant to practical life — medicine, agriculture, psychology, business management, economics, education, technology, and so on — often with dedicated institutions — government think-tanks, university research centres, business schools, policy institutes, training colleges. In *After Virtue*, Alasdair MacIntyre contends that the appeal to expertise of this sort as a guide to conduct is one of the principal outcomes of the eighteenth-century Enlightenment. They 'justify their claims to authority, power and money', he argues, 'by invoking their own competence as managers of social change' (*After Virtue* p.83).

Secondly, while expertise of this kind is grounded in complex intellectual investigations that only specialists can engage in, their advice is confined to devising methods. The modern expert, supposedly, in contrast to Plato's philosopher-king, recommends means, but never ends. These have to be chosen by others — customers, clients, or political leaders, for instance. So, on the one hand, this conception of 'applied science' attributes rational superiority to expertise over practical experience. On the other hand, it attempts to balance its claim to superiority with its alleged value neutrality. The expert, so conceived, cannot tell you *what* to do, only *how best* to do it. Thus, while human beings are *unequal* with respect to expertise, they are *equal* at the level of choice and desire.

III. Practical Reason

Practical reason construed as 'applied science', then, can tell you the most effective *means* to a given end — whether personal, political, or social — but it cannot determine what it would be wise or foolish to attempt.[1] Indeed, if practical rationality is the application of knowledge, then the concepts of wisdom and folly apply only to the means, never to the end or purpose of action. It follows from this that ends and purposes have to be established on some non-cognitive basis, not by what we know or can discover, but by what we want, or need, or prefer.

This purely instrumental conception of practical reason has a distinguished philosophical pedigree. It is expressly articulated and endorsed by David Hume, 'widely regarded as the greatest philosopher ever to write in the English language', according to one commentator.[2] In his *Treatise of Human Nature*, Hume famously declares that, 'reason is, and ought only to be the slave of the passions, and can never pretend to any other office than to serve and obey them' (*Treatise* 2.3.3.4). Some chapters later, he expands on this claim by asserting that 'reason in a strict and philosophical sense, can have an influence on our conduct only after two ways: Either when it excites a passion by informing us of the existence of

---

[1] The role of public health 'experts' during the global 'pandemic' of 2020–22 underlined the wholly abstract character of this conception. Epidemiologists, medical advisers, and above all computer modellers actively promoted a curtailment of freedom and a level of intervention in ordinary life as great as anything Plato envisaged. Furthermore, the corresponding claim of political leaders to be 'following the science' served to blur the ends/means distinction yet further, and in a way that compromised any claim to value neutrality. In effect, the 'experts', though allegedly 'advisers', acted as policy makers.

[2] Douglas C. Rasmussen in the Preface to *The Infidel and the Professor*.

something... or when it discovers the connexion of causes and effects, so as to afford us means of exerting any passion" (*Treatise* 3.1.1.12).

Hume explicitly offers his account of the practical role of reason as an alternative to Platonic intellectualism, the tendency 'in philosophy and even in common life... to talk of the combat of passion and reason, to give preference to reason, and assert that men are only so far virtuous as they conform themselves to its dictates' (*Treatise* 2.3.3.1). Part of the appeal of Hume's view is that any high-minded preference for reason over emotion resonates badly in modern ears, suggesting as it does both elitism and judgementalism. Accordingly, the neutrality of Hume's instrumentalism seems attractive, and it undoubtedly has the merit of capturing very succinctly the assumption upon which the widespread appeal to value-neutral expert knowledge rests. Here, as in many other places, Hume so successfully articulates a recurrently appealing idea that it seems obviously correct.

Nevertheless, strict instrumentalism about practical reason is no less problematic than intellectualism. To begin with there appears to be an element of contradiction. If we accept Hume's contention, then he has himself demonstrated that intellectual reflection—in the form of philo-sophical reasoning—*can* tell us what we ought to do. Philosophy tells us we *ought* to treat reason as a 'slave' of the passions. Secondly, even if we overlook the element of contradiction, it is unclear how we are to abide by this recommendation. It does not obviously fall under either of the 'only two ways' in which, Hume has told us, reason can direct action. His argument—that reason on its own is 'inert'—is meant to influence our thinking, but it has neither 'excited a passion by informing us of the existence of something' nor 'discovered a connexion between causes and effect'. It follows that Hume's recommendation presupposes some other, non-Humean, way in which reason can influence action.

As conceptions of practical reason, then, both Platonic intellectualism and Humean instrumentalism are flawed. Interestingly, this is partly the consequence of a supposition that they share. Platonic rationalism sub-sumes practical reason within the sphere of theoretical reason by making our knowledge of 'the Good' a purely intellectual exercise. Hume intends to depart radically from this intellectualistic (what he calls 'rationalist') way of thinking, and yet his instrumentalist account equally confines reason to the 'theoretical'. The only role he can assign to it in deliberation and decision-making is the impartial discovery of empirical facts and causal connections. His account thereby provides an implicit endorsement for modern 'experts' who claim to provide value neutral factual observations and causal theories for individuals and groups to use in the pursuit of personal and collective goals. In other words, while Plato's understanding of practical wisdom conceives of it as theoretical reason that motivates *directly*, Hume's conception understands theoretical reason to motivate us *indirectly*. From both points of view, strictly speaking there is no such thing as practical reason, only theoretical reason employed to practical ends.

What is needed, plainly, is a conception of practical reason that shows it to be an autonomous counterpart to theoretical reason, with a role that is more than establishing facts and causal regularities. A central figure in framing this third possibility is Immanuel Kant. Kant's principal philosophical aim (prompted by Hume) was to secure the epistemological credentials of science against the onslaught of philosophical scepticism. In doing so, however, he found it necessary to assert a strict logical division between the theoretical and the practical. The reasoning appropriate to science, by Kant's account, was of a different kind to the practical reason that guides conduct in ethics, politics, and everyday life. Hume's assertion that reason is 'inert' rests upon the observation that facts, by themselves, cannot motivate. The fact that there is food on the table only motivates me to reach for it *if* I want food. This much Kant concedes, and the concept of moral or evaluative 'truths' that Humean opponents of Platonic rationalism reject is in his eyes equally suspect. He holds, however, that the conclusions of practical reason do not have to be factual propositions. They can be imperatives—'Do this' or 'Don't do that'—commands and injunctions that are directed at myself or at others. Most importantly, patterns of reasoning that conclude with imperatives are subject to the rules of logic no less than those that conclude with factual propositions. Rejecting Platonic rationalism, consequently, does not mean that we must follow Hume and declare that right and wrong, good and bad can only be determined by needs, desires, or preferences (or power relations, as Plato's ancient opponents contended). Kant's key insight in this context is that, since human action is the rational exercise of freedom, the practical injunctions we formulate to guide it can have (or lack) a rational basis, just as our beliefs about the world can be rational or irrational.

If Kant is right about this, he has construed practical reason in a way that makes it the rational equal of theoretical reason (or 'pure' reason in Kant's terminology). Pure and practical reason are different but both are authoritative for rational beings. The 'pure' reason we employ in science tells us what we ought to believe. The practical reason we employ in ethics, politics, and ordinary life tells us what we ought to do. Practical reason does produce 'hypothetical' commands of the form 'If X is your goal, do Y.' In this mode, it is instrumental reasoning. We should notice, though, that the goals we adopt need not be determined by Humean passions or desires. Some of them are, in Kantian terms, 'assertoric'. Health and happiness, for example, are not simple objects of desire, but ends at which all human beings naturally aim. In addition to instrumental reasoning, however, there is also 'pure' practical reason. The injunctions to act that result from pure practical reason are 'categorical' because they apply to all human beings as rational agents, and are not dependent on the desires and preferences we happen to have. Examples include 'Do not tell lies' and 'Keep your promises.' Injunctions such as these override instrumental reason, and thus constitute the basis of moral obligation.

Kant's first 'critique' of *pure* reason sought, amongst other things, to establish the limits of theoretical reason. His second 'critique' of *practical* reason (along with his *Groundwork to the Metaphysics of Morals*) sought correspondingly to secure its autonomy.[3] A large part of Kant's own interest in this possibility lies in securing the rationality of morality, and most of the subsequent debate has concerned his success or failure in this regard. For present purposes, however, it is his emphasis on the autonomy of practical reason that is most significant. Suppose we agree with Kant, and against Plato and Hume, that 'practical' reason is different to theoretical reason, but no less authoritative an exercise of our rational faculties. Might this not have a further implication—that we ought to side with Hume against Plato (and other rationalists) by concluding that philosophical inquiry itself is redundant from a practical point of view? Some important nineteenth-century thinkers did infer from the autonomy of practical reason that philosophy is redundant. They thus opened the way to a radically different approach to philosophy's concerns.

IV. Radical Philosophies

Among these thinkers, Karl Marx and Friedrich Nietzsche proved to be especially influential. Though they differ in several respects, both of them

---

3   His third 'critique' is concerned with judgements of beauty. These, by his account, also involve the exercise of reason, but aesthetic judgements are neither theoretical *nor* practical. Pure beauty has the form of purposefulness, but without purpose.

held that human existence gives practical reason priority over speculative inquiry. 'The question of whether objective truth can be attributed to human thinking is not a question of theory', Marx tells us in his 'Second Thesis on Feuerbach', 'but is a *practical* question. In practice man must prove the truth, that is, the reality and power, the this-sidedness of his thinking. The dispute over the reality and non-reality of thinking which is isolated from practice is a purely *scholastic* matter.' The much quoted Eleventh Thesis extends the point: 'The philosophers have only inter-preted the world, in various ways; the point however is to change it.' In a somewhat similar spirit, Nietzsche praises the ancient Eleatics for 'the faith that their knowledge was at the same time the principle of life'. The 'ultimate question about the condition of life' is this: 'To what extent can truth stand to be incorporated? That is the question; that is the experi-ment' (*The Gay Science* §110).

Both Marx and Nietzsche differ from Kant in another important respect. Kant's *Groundwork to the Metaphysics of Morals* sets out the logical structure of practical reason, but his *Critique of Practical Reason* aims to do more than this. It purports to establish the rationality of religious concepts that do not admit of *theoretical* validation. In principle, the *Critique of Pure Reason* contends, neither philosophy nor science can demonstrate the existence of God, freedom, or immortality. Nonetheless, Kant holds, these concepts can still be given a rational foundation through practical reason. All three are to be endorsed as rationally necessary presuppositions of action. By contrast, and precisely because of their belief in the primacy of practice, Marx and Nietzsche emphatically reject religion as an object of rational hope. For Marx, religion is a manifestation of false consciousness that will fade to irrelevance once practical thinking is redirected from the passivity of other-worldly consolation to this-worldly action—the 'forcible overthrow of all existing social conditions', as the *Communist Manifesto* puts it. For Nietzsche likewise, religion is a form of false hope because 'God is dead', as he famously declared in *The Gay Science*.[4] Humanity has 'murdered' God by a centuries long process of philo-sophical criticism and scientific investigation. The metaphysical basis on which the existence of God relied has been destroyed. Yet the full implications of this destruction have still to be grasped, leaving the

---

[4] The expression itself appears in §§108, 125, and 343, but the theme pervades much of the book.

triumph of humanistic naturalism a long way off. Nietzsche laments the persistence of a servile Christian morality of human rights, as well as continuing scientific commitment to a Platonic idea of 'Truth'. He is clear that 'an edifice such as Christianity, that has been built so carefully over such a long period... could of course not be destroyed all at once' (*The Gay Science* §358), but nevertheless declares that in the light of this 'greatest recent event' — the death of God —'we philosophers and "free spirits" feel illuminated by a new dawn... the horizon seems clear again, even if not bright; finally our ships may set out again,... every daring of the lover of knowledge is allowed again; the sea, *our* sea, lies open again; maybe there has never been such an "open sea"' (*The Gay Science* §343).

What does this 'open sea' promise 'the poor, the huddled masses yearning to breathe free, the wretched refuse of a teeming shore'.[5] On the strength of Nietzsche's analysis, not very much. Christian morality (whose eventual demise he predicts) is to be rejected precisely because it promotes a herd mentality that disguises the truth about 'the dross and refuse of humanity'. The vast majority of people do not have the kind of 'free spirit' that exhibits the 'overflowing energy pregnant with the future'. Of course, the lot of 'the herd' may improve in terms of their material standard of living, which has indeed risen immensely since Nietzsche wrote this. Yet from his perspective they will continue to suffer from 'an *impoverishment of life* and seek quiet, stillness, calm seas' (*The Gay Science* §370).

Is there more hope for the poor, despite the death of God and the demise of Christian morality, if they turn instead to Marx? 'Proletarians have nothing to lose but their chains. They have a world to win', the *Communist Manifesto* says with a confidence based on Marx's anticipation of the 'overthrow of all existing social conditions' and the emergence of communism. Humanity has indeed witnessed enormous political, economic and technological change since then, but the complexity of these changes is so great that it is difficult to determine how far Marx's predictions came true and how far they did not. 'Proletariat' and 'working class' are terms that now seem dated, and Eurocentric. If Marx did think that an end to poverty was in sight, from a *global* perspective he was evidently wrong. At the same time, he was right to think that radically

---

5   This sentence is a (slight) modification of lines from 'The New Colossus' by
     Emma Lazarus, inscribed on a bronze plaque set into the pedestal of the Statue
     of Liberty in New York Harbour.

altered social conditions could and would lift vast numbers of people out
of impoverished lives by liberating them from low paid industrial labour.
The principal point for present purposes, however is this. If the future did
not exactly take the course that Marx anticipated, his influential writings
are still relevant to the third contention that shapes this book. A serious
concern with poverty cannot disregard empirical issues, however complex and intractable they may be. Marx was right to hold that the hope of
eliminating poverty and overcoming economic oppression is an issue that
must at every turn consider empirical facts about the obstacles to its
accomplishment.

If we take states officially inspired by Marxism as a guide — the Soviet
Union, Mao's China, Pol Pot's Cambodia — it seems evident that he was
wrong to suppose that the overthrow of 'all existing social conditions' is a
promising means of accomplishing this hope. What then is the alternative? What courses of action, which social organizations, and what
economic policies and political reforms offer real hope to the proletariat?
A modernized, more acceptable version of Marx answers this question
with programmes of economic aid and gradual development. Since the
publication of the *Communist Manifesto* in the mid-nineteenth century, a
large number of charitable aid organizations have come into existence,
many of them operating on an international level. In addition, most
Western governments now have extensive foreign aid programmes, and
yet more significantly, global institutions such as the International
Monetary Fund, the World Bank, and the World Trade Organization have
been created. Inspired in part by the Millennium Development Goals
formulated by the United Nations in 2000, no fewer than two hundred
relief and development organizations rallied under the slogan 'Make
Poverty History'. Can we say, then, that the world Marx envisaged has
come about, not by the revolution he anticipated, but by international
cooperation and organization?

This question evidently requires empirical inquiry of a kind no less
complex than we find in Marx's *Capital*. To answer it, we need some
understanding of the fundamental causes of involuntary poverty, and a
critical assessment of the effectiveness of the remedies adopted by
charitable causes, national governments, and international organizations.
This all requires careful factual investigation. Efficacy matters, and the
rise of 'effective altruism' as a guide to charitable giving is a result of
realizing that good intentions are not enough. If 'lifting' the poor out of
poverty is to be a reality, practical reason requires that we subject aid

programmes to rigorous empirical scrutiny. What is the financial assistance given by individuals, governments, and international organizations
actually being spent on? How much difference has the investment of
'expertise' really made?

At the same time, acknowledging the crucial role of empirical inquiry
does not warrant Marx's scorn for philosophy. Serious thinking about
human well-being cannot be isolated from the philosophical questions
with which this book is concerned, namely the concepts and principles
underlying this vast complex of organized international aid. It is not
enough simply to assume that the best hope for the poor lies in expertly
designed 'development' programmes that lead to economic growth. We
need a proper account of how the concepts of poverty, growth, and
development are to be understood. Is poverty just a lack of purchasing
power, and its mitigation, therefore, increased purchasing power? Are
poverty and wealth, and the means of transition from one to the other,
best understood in terms of economic measures such as Gross Domestic
Product (GDP)? It is possible to be highly effective in the wrong way.
Some infrastructure projects are plainly like this—first class highways to
places that no one wants to go, for instance, hospitals where equipment
lies idle for want of qualified staff, or vanity project sports stadiums. It is
always possible for the methods and strategies advocated by experts and
adopted by policy makers to be highly effective, but nonetheless wrong-
headed, resulting in outcomes that bring no real benefit.

Even more importantly, there are highly effective ways of bringing
about results that no one *ought to want*. Aid in the form of armaments, for
instance, can prove very effective as a means of perpetuating civil war
and killing innocent bystanders. Solitary confinement is a very effective
way of unhinging those who are subjected to it. In both cases, history
shows, experts in the relevant fields have devised successful technological
and psychological methods. The problem, however, is not means, but
ends. These are ends no one ought to bring about. Franz Stangl was
officially honoured for his highly effective transformation of the death
camp at Treblinka, and indeed no one could fault the means. Yet they
were means to an end—genocide—which, like conflict and madness, no
one ought to bring about. The value of empirical inquiry into efficacy, we
should conclude, has to be assessed in the light of reflectively considered
aims and ideals. Practical reason, consequently, is as much concerned
with the critical examination of goals as it is with investigating the
methods by which they are pursued. So, *pace* Marx, moral philosophy still

has an important role to play. Understanding the world is often an essential preliminary to changing it for the better.

Precisely this point needs to be made about 'development goals'. The successful pursuit of the UN's 'Millennium Goals' (and their 'sustainable' successors), or international agreements designed to stimulate economic growth, or the promotion of democratic institutions for good 'governance', all constitute 'development' only if they are the right goals to pursue. No one denies that economic growth and personal prosperity, political stability, and individual freedom are significant components of human wellbeing, or that empirical studies of cause and effect are key to securing them. Even so, there are related, but no less important, issues to be investigated. While freely pursuing personal prosperity in a stable society is undoubtedly valuable *in the abstract*, its *actual* value turns crucially on whether a life accurately described in this way is a life worth living. Mere subsistence, after all, fits this description. What matters is *content*, not just *conditions*. The same observation applies to relatively prosperous lives. The suicide rate in wealthy Nordic countries is unhappily high, while in poverty-stricken Haiti, for example, it is almost zero. Quite what this shows is debatable, but at a minimum it alerts us to an important possibility: the connection between material wellbeing and a life worth living is not a straightforward one. Consequently, empirical assessment of the effectiveness of programmes directed at economic development cannot be divorced from a philosophical critique of whether, and in what ways, such development is beneficial.

One useful way of stating the point is to contrast wealth and poverty with enrichment and impoverishment. Increases in wealth are not always enriching. Conversely, poverty does not always impoverish. The point of these contrasting terms is to enable us to see that, paradoxical though it may sound, wealth can sometimes impoverish life — morally and spiritually — while relinquishing wealth may lead to its enrichment. The distinctions between poverty and impoverishment, wealth and enrichment, will be returned to in subsequent chapters. At this point, their introduction is important because it naturally leads to a preliminary consideration of the place of religion in the philosophy of development.

V. Religion

By and large, when it comes to assisting the poor, the conceptions of 'better' and 'worse' that operate in the modern world are materialistic. The hopes they express and embody are hopes for measurable improvements in income, health, education, and security. This contrasts sharply, at least on first appearance, with the ambition of nineteenth-century Christian missionaries who sought to improve the lives of poor people by bringing them the Gospel. Once again, the UN's Development Goals are not only an indicator, but a faithful reflection of what is now widely taken to be obvious — the poor will best be helped by being made wealthier. Many factors have produced this consensus, no doubt, but two are of special interest here. First, goals like these are especially well suited to reliance being placed on expertise of the kind described in the previous section. This is partly because they readily accommodate comparative *measurement*, and partly because they appear to be 'neutral' — in the sense of 'uncontentious'. Who is likely to dispute the value of greater material benefits? The second factor is the changing position of religion and the rise of naturalistic humanism. Both Marx and Nietzsche are significant here. Their advocacy (in Nietzsche's phrase) of a 'revaluation of all values' was directly connected to their rejection of metaphysics and religion. Humanity has been freed from quiescent other-worldliness, and must now actively secure its own salvation, which is to say, determine its own goals and the means to them, whether collectively or on an individual basis. Organizations as varied as Oxfam, the Gates Foundation, the United Nations, and the International Monetary Fund have all been founded with something like this thought in mind.

Other important nineteenth-century thinkers were less strident in their criticism of religion than Marx and Nietzsche, but their message is effectively the same. John Stuart Mill did not denounce supernaturalism, but he did press the case for a 'religion of humanity' that would supplant the Christian religion and constitute a better basis in which the hopes for future generations could rest. In New England, the post-Christian teachings of Emerson and Thoreau were more mystical than Mill's, yet despite this difference, the name by which they became known — 'Transcendentalism' — is seriously misleading. There is nothing 'transcendent' here, only a deeply humanistic search after meaning.

All these thinkers can be thought of as resolving a tension we encounter within Kant's conception of practical reason. On the one hand, Kant insists upon the autonomy of practical reason. On the other, he makes the cogency of practical reasoning depend upon metaphysical presuppositions — the existence of God, the freedom of the will, and the immortality of the soul. Marx and Mill take the autonomy of practical reason to be grounds for abandoning religion as any sort of hope, while

Nietzsche explicitly and emphatically rejects the three concepts that Kant's second *Critique* aims to revitalize. Neither Marx nor Nietzsche (nor Mill, probably) expected the intellectual refutation of supernaturalist theology to result in the rapid disappearance of religion. On the contrary, they thought that learning to live in a 'this-worldly way' is a complex and arduous task that is likely to take a long time. While Nietzsche is quite clear about this, Marx is less so, but his claim that religion is an other-worldly 'opiate' implies as much. The term 'opiate' has often been interpreted as dismissive. What Marx means to acknowledge, however, is the *valuable* role that religion plays in offering the poor and oppressed genuine psychological relief from mental and material suffering. The promise of heaven may be *illusory*, but it can nevertheless mitigate *real* pain. Yet the true solution to the problems of the poor is not to be found in an opiate to *dull* the pain of their existence, but in material improve-ments that will eliminate its *causes*.

The 'opiate' of religion, we can agree, is not always benign. If Marx is right, the belief in heaven is more than a false proposition that might have been true. In addition, it is a belief with practical consequences. Just as Nietzsche thinks that the '*ressentiment*' of 'the herd' gives an opening to a self-serving priestly class, so Marx thinks that religion's ability to console the poor makes them vulnerable to exploitation by the rich and powerful, whose ideological servants are the priests and theologians. By turning the attention of the poor to another world, they successfully deflect them from practically effective actions that would overthrow the system and thus undo poverty's real economic and political causes. In this way, religious (and ideological) 'hope', paradoxically, militates against real hope.

This, at any rate, is what the Marxist picture contends, and it is easy to cite instances of material advancement that appear to bear it out very clearly. At one time, for example, people placed their hopes for health in saying prayers, wearing amulets, obtaining holy relics, visiting sacred sites, and invoking the protection of gods and saints. Once modern scientifically based medicine began to make real progress, it is plausible to think, these 'folk' remedies of religion gradually disappeared, and priests were replaced by physicians. There is evidently some truth in this, and if poor people still turn to religion, this way of thinking suggests, it is only because they cannot afford the drugs and surgical procedures that much wealthier people have found to be far more effective. Similarly, or so it is easy to imagine, agrarian processions, prayers for rain, public fasts, and the sacrificial offering of 'first fruits' were practices intended to ensure good harvests, give protection from the elements, and avert famine. The rise of agricultural engineering, science-based farming, the use of chemicals as fertilizers and pesticides, rendered these practices strictly useless. If they persist here and there, which they do, this is either superstition, or an aesthetic pleasure in the quaint and intriguing residues of times past.

This sketch of the redundancy of religious practices accords with the general theme of Hume's *Natural History of Religion*, published in 1757. Hume argues that 'the first ideas of religion arose… from a concern with the regard to the events of life, and from incessant hopes and fears, which actuate the human mind' (*Natural History of Religion* p.139). These hopes and fears are fuelled by ignorance about the way the world works. As our knowledge of nature grows, our control of affairs increases. As a result, our fears are mitigated. We become better and better able to protect ourselves from the things we fear. We find the means to realize the things we hope for, and as a result superstitious religious practices die away. The growth of knowledge, Hume firmly believed, will lead to a decline in religion.

It is a striking fact that while this scenario has seemed immensely plausible to very many people, history has not confirmed it. In the 250 years since Hume wrote, science and technology have flourished beyond his most enthusiastic imagining, and yet religion has not disappeared. People continue to pray and to worship, and to do so for highly practical reasons often. Even in countries with the most advanced healthcare, such as the United States, prayers for healing remain a common practice. It is true that the Christianity with which Hume was most familiar in his native Scotland has a very tenuous hold there now, but this collapse is relatively recent[6] and cannot be correlated with increasing knowledge in the way that the *Natural History of Religion* might incline one to suppose. Besides, though the condition of religion in contemporary Scotland is similar to its condition in other parts of Europe, this is not true of the world as a whole. On the contrary, over the last quarter of the twentieth century, all the major religions underwent some measure of revival — in wealthy places as well as poor — though this upward trend seemed to slacken in the first decades of the twenty-first century.

---

6   See Callum Brown, *The Decline of Christian Britain*.

In a letter written relatively late in life,[7] Hume looks forward to a world in which 'all the Churches shall be converted into Riding Schools, Manufactories, Tennis Courts, or Playhouses', adding that, old though he is, he expects to see this condition much advanced before he dies. Curiously, however, while he may have hoped for religion's demise, it seems he did not really expect it. At the end of the *Natural History* he reiterates the maxim that 'Ignorance is the mother of Devotion', and that the religious principles which have prevailed in 'most nations and most ages' are more like 'the playsome whimsies of monkeys in human shape' than the 'asserverations of a being, who dignifies himself with the name of rational'. Yet, he adds, 'look out for a people, entirely destitute of religion: If you find them at all, be assured that they are but a few degrees removed from the brutes.' The phenomenon of religion, he concludes, 'is a riddle, an ænigma, an inexplicable mystery' (*Natural History of Religion* pp.184–5). In other words, however absurd religion may appear, it has roots in human nature that are too deep for scientific and economic advancement to eliminate.

My concluding philosophical claim in this book runs counter to Hume's scepticism. Religious engagement with the world, I shall argue, is deeply practical. Its principal interest is in how we ought to live, not what we ought to believe, though the two are obviously connected. People's religious beliefs do influence the ways in which they conduct their lives. Hume is right, however, that the relation is not as straightforward as it is often represented. Religionists and their critics (including Hume, though not Nietzsche) often share an intellectualist prejudice that treats religious doctrine as the basis of religious practice. The widespread Christian use of creeds and confessions tends to mislead in this regard, and sustains a mistaken way of thinking that conflates religion with theology and thereby lends special importance to intellectual criticism. Yet it is contrary to most people's *experience* of religion. The actions of ordinary believers are only very rarely the outcome of an exercise in 'speculative' reason of the kind that theologians engage in. In the main, their religious life is constituted by practices of prayer, worship, ritual, and so on, in which they engage with others on a regular basis. These are not practices that they have devised on the basis of what they believe, as, say, dietary prescriptions might be derived from a knowledge of nutrition. Rather,

---

[7] Published in *Philosophy and Religion in Enlightenment Britain*, pp.256–7.

these are corporate and communal practices, into which individuals are inducted, often from childhood. Though they often have accompanying beliefs and concepts, the character of these is importantly enriched and enlarged by inherited artistic, musical, and architectural expression.[8] The inherited, communal, and corporate character of religion properly so called distinguishes it from 'spirituality' which more usually names an individual pursuit—a spiritual equivalent to fitness training perhaps. The difference explains how it is possible for contemporary sociological surveys to show 'religion' in decline but interest in 'spirituality' rising. An important characteristic of the sort of 'spirituality' that these surveys reveal is its essential 'quietism'. That is to say, it eschews corporate activity, and takes the form of subduing or stilling practical action in order to facilitate mystical 'contemplation' on the part of the individual.

If it is the case that corporate and communal practice is foundational to religion, it is nevertheless true that both theological debates and mystical movements have had important roles to play in the history of all the world's major religions. Emphasizing the practical nature of religion is not meant to deny this, only to invite a reconsideration of the relation between belief and practice. There is a strong argument to be made in support of the contention that theological doctrines and contemplative exercises are not the *basis* of religious practice, but reflective of it, in something like the way that the rules of grammar reflect, rather than determine, linguistic practice. The argument is not one that we need to engage with here, however. For present purposes, there is independent reason for focusing on religion as a practice. It is the activities of prayer, worship, and ritual that figure more far deeply in the ordinary lives of the poor than either theological reflection or the search for mystical experience. Relative poverty is part of the explanation, no doubt, because a sophisticated intellectual activity like theology requires greater wealth and leisure than poor communities can usually afford, and while even poor societies generate monks and mendicants, it is obvious that full-time devotees of this kind must always be a small minority. Sustaining life by begging, no less than devoting oneself to theology, is impossible for a majority. The main question to be addressed in the present context, then, is this. Are the practices of prayer, worship, and ritual, in which poor

---

8   I elaborate these claims at greater length in *Wittgenstein and Natural Religion* Chps 8 and 9 (Oxford University Press 2014).

people can be found to engage, importantly valuable elements in the best kind of life they can hope to lead? Or are Marxists right when they allege that the value of such things lies in their power to dull the pain of an existence whose real hope lies in economic and political transformation, and that, as Hume and Nietzsche hold, poverty and ignorance serve to sustain the psychological impulses that give rise to religion?

Next Steps

The next few chapters address this question by building on the philosophical conclusions of this one. Their main aim is to develop a different and more illuminating way of thinking about the lives of poor people. A key task lies in integrating meaningful hope and empirical realism. Such integration has an interest extending well beyond lives that are lived in poverty. It relates directly to the hopes of everyone who expects to lead what we can call an 'ordinary' life. Biographical authors, understandably, usually focus on exceptional lives—political leaders, military commanders, artistic geniuses, scientific or technological innovators, great explorers, and record-breaking sports men and women—because their lives are more likely to interest readers. But living an exceptional life cannot rationally be an ambition for the vast majority of people. Consequently, the first step in the task of integrating hope and reality must that of framing a philosophy of *ordinary* life. That is to say, we need a cogent and coherent account of how the lives of *unexceptional* human beings may integrate personal subjective satisfaction with evaluatively objective meaningfulness.

Chapter Two

Framing a Philosophy of Ordinary Life

The previous chapter concluded that rational agency, the capacity for reflection on the ends and means of action, is the foundation of our common humanity. Whereas nowadays we tend to think that 'practical' refers to questions about means, for the Scottish Enlightenment philosophers, by contrast, 'practical ethics' meant thinking about ends. Accordingly, when Thomas Reid lectured on practical ethics to his students in eighteenth-century Glasgow, he took this as his basic orientation.

> It is the prerogative of Man in his adult state to be able to propose to himself and to prosecute one great End in Life & by this to reduce the whole of his Life to a connected System making every part of it subservient to his main End and regulating the whole of his conduct with a view to that. The brutes are incapable of this: they are necessarily (sic) carried away by the appetite or Instinct which {is} strongest at the time without any view more distant than its Gratification. We have a Superior Principle given us by the Author of our Being, by which we can, from an Eminence as it were, take a view of the whole Course of human Life; and consider the different Roads that men take & and the Ends to which they lead.
>
> When we thus take a general view of human Life we can not but perceive that some Roads we may take lead to Ruin and infamy, others are mean and below the dignity of our natures… (*Practical Ethics* p.32)

Practical ethics, in this sense, abstracts from the particulars of our normal needs, usual tasks, and immediate desires. It invites us to consider the meaning and value of ultimate ends—which experiences are most *worth* having, which goals are most *worth* accomplishing, and so on. Conceived in this way, 'practical ethics' is a branch of philosophy and takes us to a level of thinking beyond that of everyday decision-making. Here we encounter again the crucial difference Reid identifies between humans and 'the Brutes'. This difference goes beyond older ways of thinking which regarded animals as either physical machines or biological systems. Compared to fish or insects, say, many mammals have a rich conscious life. Dogs, bears, horses, dolphins, for instance, are centres of consciousness whose mental and emotional life is stimulated by the perception of things that interest them, please them, frighten them, or anger them. It follows that *consciousness* is not what distinguishes humans from animals, and since some animals appear to be aware of themselves as distinct centres of consciousness, arguably it is not *self-consciousness* either. But for all their mental and emotional sophistication, what they lack is *reflective* self-consciousness. When an animal is not alarmed, or hungry, or fearful, or in pain, its behaviour falls into a regular pattern—foraging, resting, copulating, and so on. It follows this pattern instinctively because it does not have the ability to reflect upon it by imagining and evaluating alternatives. Still less can even the cleverest of animals ponder the significance of their experience. Those that have eyes can be influenced, but cannot be *inspired* by what they can see. They see the sun go down and this may prompt them to take shelter. But they cannot, as we can, choose to stand and watch it for a moment just because it is beautiful. Conversely, they cannot be bored by their experience. Animals do not suffer *ennui*—the dissatisfaction arising for a sense that a well fed, pain-free, peaceful life is not enough. Consequently, animals cannot long for something special to enhance and enrich their instinctual routine. When their lives go well, they simply live them, and no question as to the meaning or value of those lives arises.

By contrast, human beings can experience dissatisfaction with the course of life, even when they are comfortable and prosperous. People long for something to inspire them, and their capacity for rational reflection enables them to pursue goals in the hope of making their lives more interesting or exciting or challenging. A key element in this is the ability to *imagine* alternative futures, and this is what the metaphor of 'dreams' refers to. Exercising this power of imagination leads ineluctably to the sorts of question that Reid, in different terms, wanted his students to ask. 'What should my dream be?'

A commonplace answer is: 'To be rich and famous.' At best, though, this is simply a placeholder. If my dream of wealth is realized, I have still to decide what to spend my riches on. If fame beckons, I still need to decide what it would be good to be famous *for*. There are famous saints and famous serial killers, and 'celebrities' whose fame amounts to nothing more than being well and widely known. It is in these questions about the *object* of wealth and fame that we encounter the subject matter with which Reid wanted his students to engage. Which 'ends' in life are most worth having? What hopes ought we to have? Since these are questions that *any* human being can ask, they provide a good starting point for framing what I shall call a 'philosophy of ordinary life'.

A philosophy is not a plan or project. Rather, it is an understanding of what critical reflection on the purposes of life involves. It properly begins when we abstract still further, and consider the different *kinds* of things on which our hopes and dreams can fasten. For instance: I hope for some special experience—that one day I will get to eat truffles, that I will hear the world's greatest tenor, that I will visit Niagara Falls. I hope for some special accomplishment—gaining a university degree, writing a novel, successfully running a restaurant. I hope for some special relationship—to fall in love, have children of my own, make a friend of someone I have met recently. These simple examples show that aspirations fall into different categories. Characteristically (as in this list) we hope for good experiences, significant achievements, and personal relationships. The three kinds are neither exhaustive nor exclusive. Indeed, further investigation will show that experiences, achievements, and relationships are importantly connected. Furthermore, they are often modified within the contexts of work and recreation. A philosophy of ordinary life is what emerges from the exploration of these concepts and their interconnectedness. Its aim is to establish the ways in which experiences, accomplishments, and relationships are most satisfactorily combined within a single human life. Their successful combination is what constitutes a biography, that is to say, a meaningful life story. Stories have a narrative structure, and it is with the shape of this narrative that the philosophy of ordinary life is ultimately concerned. For the next few sections, however, we will treat these different dimensions separately.

I. Experiences

It is natural when we first start to think about what kind of life it would be good to have to conceive of it in terms of possessions and experiences —things we would like to own and experiences we would like to enjoy. However, it is not necessary to treat possessions independently of experiences because, leaving aside some pathological psychologies, what is valuable about possessions is the experience of enjoying them, not the simple fact of owning them in itself. There is not much to value in owning a sports car, for instance, if ownership does not bring with it the pleasure of *driving* the car, seeing it parked in front of my house, or witnessing the admiring glances of others, and so on. Owning a car that is never driven, seen, or admired is no better than owning no car. Value derives, then, from the experiences my possessions enable me to have. But where precisely does the value of an experience lie?

An ancient, recurrent, and enduringly attractive philosophical doctrine known as 'hedonism' finds the answer in pleasure and enjoyment. Experiences add value to our life because we enjoy them; they give us pleasure. This is a conception of the good life propounded by some of the Sophists with whom Socrates argues in many of Plato's dialogues. Something similar underlies most versions of utilitarianism. As an ethical doctrine, utilitarianism holds that the best action is the one that serves the greatest happiness of the greatest number of people. The most forthright exponent of this doctrine was Jeremy Bentham, but it is John Stuart Mill, building on Bentham's legacy, who gave utilitarianism a more philosophically sophisticated and more widely discussed articulation. Mill holds that wellbeing is identical with happiness, and that happiness is the successful pursuit of pleasure (and avoidance of pain). In pursuit of this ideal, and for the purpose of practical guidance, utilitarianism has to make calculations and comparisons between possible actions, so both Bentham and Mill also have to suppose that pleasure or happiness is quantifiable in some way. Bentham explicitly develops a 'felicific calculus' that aims to do this.

The central terms Mill uses — wellbeing, happiness, pleasure — admit of some variation in interpretation. Many people have argued that they do not fit together as easily as Mill supposes. Others have argued that no sense can be made of the idea of 'measuring pleasure', and have proposed instead that the hedonic element be dropped. In response, still others have tried to preserve the consequentialist structure of utilitarianism by replacing the concepts of happiness and pleasure with an entirely neutral concept of 'preference satisfaction'. There is now a vast literature on hedonism and especially modern utilitarianism, but for present purposes several of the most interesting and important debates can be set aside. The terms 'pleasure', 'enjoyment', and 'happiness' can be used interchangeably, and the matter of measurement ignored, because to investigate the role of enjoyable experiences in framing a philosophy of ordinary life, we need only consider three philosophical problems.

The first, and most fundamental, turns on the question whether pleasure is actually an intrinsic value. Obviously, if it is not, then valuable experiences cannot be valuable in virtue of being pleasurable. Since people are so readily motivated by the prospect of pleasure, it seems very odd to question its intrinsic value. Nevertheless, a doubt arises as soon as we note the existence of sadistic pleasures. It is matter of common knowledge that some people genuinely get pleasure from hurting and humiliating others, often very severely. Why would anyone, faced with such cases, hold that there is any value in the pleasure experienced by sadists? A common response to this challenge replies (as the ancient Sophists did to Socrates) that, whether we like to admit it or not, the sadist derives the same subjective value from hurting people as the saint does from helping them. That is to say, pleasure is a *subjective* value, and for the sadist torturing and tormenting others is thus a valuable experience.

On reflection, though, this response accomplishes nothing. It amounts to a simple re-assertion of what was said at the outset, namely that some people get pleasure from the sadistic treatment of others. No one denies that sadists enjoy their sadism, if that is what 'subjective value' means. The question, rather, is why we should attribute any objective value to the fact that they do. Actually, this is as much a question for the sadist as for anyone else. Acknowledging the pleasure that they find themselves getting from inflicting pain on others, sadists might well ask, 'Is this the sort of pleasure I really want to have?' The question seems perfectly intelligible. Its intelligibility implies, however, that there is a test by which both sadists and non-sadists can *judge* the value of the subjective pleasure, a test which, by implication, it could fail.

Mill tries to address this problem by drawing a distinction between 'higher' and 'lower' pleasures, and in expounding it he makes use of some elements of Bentham's calculus—the differences in intensity, duration, and so on between different kinds of pleasures. However, even if such a distinction can be made, there is no guarantee that sadistic pleasures would fall on the 'lower' side. Mill does not address this issue himself. His concern is to rebut Bentham's willing acceptance of the somewhat philistine view that, when it comes to pleasure, the simple game of push-pin is as good as the most elevated poetry. But can Mill's higher/lower distinction be sustained? There seem to be only two possibilities, and neither will work. Either poetry is a *quantitatively* 'higher' pleasure than pushpin, or it is *qualitatively* 'higher'. An appeal to quantity accomplishes nothing because it requires the pleasures to be fully commensurable.

'Higher' and 'lower', on this understanding, are different pleasures in just the same sense that 10 and 100 are different numbers. There is no difference in *kind*. To get the same amount of pleasure, we just spend more time on pushpin than on poetry.

Mill himself does not appeal to quantity. He takes the difference to be qualitative. He invokes the opinion of people who have experience of both 'lower' and 'higher' pleasures and are thus in a position to judge between them. Which would they prefer? This is of course strictly a question of fact. Mill produces no actual evidence of what the general opinion is among people who have, for instance, played pushpin and read poetry. But let us assume that a survey of such people shows them to prefer poetry. What entitles us to infer that this judgement is based on comparing the amounts or kinds of pleasure they derived from the experience? Why is the explanation not personal preference for poetry over pushpin on the part of the person delivering the judgement?

There are further moves that could be made in the hedonist's defence, but we need not pursue them, because even if we concede, contrary to the preceding analysis, that the pleasure derived from an experience is what makes that experience intrinsically valuable, a second philosophical problem arises. The principal topic in which we are interested here is hope. What should I hope *for*? Answering this question requires me to choose between future possibilities. How would the value of pleasure facilitate this choice? The most we can appeal to is *anticipated* pleasure. Yet experiences that we expect to be pleasurable do not always turn out to be so. The case of lottery winners shows precisely this. The poor person who uses scarce resources to buy a lottery ticket may plausibly *anticipate* that a win will result in a far more enjoyable life. Often, though, the reverse is true. For a variety of reasons, lottery winners can find themselves leading miserable lives. 'Happy' lottery winners do exist, but they seem to be a small minority. The philosophical point is that pleasure, if it does accompany the outcome, is contingently, not intrinsically, related to it. It is certain, let us say, that I hope to win the lottery, but my hope cannot be grounded in the pleasure this would give me, since, depending on how things turn out, it may not give me any. And if, though I win, for some reason I get no pleasure from this, then it is valueless. In this respect, contingent value contrasts with intrinsic value. Suppose I am hoping to win in order to fund a legal appeal on behalf of someone unjustly imprisoned. If I am able to do this, it will undoubtedly please me greatly, but that is not where the value of the win lies. Perhaps I do win and the money funds a successful appeal, and yet because of some depressive illness, I can take no pleasure in this success. The intrinsic value of the win nevertheless remains. Justice has been done whether or not this gives me pleasure.

The distinction between intrinsic and contingent value is crucial. In order to act rationally in the pursuit of my hopes and dreams, whatever they may be, I have to consider future prospects both in terms of the *likelihood* of the intended outcome, and the *value* of that outcome. If I have virtually no chance of winning, it is irrational to squander the little I have. If I do have a good chance of winning, I still need to be sure that there will be real value in my success. I *cannot* know this, if the value lies in the pleasure I will take in the outcome, because, when the time comes, I may not take any pleasure in it. The dead can take no pleasure in post-mortem lotteries that they have won, but their winning can still benefit others. What I need to know is that the outcome, however I come to regard it (if I am there to regard it at all), has value in and of itself.

A possible rejoinder lies in the thought that to make my gambling rational, it is enough if I will *probably* take pleasure in the outcome. Why do I need certainty here? Nothing in this life is certain, after all. The point is well taken, but it does not serve to avert the underlying problem. We cannot rationally rest our hopes on the mere prospect of pleasure or enjoyment. How do I know what I will probably enjoy? The best answer is previous experience. I have enjoyed such things in the past. But hoping, especially on the part of the poor, is often hoping for something quite different—a better life. That raises a question. What should my attitude be to the prospect of *new* experiences? Someone recommends a movie, let us say, with the words 'You would enjoy it.' This prediction properly becomes a recommendation when they add, 'It's well *worth* seeing.' Contrary to the contentions of the hedonist, then, the real value of an experience can be independent of any pleasure it gives us. So, the question of what it is rational to hope for is really this: what experiences are *worth* hoping for? Whatever we *do* hope for, the more important question is what we *ought* to hope for.

To answer this question, we need some standard of 'worth' independent of our hoping. What would such a standard look like? The foregoing argument suggests that the value of hoped for experiences must be grounded in the character of those experiences rather than the psychological and emotional impact they have on us. It is what the experience *is*, not *how we feel about it* that matters. Philosophical hedonism rejects precisely this claim, of course. The value of an experience, the hedonist contends, *must* lie in the pleasure, enjoyment, or desire satisfaction of the person whose experience it is. Facts in themselves do not motivate, and this applies to facts about actual or prospective experiences. If the prospect of an experience is to motivate action, it must in some way connect with our internal subjective states.

Hedonists are in good philosophical company when they advance this contention because one of its best known proponents is David Hume. As the previous chapter noted, Hume's *Treatise of Human Nature* declares that 'reason alone can never be a motive to any action of the will... [and] it can never oppose passion in the direction of the will' (*Treatise* 2.3.3.1). Hume claims that, in putting forward this view, he is rebutting 'the greatest part of moral philosophy, ancient and modern' (ibid.). So successful has he been, his account of reason, emotion, and the will is now orthodoxy in many philosophical circles. Yet to insist that subjective psychological states are essential to the value of an experience is to open up a devastating possibility. If the psychological state in question could be simulated, why would there be any need for the experience itself at all? Robert Nozick raises this question with a celebrated thought experiment.

> Suppose there were an experience machine that would give you any experience you desired. Super-duper neuropsychologists could stimulate your brain so that you would think and feel you were writing a great novel, or making a friend, or reading an interesting book. All the time you would be floating in a tank, with electrodes attached to your brain. Should you plug into this machine for life, preprograming your life's experiences? If you are worried about missing out on desirable experiences, we can suppose that business enterprises have researched thoroughly the lives of many others. You can pick and choose from their large library or smorgasbord of such experiences, selecting your life's experiences for, say, the next two years. After two years have passed you will have ten minutes or ten hours out of the tank, to select the experiences of your next two years. Of course, while in the tank you won't know that you're there; you'll think it's all actually happening... Would you plug in? *What else can matter to us, other than how our lives feel from the inside?* (*Anarchy, State and Utopia* pp.42–3)

Nozick's answer to this final question is threefold. First, we want to have done certain things, not just have the feeling of having done them. Second, we want to *be* a certain sort of person, and to stand in real relationships to others. Third, we want to be in contact with a reality beyond the world of human constructs. The trouble with the experience machine is that it robs us of all these things. I have long hoped, let us say, to climb Mount Kilimanjaro and watch the sunrise from the top. The technology of the experience machine, with a very high degree of fidelity, can generate the thoughts, feelings, sensations, and emotions that I would have if I did actually climb Mount Kilimanjaro and watch the sunrise. I can thus have the pleasure of fulfilling my hopes, without any of the costs and dangers that go with actually doing so. The problem is that, even though I had pleasure indistinguishable from the pleasure the activity itself would have given me, I would not, as a matter of fact, have made my hope a reality. I would not have climbed Mount Kilimanjaro, or have proved myself to be a person with the courage, skill, and persistence to do so. Nor would I have seen the sun as it rose. Instead, I would have been subject to an illusion that, however pleasurable, actually robbed me of my hope. Thanks to 'super-duper neuropsychologists', the imaginary experience machine can do some amazing things. The one thing it cannot do, though, is realize my hopes. And insofar as it induces in me the belief that those hopes have been realized, it has condemned me to a deluded existence. Experience, then, is valuable only insofar as it is connected to reality. This brings us to the second concept a philosophy of ordinary life must incorporate — achievement.

II. Achievements

Contrary to any impression the previous section may have created, valuable experiences constitute an important element in making an ordinary life worth living. The arguments just rehearsed do not count against this. What they show, rather, is that experiences are valuable only insofar as they are connected to reality. To *imagine* that I have done something valuable may give me pleasure, but it is evident that the value of the pleasure I get from imagining this is quite different, and entirely parasitic, on the value of actually having done it. Fantasizing about how my life might go if I won a lottery can be fun, but fantasy is not enough if I am hoping that this is what the future will actually hold. Nozick's experience machine is simply a graphic way of making this point. Imagination has an important role to play in human life both at the level of the individual and society. As was observed earlier, it is by the use of imagination that we are challenged and inspired to strive for a more valuable and meaningful life. Furthermore, imagination can serve more immediate ends, not only by raising real hopes for the future, but by stimulating inventive ways of trying to fulfil them. Still, this fact remains. However pleasurable, *imagined* experiences fall short of 'the real thing'.

The common practice of referring to our hopes as 'dreams' is potentially misleading on this point. If my future is to contain worthwhile experiences, these are experiences I must *have*, and not merely *dream* of having. There is thus a necessary connection between the value of an experience and the achievement it represents. Still, acknowledging this is not an advance in thinking about what is valuable in human life. It simply leaves us with another version of the question we had about experiences. What *achievements* are truly worthwhile? The existence of sadistic pleasures raised a question about the value of pleasure and enjoyment. Similarly, the existence of *trivial* accomplishments raises a question about the value of achievements. We know that people can devote a great deal of time and effort to trivial tasks. These are among the indefinitely many things we *might* accomplish, so we need some criterion by which tasks we set ourselves are *worth* accomplishing.

Familiar suggestions appeal to skill, difficulty, and rarity as criteria of worth. If something is hard to achieve, that makes it worthwhile. Moreover, if very few people have accomplished it because it requires long practice as well as skill, then this adds to its value. Or so it is plausible to believe. Yet the *Guinness Book of World Records* provides plenty of counter-examples. For instance, it has included amongst its record holders a man who mastered the skill of smoking several cigars while simultaneously imitating bird calls. This difficult achievement was the result of many years of persistent practice. Since no one else showed the same persistence, his achievement greatly exceeded that of anyone else who had attempted something similar. It follows that this man's achievement met the criteria of being difficult, skilful, and rare. Yet none of these features, it seems right to say, does anything to alter its essentially trivial nature. Impressive though it may be in its way, it cannot be called *worthwhile*. Consequently, skill, difficulty, and rarity do not provide a satisfactory answer to the question of what makes one thing worth achieving and another not.

Utilitarianism offers an alternative, and plausible, suggestion. A worthwhile achievement is one that benefits others. This seems hard to deny. The record-breaking cigar smoker, surely, would have spent his time better if he had devoted it to improving the lives of others—finding a medical cure for a debilitating disease, inventing inexpensive forms of heating and cooling, or developing disease resistant crops, for example. Intuitively these do indeed seem far better things to have accomplished. Who could doubt the value of enabling people dogged by poverty, sickness, malnutrition, and danger to lead lives that are long, healthy, well-nourished, and safe.

The strength of this argument lies in its appearing to appeal to something indisputable. It draws on a widespread consensus underlying the activities of many governments and aid agencies—that improving the health and welfare of others is sufficient justification for what they do. Whether they are right about this is a topic for extended treatment at a later stage. For the moment let us accept longevity, health, education, and so on as real marks of a good life. Even assuming this to be the case, making benefits of this kind the standard by which to judge the value of an achievement confronts a debilitating circularity.

Imagine that I am blessed with health, energy, education, and a good income, and therefore free to do something valuable. I choose to work voluntarily with a development agency, and secure a major improvement in the material lives of poor people. Understandably, I take pride in my achievement. But have I now found a goal at which good lives should aim? The daily struggle for simple survival, let us suppose, has hitherto prevented the people I have helped from asking a question they can now address. 'What worthwhile things shall we use our newfound freedom and prosperity to do and to be?' Can I recommend that they answer it in the way I answered it? If they, in their turn, work for the betterment of the poor that is no doubt a good thing, but the problem of circularity is evident. Material betterment, this example reveals, is not a *criterion* of worthwhile activity; it is a *condition* for it. Though I rest content with having benefitted others, that does not show I have answered question 'what makes an activity worthwhile?' I have simply delegated it to the next set of beneficiaries.

Where else might we turn in search of an answer? One possible source is Aristotelianism. In the *Nicomachean Ethics*, one of moral philosophy's most influential works, Aristotle supposes that human beings have a distinctive nature and that 'living well' is 'acting excellently' in accordance with that nature. Just as the proper aim of any flute player is to be a *good* flute player, so the aim of every human being is to be a good instance of their own kind. This means realizing *human* excellences, which is to say, bringing the abilities and aptitudes that are distinctive of the species to their fullest development. Stated abstractly in this way—and leaving aside any complications generated by the outmoded biology that lies behind this idea—the Aristotelian conception may sound platitudinous, a solemn affirmation of what everyone knows. There are contexts, though, in which platitudes are a strength, and this is one of them. Aristotle wants his ethical prescriptions to rest on a completely uncontentious description of the kind of creature that we are. That is the firmest foundation they can have, and the platitudes gain substance from an elaboration of the features characteristic of human beings.

Human beings typically form families, develop friendships, run businesses, organize and govern communities, invent and employ technology. They make music, tell stories, play games, conduct religious rituals. They educate their children, participate in political affairs, frame explanations of natural phenomena, create beautiful artefacts of various sorts, and engage in philosophical and ethical debate. Undergirding this impressive range of activities is their unique capacity to reason, about both practical and speculative questions. This Aristotelian contention plainly resonates with Reid's conception of 'practical ethics', but at this stage, and in line the argument of the previous chapter, the point to emphasize is this. Practical reason underlies the pursuit of success and the avoidance of failure in *all* these activities, and hence to the assessment of mediocrity and excellence. It is thinking well that makes living excellently possible, with thought and action integrated across the range of activities that are distinctively human. A human life lived well is thus a manifestation of practical wisdom.

One strength of the Aristotelian ideal (as opposed to the Utilitarian) is that 'excellence' is an incontestable standard for anyone seeking worthwhile activity because it cannot intelligibly be rejected. Whatever the activity, excellence is better than mediocrity. This indisputable principle, however, is too abstract to direct concrete activity. Since it has universal application, it does not actually tell us what to do. To give it content and prescriptive power, consequently, we must relate it to specific activities. What counts as playing a game excellently, for instance, has to be spelled out in terms of what that game is. Some games require speed and dexterity, others require memory and strategic thinking. To play the game well is to be actively excellent in one set of respects. A different set will be critically important for a different game. The point can be generalized. People who aim to excel in a particular science, say, have to become knowledgeable about *that* science and acquire the necessary knowledge and skill relevant to it. Mastery of a science, however, is more than the possession of knowledge and the acquisition of skills. It is the degree of wisdom with which knowledge and skill are deployed that determines whether someone is a failed, mediocre, good, or brilliant scientist.

It is a notable feature of the Aristotelian conception that it construes judgements of excellence as matters of fact. Consequently, assessing the value of the life someone has led is a matter of truth and falsehood. Whether someone has been a first-class athlete, a significant composer, a successful surgeon, and so on are all questions admitting of objective answers. Either someone has, as a matter of fact, succeeded in becoming a first class in their chosen occupation, or they have not. Neither my likes and preferences nor theirs can alter that. If Aristotle is right, Humean emotivism is wrong. Things aren't made good by having subjective approval 'projected' on to them. Practical reason, as Aristotle understands it, connects feeling and action in a way that neatly circumvents Nozick's 'pleasure machine'. The positive psychological experience we identify as 'pride', for instance, is valuable only insofar as it is focused on a proper object, that is, something excellent that has actually been accomplished. To experience feelings of pride in the absence of excellence is to be deluded. The mere fact that *subjectively* I enjoy the life I lead is not enough to rescue my life from corruption or triviality. Wicked and superficial people often take satisfaction in what they do. This does not serve to make them any less superficial or wicked.

It is a further advantage, however, that on this Aristotelian conception, a truly worthwhile life is not something that has to be pursued in opposition to pleasure. Against the instincts of those whom Adam Smith called 'gloomy moralists', human beings can expect to take great pleasure in a life lived well. The good friend *enjoys* his friendships. Tennis players enjoy tennis, and the better they are (generally speaking) the happier they are. Conversely, musicians, scholars, chefs, and scientists are understandably unhappy when they fall short of excellence in their chosen profession. Subjective pleasure and objective excellence, then, are not in competition. To appreciate how they can properly be combined, we must abandon the hedonistic idea that pleasure is a distinct psychological experience arising from the activities we engage in, and think of it as something integral to those activities. The pleasure I take in what I am doing is intensified when I do it well and diminished when I do it badly. People do sometimes take delight in a mediocre performance, but when this is the case it is a result of ignorance, deception, or flattery. A rationally well-ordered life is a coherent whole in which reality and experience, success and satisfaction, are integrated.

Aristotle's account of what makes a life worthwhile has been adopted, endorsed, and elaborated by a wide range of thinkers in ethics, politics, and religion. However, taken as the basis of a philosophy of *ordinary* life, it has this crucial weakness. It is, in the strict sense, an *aristocratic* conception, one that by necessity eludes the majority. The truly worthwhile life, if Aristotle is right, will always be exceptional, something that only a relatively small proportion of human beings are ever able to achieve. Consider again the case of athletes. The ultimate mark of the athlete's achievement is winning the race. In order for there to be winners, however, there must be losers. Simply running the race is a worthwhile activity only to a limited degree because the value of participation cannot compensate for failure. While someone might understandably be pleased just to have crossed the finishing line as a 'personal best', there is no proper satisfaction to be gained from having come in last. Similarly, though music making at almost every level is a worthwhile activity in which to engage, only excellent musicians realize the *full* value of this activity. Mediocre (or merely 'good') singers and players — who constitute the majority of course — often enjoy themselves, but at the same time acknowledge how far they fall short of what they would hope to achieve. This truth is even more evident in the case scientific achievements. Nobel Laureates are the gold standard of scientific excellence, but it would be irrational for all except a tiny proportion of highly professional scientists to make a Nobel Prize their goal.

These examples demonstrate how the Aristotelian conception of 'the good life' must regard *ordinary* lives as, at best, predictably failed attempts at excellence. In the pursuit of excellence, it is winning the prize that matters, and by the nature of the case, not all can have prizes. Aristotle, it seems likely, would have accepted this implication. He lived in a world where the lives of slaves, servants, the poor, women even, were *expected* to fall short of human excellence, and it is likely that he took the relative worthlessness of ordinary lives to be an evident fact of life. Adopting the Aristotelian ideal means endorsing an 'aristocratic' ethic, and thus siding with Nietzsche in affirming the radical inequality of human beings.

Such an ethic is incompatible, plainly, with modern affirmations of human equality. Nietzsche's critique of post-Christian modernity expressly acknowledges this. Nietzsche rightly sees that as a claim about empirical reality, the assertion of human equality simply flies in the face of the facts. Talents and accomplishments vary greatly. A small proportion of people are highly talented and can claim impressive accomplishments. The vast majority, on the other hand, display no special gifts or accomplishments and lead mundane lives. Declaring human 'equality' to be a moral ideal, from this perspective, is both false and self-deceived. In his own time, Nietzsche was not alone. In a similar spirit, though a slightly different context, the American 'transcendentalist' Ralph Waldo Emerson denounced philanthropic efforts to assist the poor. 'The worst of charity', he wrote, 'is that the lives you are asked to preserve are not worth preserving.'[1] Nietzsche's ideal of the *Übermensch*, like Aristotle's ideal of the *megalopsychos*, is based on the assumption that excellence stands out. Accordingly, it is something that ordinary people will never achieve. It would be foolish, therefore, for them to aspire to it, and by the same token damaging for them to be encouraged to do so.

Aristotelian excellence, we may conclude, could at best be a reasonable hope only for a very small proportion of poor people. Occasional exceptions apart, Aristotle firmly believed the poor cannot reasonably expect to lead good lives. They do not have the resources, the education, or the leisure necessary to do this. Accordingly, the only philosophy of *ordinary* life that an 'aristocratic' conception such as Aristotle's or Nietzsche's could sustain is the fulfilment of inferior status within a hierarchical society. People who lack any real prospect of human excellence should be given the advice Plato effectively gives the denizens of his *Republic*. They ought to admire the superiority of those more gifted and accomplished than themselves, and can take *vicarious* satisfaction in supporting their achievements. The best they can hope for in their own lives, however, is to fulfil the inferior social role to which their limited natural endowments confine them.

III. Relationships

Such a conclusion creates a significant difficulty for the account of human equality developed in the previous chapter. Social inferiors exercise rational agency in carrying out their appointed tasks no less than the social superiors who assign those tasks, and practical wisdom is indispensable to performing their functions well. Our 'common humanity', accordingly, does not render us equal, since it is compatible with gross social inequality. This follows, however, only if overlook the importance of personal relationships.

'Aristocracy', strictly, means 'rule by the best' and it implies, as Nietzsche saw, a rejection of the egalitarianism that the ideals of

---

[1]   Quoted in Linsey McGoey, *No Such Thing as a Free Gift* p.12.

democracy and human rights aim to secure. It rests on the pursuit of 'excellence' as a criterion of worth, and that is why it is sometimes called 'perfectionism'.[2] As a philosophy of the good, its strength lies in the fact that excellence is something it makes no sense to reject. Yet alongside this evident strength, there is a significant limitation. The pursuit of excellence must be focused on activity and achievement, and, just as we found reason to reject 'experience' as the sole constituent of the kind of life we might hope for, so there is reason to hold that 'experience *plus* achievement' does not capture all the key elements of a valuable and meaningful life. Human lives are also marked, and marred, by the relationships in which people stand to each other. Indeed, this is a dimension of existence that the commonplace language of 'dreaming' implicitly affirms, since I can hope, as many do, 'to meet the person of my dreams'. More prosaically, perhaps, I can hope that in the future I will have 'a family of my own'.

By turning our attention to relationships, we not only identify a third element in human wellbeing, but introduce an important counter, both to the psychological egoism that results from too great an emphasis on the value of 'experiences', and to the necessarily hierarchical ordering of 'achievements'. Human beings live their lives within social structures. Some of these they may or may not choose to belong to—clubs, societies, churches, trade unions for instance. Others, though, they are born into— families, neighbourhoods, political communities. This means that relationships between people are both inescapable and essential. Furthermore, as parents, children, brothers, sisters, friends, companions, neighbours, and so on, human beings share a commonality that is broadly indifferent to relative wealth, status, and talent. Love or friendship between two human beings is not *conditional* on their respective prosperity or social status. On the contrary, when such considerations come into play, the relationship is subverted. Attention to the 'born-into' relationships introduces a dimension of human equality that is properly described as 'natural'.

When (to paraphrase Thomas Reid again) I start thinking of my life as a connected whole, and try to make its various parts subservient to one main end that might regulate my future conduct, I certainly pay attention to the experiences I hope to have and the successes I hope to achieve.

---

[2] This name is a little misleading. The pursuit of excellence is compatible with the familiar observation that 'the perfect is the enemy of the good'.

Alongside these, however, are relationships with other people, both those into which I am born and those I hope to form. Love, friendship, collaboration, community, and citizenship all matter to the ends I choose to pursue. While shared experiences and common achievements are important in most human relationships, the relationships themselves cannot be *reduced* to these.

For example, 'love' motivated by anticipated benefits is not love at all. Indeed, when it comes to sexual relationships, this is how love and lust are to be distinguished. Similarly, if I value my friends because of the professional benefits my friendship with them might bring me, or the personal goals it will enable me to accomplish, the 'friendship' is defective, a sham of sorts. The most important relationships are essentially reciprocal, and without this reciprocity they lose the value they might have had. Unlike experiences and achievements, the worth of human relationships is importantly egalitarian. Love between the wealthy is not more valuable or humanly significant than love between the poor. That is why 'love in a cottage' makes just as good a topic for a novel or a play as 'love in a castle'. Joy at the birth of child, grief at the death of a parent, distress at the break-up of a marriage are solid evidence in favour of the claim that there is a dimension to human life whose value has nothing to do with excellence in achievement.

It is less easy to see, but nonetheless true, that this value cannot be explained in terms of valued or valuable experiences either. The phenomenon of grief illustrates this especially well. Great grief is a profoundly negative experience. No one *willingly* undergoes or it seeks it out. Yet at the same time, it is one of the most meaningful aspects of human life. Its importance lies not in the experience, which by the nature of the case is intensely painful and distressing, but in what it signifies. If I grieve deeply at someone's death, it is because my relationship to them was of great value; if I do *not* grieve, it is because the relationship was for the most part a casual one. When someone exhibits intense grief at the death of a student or colleague, say, this is evidence that the relationship was more personal than professional. Love and grief are positively correlated. The greater the love, the greater the grief; the less the grief, the less the love.

Correlations like this show that relationships are more foundational than either experiences or achievements because they relate more directly to the meaning of a human life. This is demonstrated by the contrasting degree of significance that experience, achievement, and relationships are accorded in serious literature. Many good books and epic poems describe exciting journeys and glorious battles, just as first-rate histories record great inventions and recount highly successful expeditions. It is an interesting fact, though, that with a few exceptions, the great 'classics' do not fall into either category. For the most part, the enduring interest of poems, plays, and novels—across many times and places—lies in the human relationships they explore. The novels of Jane Austen are especially striking in this regard. Though widely admired as some of the finest works in English literature, her stories contain virtually nothing in the way of unusual experiences, dramatic adventures, and exceptional achievements. It is a complaint among younger readers, in fact, that 'nothing happens'. This is true. Like Austen herself, all the characters who populate her novels lead very limited lives, conducted within a remarkably narrow social and geographical compass. Since nothing very much ever *happens* outside the established social round, we are left with a question about where their proven interest lies. What is it that places them in the forefront of English literature? The answer lies in the characters Austen invents, and the relationships between them that she depicts and analyses. The two are interconnected, of course. The development of the characters is a function of the relationships in which they stand to each other, and it is a mark of the shallowest characters she brilliantly dissects that they are those least capable of change and development. Austen is especially good at revealing the way in which self-satisfaction closes the mind and stifles the soul.[3]

A similar point can be made about Shakespeare's plays. The 'happenings' that these recount are certainly much more dramatic than anything in Austen. They are replete with battles, shipwrecks, conquests, assassinations, suicides, and murders. Yet it always turns out that these are principally important, not in themselves, but as the setting for memorable characters and complex relationships. Historians can tell us, perhaps, about what it would have been like to experience the Battle of Agincourt, and explain the cause and consequence of the victory over the French that the English secured there. Both themes make their appearance in Shakespeare's *Henry V*, but this is not what lends his drama enduring interest. The 'real' themes in Shakespeare are jealousy, ambition, love,

---

[3] Alasdair MacIntyre discusses the philosophical significance of Austen's novels at length in *After Virtue* Chps 14 and 16.

devotion, betrayal, vanity, and so on. It is these themes that make it possible for the plays to resonate with audiences whose lives and circumstances are centuries apart. Their ability to do this, however, is not to be explained in terms of the experiences or achievements they dramatize. Rather, the experience and achievements the plays enact in poetry and drama are brought into the sphere of *meaning* by their connection with such character traits. The traits, we might say, suffuse the experiences and the achievements. This suffusion is the key to their dramatic power. It can elevate or poison the experiences; it can enhance or undermine the achievement. In other words, it has the ability to make or mar the lives of the *dramatis personae*.

We are now in a better position to see how experiences, achievements, and relationships need to be interconnected. Worthwhile lives include valuable experiences, and almost all human beings have the inclination to accomplish things that matter to them. Yet taken on their own, neither experience nor achievement can constitute an adequate philosophy of ordinary life. That is not just because, as the imaginary 'experience machine' shows, too great an emphasis on valuable experiences risks collapsing into solipsism, or because goals that are very difficult to achieve can still be trivial. Rather, since relatively few lives include extra-ordinary experiences and exceptional achievements, any philosophical explanation of how the lives of unexceptional people can be of intrinsic value both to them and to others must make relationships matter most. Relationships can make ordinary lives as rich (or as impoverished) as the lives of the most exceptional people. Conversely, the most celebrated and award-winning achievements can lose all their allure with the loss of a relationship.[4]

If this is true, aren't the examples from Shakespeare, and from literature more generally perhaps, somewhat misleading? Surely what makes Shakespeare's principal characters so remarkable—Othello, Lear, Hamlet, Lady Macbeth, Leontes, Henry V, and so on—is that they are *not* ordinary. They are caught up in highly dramatic events—affairs of state and natural disasters—and their failures, as well as their achievements, are monumental. Their lives are driven, and destroyed, by 'grand' passions.

---

[4]   This appears to have been the case for the exceptionally accomplished and successful designer, Alexander McQueen, whose name remains a watchword in fashion. In 2010, despite his reputation and success, and following the death of his mother, he took his own life.

How then can they be illuminating examples in thinking about 'the hope of the poor'? Almost without exception the 'ordinary' people who appear in Shakespeare's plays—household servants, gravediggers, messengers, beggars, and so on—are either largely inconsequential, or used as comic foils to the main dramatic action.

Further reflection shows, however, that there is a deep commonality to be found between Shakespearean lives and ordinary lives. It resides in the fact that jealousy, ambition, love, devotion, betrayal, and vanity, integrity, generosity, courage, forbearance, and intolerance, can all be as evident in ordinary lives as they are in the most exceptional lives and dramatic circumstances. The centrality of rational agency which was defended in the previous chapter is a strictly *formal* conception of what it is to be a human being. It is character traits that give content to our common humanity. They do so precisely because they can be expressed, and exhibited, in *any* human relationship. Whether they are rich or poor, powerful or powerless, accomplished or naïve, people share, and show, the same human nature. It is here that the connection with rational agency is to be found. A philosophy of ordinary life lends importance to the suffusion of love, jealousy, and so on because these traits have the capacity to transform, damage, and destroy. Generosity of spirit can transform the humblest action; mean spiritedness can destroy the finest prospects; it is practical wisdom (and the lack of it) that determines which of these outcomes will prevail.

Between ordinary lives and the heroes and heroines of literature there is this difference, certainly. Even the greatest plays and novels aim to be entertaining stories, and while it is common to speak of the course of anyone's life as their 'story', by the nature of the case only in a very few instances is it likely to be an especially entertaining or engrossing one. Lives other than those of saints and heroes do sometimes make compelling stories, but the vast majority of lives do not. The average *biography*, we might say, does not warrant an *obituary*. For all that, every human being does have a 'life' that can be recounted—experiences, accomplishments, and relationships connected within the temporal structure of birth, childhood, maturity, and death. Moreover, their essential nature as rational agents allows them to shape that 'life', because rational agency implies a freedom that merely organic beings do not enjoy. An important question asks how the shaping of life is to be given unity. What integrates the variety of experiences, accomplishments, and relationships into a whole? The answer, I shall claim, is 'vocational dwelling', but what this means must wait for a later chapter.

First, a different topic needs to be addressed. Freedom of action is not freedom from every and any kind of condition. It would be absurd to suggest that rational agents are free to fashion the world in accordance with their desires and wishes. At a minimum, decisions about how to live must take context into account. This context is part biological—variable food supplies, climatic conditions, prevalence of disease—and part historical—the social, cultural, and political conditions into which each individual is born. Since circumstances are so variable, there is a limit to what can be said in general about the context of existence. Still, all human beings find themselves in what is traditionally referred to as 'the human condition'. This is the subject of the next chapter.

Chapter Three

The Human Condition

In Chapter One I defended the (broadly Kantian) idea that we should locate the distinctiveness of human beings, and their fundamental equality, in their capacity for rational agency. The term 'rational agency' may sound abstract and intellectualized, but it refers simply to choosing between possible courses of action in the light of norms and values, both immediately and as part of a short- or long-term strategy. Rational agency is most fully manifested in practical wisdom, which is to say, deliberation that draws on knowledge and skill acquired through past experience, as well as imaginative anticipation of future events. To say that rational agency in accordance with practical wisdom is the basis of our common humanity is not to observe or describe how human beings generally behave. Rather, it is to present a normative ideal, an aim and aspiration of how human beings ought to behave. The relevant contrast is between 'rational' and 'non-rational', not between 'rational' and 'irrational'. This is a point worth emphasizing. To the degree that human beings act rationally, they act wisely. To the degree that they act irrationally, they act foolishly. In both cases they exhibit their rational agency, because non-rational creatures cannot act foolishly any more than they can act wisely.

Irrational behaviour is a form of miscalculation, though not necessarily grounded in straightforward error. It may result from prejudice, superstition, envy, social conformity, or political manipulation, but importantly these are all motivations that only human beings exhibit. In many historical contexts, ranging from the Salem witch hunts through the First World War, Nazi Germany, and Soviet Russia and the global response to Covid, human irrationality can show itself on a massive, collective scale.[1]

---

[1] Mark Woolhouse's 'scientific memoir' of the response to COVID-19 is significantly entitled *The Year the World Went Mad*.

Yet this is no less a demonstration of our agency. No other animal is capable of anything as bad.

I. Practical Wisdom

Intriguingly, mass irrationality often reflects the undue influence of supposed 'expertise'. Such is our belief in historical 'progress', we find this easier to acknowledge with respect to the theological and astrological 'experts' of earlier times and more 'primitive' cultures, than modern 'scientific' experts with their computer models. In fact, the two are much harder to differentiate than is generally supposed. A more important point to make, however, is that though practical wisdom relies in part on empirical knowledge, in general it owes very little to formal expertise, even when this is based on systematic scientific investigation. Like the language we speak, the knowledge we need to make wise decisions is something we pick up and pass on as part of a common stock. The prominence of medical science in modern life has inclined us to think otherwise, since it has (largely) displaced 'folk' medicine. Yet, while it is true that the study of anatomy and physiology has taught us a lot about health and diet, freedom from physical or mental impairment is no guarantee that we will more fully realize the rational agency that con-stitutes our common humanity. Being truly human means more than organic, or even psychological, health. It is an ideal that both underlies and directs elementary socialization, formal education, and personal development. Moreover, as a norm, it always leaves open the possibility that human beings can be 'de-humanized'. The developing child, standardly, is on a trajectory whose proper end is maturity as a fully human being. Yet unhappily it is the case that the way others treat us, and the choices we make, can leave the individual with a very limited or distorted intellectual, emotional, and moral life. Abilities, aptitudes, and sentiments that ought to constitute mature humanity may fail to materialize, or may degenerate, leaving a human being dominated by basic instincts, unmediated emotions, egoistical desires, and a narcissistic view of the self.

It is common to describe human degenerates (in this sense) as having become 'animals'. Yet even the most 'brutalized' people remain, obviously, members of the species *Homo sapiens*. This is further confirma-tion that in this context 'human' and 'animal' are moral, not biological, concepts. Conversely, of course, even in the most adverse circumstances, individuals may successfully resist de-humanization and, despite every plausible prognostication, succeed in affirming their true humanity. Slave narratives often recount this impressive phenomenon, thereby revealing how the human spirit can transcend distorting conditions and overcome the many respects in which a life has fallen far short of Aristotelian 'flourishing'.

Still, even if we think of 'human nature' as a moral rather than a biological concept, practical wisdom must take account of the fact that humans are evolved biological organisms. A flourishing human life is normally one that adequately accommodates both our evolved physiological nature and the natural world that surrounds us. From the point of view of practical wisdom, the truth that we are 'dependent rational animals'[2] is not a result of relatively recent discoveries of evolutionary biology. Human experience tells that we are organic beings with physiological needs like other animals, and reliant on the world around us. In light of these needs, our environment can be divided into two abstract categories — those things that are aids or threats to organic life, and those that are not. We need to drink. This makes springs, rivers, and wells especially valuable to us, but not the vast amount of water in the sea, since it is no use to us for this purpose. We need to eat, but we must not eat hemlock. We are prone to injury, which means that sharp and heavy objects are potentially dangerous in ways that light and soft ones are not. We need protection from extremes of heat and cold, but only some materials have the properties that make them useful for the construction of shelter and the manufacture of clothing. We are vulnerable to some diseases but not all, and this makes certain habitats healthier and less dangerous than others. And so on.

Since the days of the Sophists with whom Plato argued, a sharp distinction has often been drawn between 'facts' and 'values'. Yet terms such as 'healthy', 'dangerous', 'nutritious', and 'poisonous' undermine this familiar distinction. At one and the same time they convey facts about the world — water quenches thirst — and evaluate those facts — fetid water is no good. Within certain parameters, our biological needs are 'givens' that determine the practical relevance of the world. The things that count as physical dangers and nutritious foodstuffs reflect our organic nature, and thus reveal two of the many ways in which our dependence on the natural world is the same as that of other animals. Plants are no less

---

[2] This is the title of a relevant book by Alasdair MacIntyre.

vulnerable to disease than we are, and like us need both moisture and nutrition. So we may say that all living beings share a common 'condition'. This is why an analogical expression taken from the world of plant life — *flourishing* — is so widely and easily applied to human beings. On the other hand, while there are these important considerations, 'the human condition' properly understood points us to a context that is far wider than, and markedly different to, that of other living things. While human beings are biological organisms, from birth to death their lives share a common *non-biological* pattern. At one level 'growing up' is something all organisms do, but in the case of human beings it refers to far more than physical growth and biological development. The route to human maturity has a crucially social element. It requires the acquisition of deliberative and communicative power as a means of adaptive incorporation into a circle of personal relationships. A human being whose organic development is complete may nevertheless remain immature in certain respects. That is why it is possible to use the expression 'Grow up!' as a rebuke.

The circle of relationships into which the maturing individual is drawn steadily widens. The newborn baby is first aware only of its mother, then an extended circle of family and friends, then the neighbourhood in which it lives. Somewhat later, generally, the child becomes aware of a still larger entity — the circle of educational, commercial, and political relationships called 'society'. With a few exceptions, for most human beings society is a circle of *strangers*. That is to say, it comprises people with whom we are not personally acquainted, but with whom we are nevertheless importantly related through language, history, education, law, commerce, and politics. Large numbers of perfect strangers meet in markets, for example, but they still find themselves negotiating and coordinating their needs and interests with each other in ways that generate consequent obligations and opportunities.

The families, tribes, or neighbourhoods into which we are born are not of our own choosing and to this extent are as much 'given' as physical and biological constraints. At the same time, individuals are often able to shape them to some small degree in order to accommodate person-specific interests and desires. Those who live and work in the same small neighbourhood are constantly, usually imperceptibly, accommodating themselves to each other. In extreme circumstances people may be compelled, or choose, to abandon home and family. This, indeed, is the distinguishing mark of refugees and migrants who are separated from the communities into which they were born because they have decided (or been driven) to leave them behind. The larger 'world' in which most urban dwellers find themselves is also one they had no part in making, but it is also one they cannot tailor to their liking.

Both these worlds are 'givens' that we have no choice but to accept. Existentialist philosophers have noted the distinctively human phenomenon of suicide, the ever-present possibility of *exiting* the world. What is strictly impossible however, is *relinquishing* the world. This holds true as much for hermits as for the most sociable of people. It is an inescapable fact of life that the human condition is where I *must* live, if I am to live at all. Furthermore, the natural and the social cannot be separated from each other and it is the human condition that seamlessly connects them. Though the distinction between 'natural' and 'social' can be a useful abstraction, in the reality of our experience, the social and natural aspects of our lives are integrated into a single life for which anthropologists have coined the helpful term 'dwelling'.[3]

Human activity must be organized in acknowledgement of our nature as organisms, but this activity is wrongly construed as a reaction to natural necessities. Rather, in deliberate action what we need, and how we meet that need, are combined in a transformation. Consider the example of bread, widely used as a symbol of basic necessity. For all its symbolic simplicity, the making of bread is in fact a highly complex operation. In the course of growing grain, milling flour, mixing it with other ingredients, and baking it, the 'natural' ingredients that the process uses are completely changed. At one level of description, bread is properly described as food of a very simple kind. More closely considered, it is the sophisticated product of a remarkable exercise in human ingenuity.

Bread is just one illustration of how radically the satisfaction of basic human needs differs from the activities of other creatures in their search for nutrition. As a biological organism, my body requires the nutrition that bread can provide, but the practice of making, selling, buying, and sharing bread goes far beyond what our biology requires. All these are activities in an unmistakably *human* world, so that participation in them sets us apart from the animal kingdom. The careful study of animal

---

3 See Tim Ingold, *The Perception of the Environment: Essays in Livelihood, Dwelling and Skill* (2000). Some of the themes from these essays will be considered again in Chapter Seven.

behaviour has often undermined attempts to make 'reason' or 'tool making' or 'language' the anthropological difference that sets human beings apart, because the behaviour of other animals—not just chimpanzees, but creatures as varied as dogs, pigs, crows, and elephants —can be strikingly intelligent. Nevertheless, no other animals cook the food they find, and this makes cookery an especially telling indicator of the way in which human beings have set themselves apart from other species. Humans integrate their organic needs and felt desires with natural resources, thereby calling into existence a single 'world' of experience that is not the world of any other creature. Eating and drinking are no less biologically necessary for human beings than for other animals, but human activity has transformed the means by which they are satisfied. In German, the difference is incorporated in the language—'essen' when humans eat, 'fressen' when animals do. Of course, a human being can eat ravenously like an animal, but this just serves to show yet again that 'being human' is not a matter of biology.

The same point can be made about dress. What other creature has secured protection from the elements by creating fabrics, still less the extraordinary range and quality of fabrics and profusion of styles that constitute the world of human dress? The Bible invites is to 'Consider the lilies of the field, how they grow: they neither toil nor spin, yet even Solomon in all his glory was not arrayed like one of these' (*Matthew* 6:28.9). The text is making an important point about materialism, but for all that, 'arrayed' when applied to a field of flowers remains the extension of a concept that has its home in human life. Solomon could try (perhaps misguidedly) to vie with the lilies of the field; the lilies could not vie with him.

In this way the 'world' is neither a natural environment nor a social organization. It is an inseparable integration of the two. The social element is not any less independent of us than the natural, because it too is something into which we are 'thrown' (to use Heidegger's useful term). Still, while not of our making, it is not a wholly alien environment either. Having been shaped by a long history of human effort, ingenuity, and purpose, it is a fit habitation. Our lives are conditioned by limits, demands, opportunities, and challenges that we cannot ignore, and that we must somehow accommodate. These conditions, on the other hand, are themselves the outcome of indefinitely many previous human accommodations. That is why it is right to identify the world in which we live as 'the *human* condition', a place in which we are both compelled and able to make our 'dwelling'.

Sometimes people identify the 'world' with the earth as a biosphere or the cosmos as a physical system. They are then misled into thinking that the natural sciences give special insight into how we must live. This is a mistake. The 'world' is neither earth nor cosmos, but the context within which we must pursue life. This makes knowledge of its character an essentially practical matter. Newborn infants, unlike all other neonates, have no ability to secure the things that are essential for their survival. The remarkable degree to which they are vulnerable means that their only hope lies in the providential actions that other humans perform for their sake and on their behalf. From the moment of birth, what happens to infants and how they fare is the outcome of deliberative action, but not on the part of the infant. The modern form of rationalism that looks to science and technology for solutions to practical problems can make us forget that human beings were able to care successfully for their young long before systematic inquiry taught us anything about nutrition and hygiene. Practical deliberation, whether on our own behalf or on behalf of others, is an inescapable aspect of action, and thus a feature of human life in every time and place. Science and technology owe their existence to practical reason, and practical wisdom is necessary to control and assess their value. This truth is importantly at odds with the idea that practical reason can be significantly improved if it is made more 'scientific', an idea that has had currency and influence since the eighteenth century, and one to which we will return in the next chapter.

Children become deliberative agents at a very early stage, and they learn to do many things without much reflection—speaking a language, for instance. When, like the students Reid was addressing, they do reach sufficient maturity to engage in critical reflection, they can begin to formulate more extended plans and projects. Acting, choosing, delibera- ting, and especially planning all require that we have some grasp on how, and to what extent, the human condition is supportive or hostile to our actions, plans, and projects. Such a grasp requires that we possess a *con- ception* of the world in which we find ourselves. This is not a *theory* of any kind, but what Wittgenstein calls, in a slightly different context, a *picture* of the world. 'My picture of the world', he says, is an 'inherited back- ground' and 'the propositions describing [it] might be part of a kind of mythology'(*On Certainty* §§94–5). Such a 'picture' is generally implicit rather than explicit, and, as Wittgenstein's allusion to mythology suggests, it may be embodied in stories and fables. Nevertheless, what-ever form it takes, the possession of such a conception is essential if we are to act. That is because such a conception gives us a practical orienta-tion to the human condition. Here again we can note a difference from other animals. Guided by feeling, instinct, and habit, they act responsively to the world, often very successfully; but they have no conception of it.

How are we to frame such a conception? And by what standards is its adequacy to be assessed? In one sense, no answer is required to the first of these questions. Our understanding of the human condition is, as Wittgenstein's says, a background that is *inherited* — through the language we learn, the practices we master, and the knowledge that we acquire. Wittgenstein, who deploys this concept for more narrowly philosophical purposes than those that concern us here,[4] thinks that we logically *cannot* satisfy ourselves of the 'correctness' of our 'picture of the world' because there is nothing against which we could measure its correctness. At one level, this seems right. Our understanding of 'the human condition', like the language we speak, is something we simply find ourselves possessing. It is impossible that it should be otherwise. Yet this does not put it beyond either criticism and revision. Let us agree with Wittgenstein that it is absurd to suppose we could invent our 'picture of the world' *de novo*. That is what he means by calling it 'mythological'. Yet the pertinence of this description does not license the erroneous inference that we cannot meaningfully articulate, examine, affirm, and abandon specific elements within our inherited picture of the world.

II. Pictures and Myths

In contemporary English, the term 'myth' often implies falsehood. A myth, in this narrow sense, is a belief, usually about the past, that is not borne out by the evidence. This narrow sense, however, fails to capture the real character of the great mythological stories that have been told and re-told over thousands of years. These myths are not, and were never intended to be, narratives based on historical evidence. The ancient Greeks did not think the stories they told about the gods on Olympus were 'literally' true, and the Norse myths were never understood to be historical in the way that we now conceive of history. Myths about

---

4 I discuss these issues at length in *Wittgenstein and Natural Religion* (Oxford University Press, 2015).

ancient gods are not erroneous histories, because they are not histories at all.

It follows that understanding the power and importance of myths in this broader sense is not a matter of assessing their historical accuracy. In general, it is more profitable to think of myths as 'living' or 'dead' rather than 'true' or 'false'. What is of greatest interest about them is whether, and in what ways, they continue to be relevant to human lives. *Living* myths are those that capture a thought or idea that seems to say something illuminating about the human condition. *Dead* myths are those that, whatever other interest they may have, no longer do this. So, for instance, the spiritual world of Yggdrasil and the Norse gods is now no more than a source of entertaining fables. Some of the ancient Greek myths, on the other hand, can still 'speak' to modern ways of thinking. Consider the myth of Sisyphus. Homer recounts this myth several hundred years before the birth of Christ. Yet nearly three thousand years later, Albert Camus could publish an essay with this title, thereby revealing its continuing resonance for twentieth-century ways of thinking about life and meaning. Sisyphus, king of Corinth, is punished by the gods for self-aggrandizement. Forced to roll a huge boulder uphill only to watch it roll back, he is condemned to repeat this action for eternity. The myth provides Camus with a powerful image of human life as filled with futile toil, and thus illuminates some of the existentialist themes with which he was concerned.

The story of Prometheus is another Greek myth that continues to resonate with us. It paints a not dissimilar picture of life, though with an interesting further twist. Prometheus, the Titan god who creates humankind, does so, not with the blessing, but in defiance of Zeus, king of the gods on Mount Olympus. Prometheus bestows benefits on the race he has created, one of which is fire. But this particular benefit has to be *stolen* from the home of the gods. While the myth of Sisyphus depicts the human condition as one that is indifferent to the efforts and hopes of human beings, the story of Prometheus goes a step further, construing the world as essentially hostile to human efforts and hopes. It is this second, darker, conception that the great Greek tragedies of Aeschylus, Sophocles, and Euripides reflect. They rely on the idea of a world so hostile in its nature that it can subvert and overthrow even the wisest human actions, and frustrate even the best human intentions. Pictured in this way, the human condition makes these famous figures *tragic* heroes, and it is not hard to relate to their tragic character. Shakespeare, in fact, gives memorable expression to much the same idea when, in *King Lear*, he has Gloucester say 'As flies to wanton boys are we to the gods. They kill us for their sport.'

Some versions of the Promethean myth, it is true, wrest a kind of hope by making Prometheus's defiance a symbol of the resolute determination (found in part in Nietzsche's *Übermensch*) that alone will allow exceptional human beings to accept and confront the hostility of the world. But the optimism embodied in this modified version still falls far short of the more subtle picture presented by another ancient, enduring, and even more influential myth — the story of Adam and Eve in the Garden of Eden. Unlike the Greek myths, this one has sometimes been thought to be 'literally' true, though not as often as those who reject it tend to assume. For present purposes, however, its importance — whether believed to be 'literally' true or not — is the way in which it embodies, and has served to reinforce, a picture of the human condition as essentially *hospitable* to the aspirations and actions of human beings. Originally, as *Genesis* tells the story, human beings lived in paradise — a place where a divinely created order supplied every natural need. The perfection of paradise was ruptured when Adam, or 'Man', succumbed to temptation, and sought the ultimate knowledge of good and evil that God had reserved to himself. This 'Fall' led to humanity's expulsion from paradise, and as a result, human beings were cast out into a world marked by both sin and suffering. Expelled from Eden, Adam and Eve (and all their human progeny) encounter hunger, pain, labour, frustration, envy, pride, illness, and death. This harsh world is now the place in which are obliged to live. Yet it is not without hope of redemption.

Two features of the *Genesis* myth are of special interest here. First, the hope that it holds out — even if it is one made possible chiefly by divine grace — is the prospect of transforming or transcending the human condition. Paradise cannot be restored as it originally was, but the world can nevertheless become 'home' again. Second, and more importantly for our immediate purposes, the *Genesis* story conceives of the world, both before and after the Fall, as a place with human beings at its centre. However greatly Adam and Eve may have gone astray, and however many other wonderful things God may have chosen to create, the world was *made for* humanity, and retains that character. Even though most of creation came into existence before human beings, humanity is nonetheless its crowning achievement. This pre-eminence is revealed in Adam's being given the privilege of naming the animals, and being explicitly accorded 'dominion' over them. Even after humanity's hubristic pride has prompted a cleansing Flood sweeping most of it away, this mandate is renewed to the 'saving remnant' of Noah and his descendants, for whom the rainbow becomes a symbol of perpetual hope.

Humanity's superior status within creation implies that, however burdensome life may be, and however hostile the natural environment may appear to be, the human condition is ultimately a benign one. In other words, deep down, creation works *for* us, not *against* us. If so, then human effort and aspiration can draw practical support from 'the world' since it is set up to be humanity's home. The conviction that humanity's wellbeing is the central purpose of the whole creation can lead to complacency. But it can also lead to wonder, the source of veneration. 'What is Man that that you should be mindful of him?', the Psalmist asks God. 'You have made him little lower than the angels and given him mastery over the works of your hands' (*Psalm* 8). The context makes it plain that this observation is neither intended, nor expected, to engender human pride. Its purpose is to elicit awe at the mystery of divine election.

The basic elements of this cosmological myth are shared by the three great religions of the book—Judaism, Christianity, and Islam—and by their cultural descendants. Such a cosmology is not universal, however. The alternative conception of the human condition embodied in the Greek myths alerts us to the fact that while myths are not histories, they are nonetheless subject to critical reflection. Though mythical, they aim to make sense of the world as we experience it, and so are subject to scrutiny in the light of that experience. The story of Adam and Eden tells us that the deepest structure of creation is benign. How is this idea to be squared with recurrent life experiences in which good and prudent people fail miserably, while wicked and foolish people not infrequently prosper?

> Were a stranger to drop, in a sudden, into this world. I would show him, as a specimen of its ills, an hospital full of diseases, a prison crowded with malefactors and debtors, a field of battle strowed with carcasses, a fleet floundering in the ocean, a nation languishing under tyranny, famine, or pestilence. To turn the gay side of life to him, and give him a notion of its pleasures; whither should I conduct him? To a ball, to an opera, to court? He might justly think that I was only showing him a diversity of [i.e. diversion from] distress and sorrow. (Hume, *Dialogues* Part X)

This is how Hume has Philo describe the human condition in his posthumously published *Dialogues Concerning Natural Religion*. The description is not the result of systematic empirical investigation, but neither is it the outcome of imaginative invention. It is a reflection grounded in experience. The Greek myths capture this gloomy picture, and the logical point that its articulation enables Philo to make is a simple one. There does not seem to be a sufficiently consistent correlation between practical wisdom and material success to sustain the Genesis picture of the world as an anthropocentrically benign place. If the human condition were as *Genesis* depicts it, Philo contends, things would go better for human beings than they do.

Myths, then, are not histories, but they are nonetheless open to critical reflection. Yet the experiences to which they appeal are never decisive. In attempting to decide between a benign and a hostile picture of the world, the balance of evil over good is hard to calculate. Indeed, as Philo himself remarks, it may be impossible 'to compute, estimate, compare all the pains and all the pleasures in the lives of all men and of all animals'. This observation works both ways, of course. Even if we agree with Philo that experience seems to count against the idea of a benign universe, it does not thereby favour the alternative conception—a world actively hostile to human welfare and organized in ways that systematically thwart it. The *Dialogues* articulate this very thought.

> There may be *four* hypotheses framed concerning the first causes of the universe: *that* they are endowed with perfect goodness, *that* they have perfect malice, *that* they are opposite and have both goodness and malice, *that* they have neither goodness nor malice. Mixed phenomena can never prove the two former unmixed principles. And the uniform and steadiness of general laws seem to oppose the third. The fourth, therefore, seems by far the most probable. (*Dialogues* Part XI, italics original)[5]

In short, Philo (and Hume probably) concludes that nature's moral *indifference* is the only rational conclusion to be drawn from the evident mix of good and evil that we find in the world. This means that the human condition plays no active role in either human prosperity or human adversity. It simply is what it is. Our only choice is to make the best of it according to our lights and opportunities.

III. Geocentrism and Anthropocentrism

Hume was writing at a time when most people still took the *Genesis* picture of the human condition very seriously. He was not, however, a solitary voice. His scepticism reflected important intellectual movements,

---

5   I discuss the problem of evil at length in *Evil and Christian Ethics* (Cambridge University Press, 2001).

especially in physics and astronomy, that had slowly been undermining the intellectual hegemony of Christian theology. It is important to distinguish, however, between *anthropocentric* and *geocentric* conceptions of the world. Our eyes appear to tell us that the sun goes around the earth, so it is a natural assumption that the earth is at the heart of the solar system, and by extension, the centre of the cosmos.

Ancient astronomers had not always made this geocentric assumption. As early as the third century BCE, the Greek philosopher/scientist Aristarchus of Samos had posited a heliocentric universe. But in early modern Europe geocentrism was a fundamental assumption. Consequently, when the astronomer Nicholas Copernicus (1473–1543) challenged it, he met with fierce resistance. By displacing the earth from the centre of the solar system, he inaugurated what soon came to be identified as a 'Copernican Revolution' in scientific thinking. Copernicus himself was not motivated by anti-Christian sentiment, or even religious radicalism. On the contrary, he served faithfully as a canon of the Catholic Church throughout his life, and his astronomical speculations were generated entirely out of his interest in resolving some long-standing puzzles concerning the movement of the heavenly bodies. It seems that it was fear of ridicule, not religious persecution, that made him hesitate to publish his heliocentric conclusions. Finally, just before his death in 1543, his book *On the Revolutions of the Celestial Spheres* appeared in print. The change in human understanding that this book eventually brought about was immense, and in Hume's day, two hundred years later, the once revolutionary alternative to geocentrism had become astronomical orthodoxy.

Some of Copernicus's contemporaries supposed, as many have since, that heliocentrism implies the demotion of humanity from the privileged position within Creation that *Genesis* accords it. This partly explains how Galileo, almost a century after Copernicus, could still be prosecuted and convicted for heresy. He was, the charge said, expressly 'following the position of Copernicus', which according to the Pope at the time was 'contrary to the true sense and authority of Holy Scripture', though this view was based on a single verse from Psalm 93, which says 'The earth is established immovably.' The condemnation did not last, and though heliocentrism was accepted, *Genesis* retained its authority. That is because the picture it paints is anthropocentric, not geocentric. The two ideas are logically distinct. There is no life on the sun. Consequently, neither the earth's stability nor the sun's centrality to the planetary system, of which earth is a small part, implies anything whatever about the importance or otherwise of life in general, and human life in particular. Astronomy has advanced enormously since the time of Copernicus, and revealed to us how tiny, relative to the cosmos, the earth is. Yet it remains the case that the most sophisticated thing in the known universe—humankind—is uniquely located on earth.

It is true, nonetheless, that the demise of geocentrism had a dramatic and widespread *psychological* effect. A century after Hume, in Gifford lectures devoted to the philosophy of theism, Alexander Campbell Fraser eloquently articulates how heliocentrism (combined with Darwinian biology) had pushed anthropocentrism aside in the way the modern mind had come to see things (and sees them still, largely). The starting point of Fraser's lectures is the question he had asked since his earliest forays into philosophy. 'What is the deepest and truest interpretation that can be put upon the world in which I found myself participating when I became percipient, and with which I have been in contact or collision ever since I began to live? Ought a benign meaning or a malign meaning be put upon it?' (*Philosophy of Theism*, p.4). On this topic the demise of geocentrism seems highly relevant.

> How can so grand a spectacle as modern astronomy puts before us be supposed by any reasoning being to have for its final cause the convenience of short-lived animals who somehow find their home on this small planet—transitory in their successive generations... as the leaves which yearly appear and disappear on the trees in the forest?... The progress of modern astronomy has been a running commentary on the local insignificance of men, when men are thought of only as individual organisms in the immensity of space. What is the human body, invisible from another planet, in comparison with the infinite material world? (*Philosophy of Theism*, p.50)

Humanity, astronomy has shown us, is set within a vast universe. Yet, incontrovertible though this demonstration may be, the further thought—or feeling—that, science having demonstrated our 'local insignificance', we must accept reality's indifference to human life, is neither implied nor confirmed by the findings of astronomy. There is no logical bar to supposing that the whole of the cosmos, however immense, finds its ultimate purpose in emergent human beings and their welfare. It is evident, nevertheless, that for many people advances in astronomy and biology have rendered the belief in an anthropocentric world—a world built around human purposes—much less plausible than it was when the earth was believed to be at the centre of the solar system. Still, the obstacle to believing in an anthropocentric world is psychological, not logical. That is why recent discussions of the 'fine tuning' of the universe and 'the anthropic principle' as an explanation of it, despite the interest and intensity they have generated, are strictly irrelevant to the question of life's value and significance.[6]

The idea of a metaphysically indifferent world long predates the discoveries of modern physics or astronomy. A picture of the human condition that had hostility or indifference written into the creation and government of the world was the theme of many myths of the classical world that had no source in astronomical observations. Similarly, what we might call 'a cosmology of indifference' is easily identified in the religions of the East. The human condition for Hinduism and Buddhism is conceived as a perpetual cosmic cycle structured by the principles of *karma* (law of consequences) and *metempsychosis* (reincarnation). These fundamental principles tie human beings to an endless round of birth and rebirth in which there is no respite. Humanity's plight, on this picture, is not wholly dissimilar to the fate of Sisyphus, and its best hope, accordingly, is *moksha*, escape from *samsara* (endless wandering) and release into *nirvana*, which is to say *liberation from being* through the *dissolution of being*.

For present purposes, we can usefully stay with the cosmological metaphysics that modern science appears to support—a universe that by its nature is indifferent to human projects, aspirations, and anxieties. An 'agnostic' (the term expressly coined in this connection by Thomas Huxley) is someone who finds neither evidence of a benign omnipotent agency committed to our greater good, nor evidence of a malevolent demon determined to thwart or destroy us. The world in which we live, from this agnostic point of view, cannot be evaluated as either good or bad *intrinsically*, but only in virtue of the things that interest and concern us as human beings. The natural world operates to our benefit or to our detriment to the degree that we make it do so. Bacteria that cause disease, for instance, are in themselves entirely neutral. They simply act as they act. Of course, using our knowledge of their behaviour, we can devise ways of protecting ourselves against them and we can fail in our attempts to do so. Success in this respect is of great value to us, and failure is costly,

---

6   A valuable collection of essays addressing many of the issues is Neil A. Manson, ed., *God and Design: The Teleological Argument and Modern Science* (Routledge, 2003).

but it would be absurd to suppose that either appears to bacteria in this way. It is even more absurd to attribute such an attitude to the vast universe that contains them.

For the moment, let us embrace this agnostic picture as an accurate conception of the world in which we live. What implications does that have for practical reason? One important point to emphasize, especially if our ultimate concern is with the hope of the poor, is that the moral indifference of the universe does not make human interests matter any less than they would if we believed otherwise. It merely says that human interests matter only to human beings themselves. The fact (if it is one) that the laws of nature are completely indifferent to our interests does not license any indifference on our own part. Nor, actually, does it do anything from a practical point of view to alter the human condition. Poverty and prosperity, health and sickness, knowledge and ignorance, all remain precisely as they were, and so does the practical problem concerning them, namely, how to ensure that the positive wins out over the negative, that wisdom is better than folly. Even if we have been psychologically compelled by the discoveries of modern astronomy to relinquish an anthropocentric conception of the world, the task of ameliorating the human condition remains. The sole practical implication is that now, in trying to accomplish it, we have only our own energy and ingenuity to rely on.

IV. The Baconian Vision

The agnostic foregoes any appeal to what we might call the inherent helpfulness of the world. Is there anything else that might aid us in responding effectively to the challenges with which the human condition presents us? The most common modern answer to this question is technological innovation based on scientific knowledge. Interestingly, this 'solution' is also a product of the revolution in ideas that undermined the picture of Adam, Eden, and the Fall. Science and religion are nowadays so independent of each other that they are often held to stand in opposition. Yet the roots of modern science, as intellectual historians have often observed, are to be found in Christian theology. The possibility of science rests on the supposition that the physical world has an intelligible structure waiting to be uncovered and understood. Without such a supposition, science is a fruitless endeavour. The origin of this crucial supposition is to be found in the *Genesis* story of creation, but as science developed, this source gradually faded from consciousness.[7]

A key figure in this intellectual development was the scientist-philosopher Francis Bacon (1561–1626). Bacon was a man of prodigious abilities, a successful lawyer and a brilliant writer who rose to one of the highest political positions in England—Lord Chancellor. In 1621, however, charges of corruption led to his fall from grace.[8] Throughout it all—struggle, success, and infamy—and especially in the forced retirement of the last years of his life, he wrote copiously on a vast range of subjects—religion, law, politics, philosophy, research, and education. His enduring reputation rests largely on *The Advancement of Learning*, two volumes published in 1605. The purpose of this book, Bacon says in a letter, was to purge learning of 'frivolous disputations' and promote 'industrious observations, grounded conclusions, and profitable inventions and discoveries' (Bacon, *The Major Works*, p.577). It is this ambition, and the vigour with which his two volumes pursue it, that made him a founding figure in modern science. Far from abandoning the picture of the world as fallen Creation, however, Bacon himself (like Isaac Newton) whole-heartedly subscribed to the picture. Indeed, his belief in the value of science was expressly underwritten by his theological conception of the world. Bacon's role in the development of science was twofold. First, his writings favoured scientific experimentation above (what he regarded as) the arid methods of logical deduction and verbal distinction characteristic of the 'natural philosophy' of 'the schoolmen' which had hitherto prevailed. Secondly, his social position enabled him to play a key part in establishing one of the first institutions to be expressly devoted to scientific research, namely the Royal Society of London.

> I do not pronounce upon anything [Bacon writes]. I set down and prescribe but only provisionally... I sometimes make attempts at interpretation... [but] what need have I of pride or imposture seeing that I so often declare that we are not furnished with so much history or experiments as we want

---

[7] A very powerful case can still be made for thinking that the intelligibility of natural science still requires theological underpinning. See, for instance, Alvin Plantinga, *Where the Conflict Really Lies: Science, Religion and Naturalism* (OUP, 2011).

[8] The case against Bacon was more likely the result of political machination than the pursuit of justice. By the standards of the time, the bribes he accepted were few and modest.

and that without these the interpretation of nature cannot be accomplished.
(*Abecedarium naturæ*, quoted in Butterfield, *Origins of Modern Science*, p.90)

This captures one of Bacon's key contentions — that the science of his day
was seriously lacking in experimental data, and without better data,
'interpretations' (i.e. theories) of nature were at best highly provisional.
The 'Baconian method', accordingly, avoided any a priori pronounce-
ments and laid great emphasis on the role of experiments in the
acquisition of knowledge.

The truth about the revolutionary nature of Bacon's method, and about
the studies of 'natural philosophy' (physics) before his time, is more
complex than this familiar story implies. Bacon's advocacy of experimentation was undoubtedly influential in the transformation that the
natural sciences underwent over the succeeding two centuries. At the
same time, previous attempts to rely on empirical observation alone and
in the absence of 'abstract' mathematical techniques had accomplished
relatively little. Moreover, the continued use of 'thought experiments',
together with the development of mathematics (above all in the hands of
Newton) proved no less significant for the advancement of science.[9]
Indeed, the history of modern astronomy clearly illustrates the need for,
and the benefit to be derived from, the interplay between theorizing and
observation. While Copernicus was primarily a mathematician and a
theorist, the next major figure, Tycho Brahe (1546–1601), was less
theoretically venturesome but devised greatly superior means of
gathering observational data than him. Without Copernicus's theory,
Tycho's data would have lacked the significance they were soon seen to
have. Without the data, on the other hand, the theory would have lacked
substance.[10]

Bacon's contrast between abstract theorizing and observational data,
then, should not be overstated. The history of science shows that both are
needed. Equally, it is no less a mistake to suppose that Bacon's advocacy
of empirical fact finding as the basis of knowledge signalled a rejection of
natural or revealed theology. On the contrary, his two important volumes
are expressly entitled 'the advancement of Learning, *divine* and *humane*'
(emphasis added) and he incorporated the fundamentals of orthodox

---

[9] See Butterfield Chapters V and VI.
[10] See Dava Sobel, *A More Perfect Heaven: How Copernicus Revolutionised the
     Cosmos* (2012).

Christian theology in a personal *Confession of Faith*. Published after his death, though composed many years before, this Confession expressly endorses the doctrine that 'God created heaven and earth... and gave unto them constant and everlasting laws which we call Nature.' These laws, Bacon held, persisted through the Fall ('the curse') 'which notwithstanding was no new creation, but a privation of part of the virtue of the first creation' (*Bacon: The Major Works*, p.108). Bacon believed, in other words, that the Fall deprived human beings of their original God-given *dominion* over nature, while leaving in place the law-governed character of the natural world. Consequently, nature remained something that humanity could still aspire to manipulate. What this needed was knowledge of the laws of nature.

Human foolishness has hitherto made us powerless to control the conditions of life, but properly conducted scientific investigation can empower us. 'The advancement of learning' would enable us not only to understand the workings of nature's laws, but to turn them to our practical advantage and so enable us to ameliorate the human condition. This is the idea that underlies the Baconian slogan (which does not seem to have originated with Bacon himself) 'Knowledge is Power' — power, that is to say, to control nature to our benefit.

If the true impact of the Baconian *method* is uncertain, there is no doubt that over time the Baconian *vision* of the human condition proved hugely influential. Aristotle had held that the most perfect form of knowledge to which the human mind could aspire is theoretical rather than practical. Science, on his account, is no less a mode of contemplation than the knowledge of God that medieval theologians sought. In modern times we might be more inclined to express this by saying that scientific knowledge is valuable purely for its own sake. Bacon's view of science contrasts with all these. Knowing and understanding the world around us is important first and foremost for what it allows us to *do*. That is the meaning of the slogan 'knowledge is power', and if it is not Bacon's own, it is nonetheless appropriately attributed to him. The power that knowledge gives us is the power to make life better for ourselves, despite the Fall. This clearly has implications for beliefs about our reliance on God and our final destiny, but it does not render them either false or redundant.

Bacon's own vision located the value of science and technology within a theological framework of thought. It was later thinkers who separated the two. In the lectures on theism previously cited, Campbell Fraser charts the subsequent rise of agnosticism. But he begins by noting Bacon's own contention that 'depth in philosophy alone bringeth men's minds to religion; for while the mind of man looketh upon second causes [i.e. physical causes] scattered, it may sometimes rest in them and go no further; but when it beholdeth the chain of them confederate and linked together, it must needs fly to Providence and Deity' (quoted in *Philosophy of Theism*, p.110). Fraser follows this quotation by citing passages from the two greatest philosophers of the period—Descartes and Locke—in which they assert both the certainty of God's existence and its indispensability for the scientific enterprise. His point is that modern agnosticism constitutes a huge shift in *scientific* opinion, and a major part of this shift of opinion is the separation of Bacon's vision of science from its original theological context. A further step in the 'liberation' of science from theology (and in the end their mutual alienation) is to be found in the rise of a widespread belief that separation from theology is essential to the full realization of the Baconian vision. That is to say, the ability of scientific knowledge to bring real practical benefits relies on its being conducted quite independently of the theological trappings it may once have had. Avowed atheism is not required, but theological neutrality is. This is a belief that Bacon himself would not have condoned, but in this respect modern science has left him behind.

V. Neo-Baconianism

The contemporary version of the Baconian vision, which I shall call neo-Baconianism, holds that a properly scientific approach to the problems presented by the human condition is possible only with the complete autonomy of the scientific enterprise from religious presuppositions. Both the natural and the social sciences are sources of knowledge, which, applied to the problems of the human condition, offer humanity's best hope, and thereby the best hope of the poor.

Some of neo-Baconianism's presuppositions can be found at work in *The Great Escape*, an important book by the economist and Nobel Laureate Angus Deaton. The 'escape' that Deaton describes and investigates is the remarkable and rapidly accelerating improvement in human wellbeing that has taken place over the last 250 years, and especially since the end of World War I. Some of the more detailed issues with which his book deals are topics for the next chapter. For now it is worth recording his view that an important stimulus for this huge improvement is to be found in the eighteenth century's adoption of the Baconian vision. Deaton believes, with Bacon, that knowledge is critically important to material progress. If we consider the 'division of credit for increases in wellbeing between income and knowledge', he says, we will find that 'knowledge is the key', and though the huge rise in incomes is undoubtedly important, 'it is not the ultimate cause of wellbeing' (*The Great Escape*, p.41).

Deaton expressly endorses the view of Roy Porter in *The Creation of the Modern World* — that the process in which he is interested was triggered at a particular historical juncture. This was a point in time

> when people stopped asking 'How can I be saved?'... and asked instead 'How can I be happy?' People began to seek personal fulfillment, rather than seeking virtue through obedience to the church... Happiness could be pursued by using reason to challenge accepted ways of doing things... and by finding ways of improving one's life, including both material possessions and health. Immanuel Kant defined the Enlightenment by the mottoes: 'Dare to know! Have the courage to use your understanding.' During the Enlightenment, people risked defying accepted dogma and were more willing to experiment with new techniques and ways of doing things. One of the ways in which people began to use their own understanding was in medicine and fighting disease, trying out new treatments. (*The Great Escape*, p.84)

As an account of the Enlightenment and its relation to the development of science, technology, and religion, this is, at best, a considerable simplification. Who exactly are the 'people' who stopped asking one question in favour of another? Perhaps David Hume fits Deaton's picture, but several important Enlightenment thinkers were practising Christians, and some of them were clergymen. Francis Hutcheson, for instance, the philosopher often hailed as the 'Father' of the Scottish Enlightenment, was a Presbyterian minister, as was Thomas Reid. Immanuel Kant's adherence to Christianity is less clear, but his celebrated essay 'What is Enlightenment?' makes freedom of thought, not the abandonment of religion, the key to enlightenment. Indeed, Kant heralds the prospect of enlightenment *within* religion as much as within any other sphere of thought, because the enemy of Enlightenment on his account is intellectual laziness, not religious belief.

Still, Deaton is endorsing a contention that has been widely advanced and no less widely accepted. Its importance in the present context is twofold. First, it neatly articulates the idea that the Baconian vision of knowledge as power really came into its own when, in opposition to the ecclesiastical authorities who defended it, it was endorsed as an alternative to the traditional theological picture of the human condition that had hitherto prevailed. Second, the fact that a celebrated economist invokes it is enough to show that the idea of 'knowledge as power' still has considerable traction in the serious study of material progress in the lives of human beings. Deaton, moreover, is not engaged in economic history for its own sake. He aims to throw helpful light, if he can, on how the lot of the poor in the twenty-first century can be alleviated and improved. It is useful knowledge that he offers us.

The first topic in *The Great Escape* is health, and how the truly remarkable decline in deaths from infectious diseases that the world has witnessed since 1700 is to be explained. An especially striking instance is smallpox. For centuries, smallpox was a scourge of humanity and the cause of innumerably many deaths, both in the course of ordinary lives and in terrifying epidemics that devastated whole populations. By the late twentieth century, it had not only been brought under control, but completely eliminated, its global eradication being formally declared in 1979. It seems that there could hardly be a clearer instance of a change in medical practice bringing about a radical amelioration in the human condition. It is important to note, however, that the case of smallpox does not quite fit the broader Baconian picture in which scientific investigation produces the knowledge that makes the difference. Deaton confirms the familiar claim that inoculation for smallpox was dramatically effective. By 1800, the number of smallpox deaths per baptism in London had fallen by half, and whereas '[s]mallpox epidemics in Boston had killed more than 10 percent of the population in the late 1600s... there were relatively few smallpox deaths after 1750.' However, the technique of inoculation is not dependent on the discoveries of science. In fact, Deaton himself observes that the dramatic decline in deaths from smallpox was (most probably) the result of adopting *variolation* (scratching healthy people with material from infected people) which, he tells us, was 'an ancient technique, practiced in China and India for more than a thousand years' (*The Great Escape*, pp.85–6). The decline, then, was not the result of the modern, much more sophisticated, technique of *vaccination*, since this was only invented by Edward Jenner in 1799.[11] A similar point can be made with respect to the decline in other infectious diseases, together with the corresponding decrease in infant mortality and increase in life expectancy that followed. While Deaton thinks that there is 'a plausible case' for thinking

---

[11] Vaccination is safer and more effective, but its full impact took a long time. There were an estimated 2 million deaths from smallpox as recently as the year 1967.

that effective innovations were 'born of the new openness to trial and error' he is clear that:

> Decreased child mortality cannot have had much to do with medical treatments, such as new medicines or drugs such as antibiotics, sulfa drugs or streptomycin for tuberculosis, in part because most of the decrease in mortality took place before such treatments were available, and in part because the introduction of the drugs did not result in any sharp changes in mortality from the diseases that they treat. The founder of social medicine, the Englishman Thomas McKeown, drew a series of famous diagrams showing for a whole series of diseases that mortality rates were falling before the introduction of the effective treatment, and continued to fall at much the same rate after its introduction. (*The Great Escape*, p.91)

So despite first appearances, these dramatic improvements in human health do not sustain the Baconian vision in quite the way that they are commonly thought to do. Just as it is not the case that religious beliefs invariably obstruct material progress, so it is not the case that the astonishing improvement in health and life expectancy the modern world has witnessed over the last three centuries can be shown to be the result of a new empowerment made possible by the rise of empirical science.

This fact is not sufficient to disprove neo-Baconianism, of course, because other contexts present further possibilities—improvements in agriculture and nutrition for example. The eighteenth century saw the creation of many societies whose aim was to promote 'scientific' farming, which is to say, a better approach to the production of crops and livestock. This ambition is another topic for the next chapter, but here it is relevant to note that the term 'scientific' in this context does not refer to specialized knowledge so much as to more systematic practical organization. Nor is Deaton inclined to give 'science' as we now think of it the greater part of the credit in this kind of context either.

> The major credit for the decrease in child mortality and the resultant increase in life expectancy must go to the control of disease through public health measures. At first this took the form of improvements in sanitation and in water supplies. Eventually *science caught up with practice* and the germ theory of disease was understood and gradually implemented, through more focused, scientifically based measures. (*The Great Escape*, p.93, emphasis added)

'Science catching up with practice' does not resonate very well with the slogan 'knowledge as power'. Still, modern proponents of the Baconian vision can accept that Deaton is right to claim that the application of science *followed* rather than *caused* the initial dramatic improvement in the human condition, while denying that this in any way weakens the vision itself.

Its key idea is this. We have it in our power to ameliorate the human condition, and we can do so most effectively by using the knowledge generated by properly scientific methods of inquiry and experimentation. Even if the detailed historical path that human progress has hitherto taken to this end does not fit it precisely, this key idea remains eminently plausible. While the Enlightenment was only a beginning, the new attitude to scientific investigation that it ushered in greatly accelerated the transformation of traditional techniques. Animal breeding and plant cultivation are good examples. Experimental and systematic artificial selection launched agriculture on a trajectory that eventually led to genetic modification, but witnessed greatly improved food production at every step. So too variolation gave way to vaccination, and increased knowledge stimulated similar transformations in other techniques for dealing with disease. These highly significant improvements are early exemplars of the major advances that scientific knowledge brought to human welfare over the course of the twentieth century. In short, it can be claimed that it is only fairly recently that neo-Baconianism has finally come into its own, showing science and technology to be far more hopeful sources for improvements in the human condition than religious rituals or traditional remedies.

It is undeniable that investigations in the natural sciences have led to many impressive inventions and innovations. New drugs, improved surgical techniques, better engineering, and sophisticated technological devices have been of immense value in the conduct of daily life and raised the general standard of living to levels that previous generations could hardly have imagined. Yet the neo-Baconian thinks we should look beyond health, medicine, and food production, and consider the actual, and potential, contributions of the social sciences to improvements in human wellbeing. In addition to public health and agricultural production, we should include innovative reforms to schools and colleges, legal and political institutions, and the adoption of enlightened social and economic policies. These developments (it is alleged) also give us reason to endorse the neo-Baconian vision, and they make it eminently plausible that the hopes of today's poor will be better served by evidence-based strategies for improvements in personal and communal life than religious hopes of salvation, release, nirvana, or heaven could ever do.[12]

This line of thought signals a further step in the transformation of thought that Bacon inaugurated. The adoption of observation and experiment in the social sciences, especially economics, politics, and sociology, also began in the eighteenth century, but gathered greater pace in the nineteenth century, over the course of which social sciences became established academic disciplines. Two important figures in this development were Karl Marx and John Stuart Mill. In his early writings, Marx sought to analyse the ways in which social organization can alienate us from our 'species being', which is to say, our humanity. In the explanation he later framed, 'ideology' played an important part. An ideology has the double function of suppressing dissident action while sustaining the interests of the rich and powerful. The ideology of 'natural rights', for instance, persuades the poor and oppressed, in the face of their manifest inequality, that everyone is equal, and gives the rich and powerful a morally high-sounding excuse for leaving things as they are. Science, on Marx's view, had indeed led to technological improvements in production that could in principle satisfy an indefinite number and variety of material human needs. Yet, poverty persisted. The explanation for this persistence lies in a mismatch between production and distribution. The structure of capitalism, according to Marx, meant that the owners of the means of production became ever wealthier because the pursuit of profit inevitably led to a decline in wages. As a result, industrial workers were unable to purchase the goods that they themselves produced. This is the 'contradiction' of capitalism as a means of production. It produces what it cannot sell.[13]

It is not only religious visions of another, and better, world beyond this one, then, that deflect attention from the dynamics of the real world in which we live. So too does the ideology of natural rights and its

---

[12] India has long had a large proportion of the world's poor, but now seems to be undergoing a significant rise in general prosperity. Edward Luce recounts this development in a book whose title conveys the Baconian vision rather neatly — *In Spite of the Gods: The Strange Rise of Modern India* (London, 2006). The book itself, however, tells a more complex story than title might be taken to imply.

[13] Though Henry Ford can hardly be regarded as a 'Marxist', the intention he is alleged to have had — namely to pay his workers enough to enable them to buy one of his cars — reflects the same thought, and aims to change things in this respect.

accompanying illusion of equality. Consequently, Marx saw his most pressing task to be that of uncovering the laws that govern economic and social relations. As noted earlier, the eleventh of his *Theses on Feuerbach* declares that 'The philosophers have only interpreted the world, in various ways; the point however is to change it.' The displacement of interpretative 'philosophy' by Marxist political 'science', in other words, was a key precondition to effective political action. But what the concept of 'ideology' is intended to reflect is the fact that even if metaphysical supernaturalism loses its credibility, and otherworldly religion is rejected, there are purely *secular* ideologies that also need to be combatted by 'science'. Ideology arises to play the role that theology formerly played. Consequently, though Marx is dismissive of Bacon himself (in the essay 'Socialism: Utopian and Scientific'), from a Marxist perspective the Baconian vision nonetheless remains relevant and critical in a world without religion.

John Stuart Mill, no less important a contributor to the development of the social sciences than Marx, is best known as a proponent of philosophical utilitarianism, a framework of calculation that makes human welfare the touchstone of social and political policy. Within this framework, the role of fact gathering is primarily instrumental—discovering how best to bring about social and economic benefits for society at large. Mill's essays 'Utilitarianism' and 'On Liberty' aim to motivate support for reforming measures by setting out the philosophical grounds on which they are based. The use of reason, in other words, can provide a secular philosophical basis for the ends, as well as the instruments of social betterment. Marx, on the other hand, thinks that ameliorating the human condition is, so to speak, 'built in' to human motivation, and needs no special arguments, because reason is necessarily grounded in practicality. From this point of view, 'theory', including the sort of moral theory in which Mill is interested, is an empty ideological abstraction that could at best have only an oblique impact on how people live. 'Social life', Marx says in another of his *Theses on Feuerbach*, 'is essentially practical. All the mysteries which urge theory into mysticism find their rational solution in human practice and in the comprehension of this practice' (Thesis VIII). Mill, however, is following a long-standing philosophical question. My *own* needs are practically motivating, but what motivates altruistic concern with the needs of *others*? And what inspires it? Utilitarianism can supply the motivation, and poetry (he says elsewhere) generates the inspiration.

We need not here decide between these two views. From the point of view of the subject of this chapter they can be combined. And indeed, they have been by contemporary advocates of what is called 'effective altruism'. As defined by Wikipedia, effective altruism is 'a philosophy and social movement that applies evidence and reason to determining the most effective ways to improve the world'.[14] Effective altruism draws on Mill's utilitarian ethic insofar as it makes human happiness and wellbeing the ultimate goal of moral action. It employs the methods and results of the economic and social sciences (both partially and selectively, it ought to be added) as important sources of the 'evidence and reason' needed to devise and critique the practical programmes and policies it endorses. The utilitarian philosopher Peter Singer has been a leading figure in 'effective altruism', but as well as a 'philosophy', effective altruism is a 'social' movement of the kind Marx thought necessary, though it is one that has been taken up chiefly by wealthy individuals and charitable foundations rather than political parties. At a conference in 2013 Singer praised Bill and Melinda Gates, along with Warren Buffet, as 'the most effective altruists in history' (quoted in Linsey McGoey, *No Such Thing as a Free Gift*, p.146), and in return Bill and Melinda Gates added a commendatory foreword to the 2015 book edition of Singer's influential essay on 'Famine, Affluence, and Morality' (first published in 1972).

While some of the controversies surrounding effective altruism will be discussed in the next chapter, the principal conclusion to be drawn here is that effective altruism embraces an implicit subscription to a thoroughly secularized version of the Baconian vision. Human beings over the last few centuries, this secularized version holds, have benefitted from a huge improvement in the material conditions of life because they have relinquished a religiously inspired quietist acceptance of the many ills that comprise the human condition. Instead they have learned to engage with natural and social sciences for the acquisition of knowledge that can be applied in a sustained and systematic way to solve the practical problems of the human condition. In many parts of the world, of course, large numbers of people still live in poverty and ignorance and remain highly vulnerable to illness and injury. However, the best hope for such people, the neo-Baconian believes, lies in programmes of economic and political development properly informed by scientifically based research.

---

[14] https://en.wikipedia.org/wiki/Effective_altruism.

Two questions arise. First, is this contention true? It seems that the most consistent approach to answering it should be Bacon's own. We can only 'pronounce' on the subject, he says, if we are 'furnished with sufficient history'. Happily, in this case there is more than half a century of history to which we can turn. Over this period a large number of organizations and agencies have initiated programmes of economic and political development, all of them aiming to be informed by science broadly conceived, which is to say, empirically based research, scientific technology, and rational management. The best-known aid and development agencies had their origins in the relief of distress, but it was not long before they took on a much more ambitious goal, a sustained improvement in the lives of the poor. For example, Save the Children was founded in Britain 1919, in response to the starvation facing children in Central Europe as a result of World War I, but it soon became an international organization that took on the broader role of improving the lives of children. Similarly, Oxfam was founded during World War II when a group of British academics raised money for the relief of famine in Greece. Subsequently it developed into a very large international confederation of charitable organizations, now with a much wider purpose—'to address the *structural* causes of poverty' (emphasis added). Following the publication of the Brandt Report in 1981, 'overseas aid' also became an acknowledged obligation on the part of the governments of many developed nations. In 2000, the creation of the Bill and Melinda Gates Foundation with an endowment of over $40 billion dollars brought a new set of players—private foundations with enormous resources. In the same year, the collaborative work of all these agencies was given a still higher profile with the adoption of the Millennium Development Goals at a Summit of the United Nations. These eight international development goals included the traditional hopes for improving the human condition—eradicating extreme poverty and hunger, reducing child mortality, combatting HIV/AIDS, malaria, and other diseases, for instance—as well as some newer aims such as empowering women and ensuring environmental sustainability. The target year for the attainment of the goals was 2015. A highly publicized effort was put into this from many quarters, though much of it, by the major agencies, may have been largely rhetorical. In 2015, the target year for their fulfilment, they were replaced by a yet more ambitious set of seventeen Sustainable Development Goals, with a new target year of 2030.[15] Naturally, there has been close attention to how much of what all these agencies have hoped for has been attained. This has proved hard to ascertain, though since the empirical questions involved are critical for the argument of this book, the topic will be investigated at length in Chapter 5.

There is also, however, a second question. Where does the modern version of the Baconian vision leave religion? Does it have any role in providing hope for the poor, and if so what is it? As we saw, for Bacon himself, the theological framework remained firmly in place. It simply had practical implications that had not been properly appreciated. Understanding the full significance of the Fall meant seizing a hitherto neglected opportunity—the systematic pursuit of empirical knowledge for the benefit of humanity. There is nothing in the Baconian vision that requires us to disparage or to abandon religion, but it is easy to trace the historical path from Bacon's initial vision to an agnostic belief in the practical importance of science and technology and the irrelevance of theology.

Religion may still have a place within neo-Baconianism, but its character is changed. If material improvement must look to science and technology, the role of religious beliefs and practices must lie elsewhere—to be a source of 'spiritual' value by generating and sustaining 'meaning', for instance. Regarded in this light, the arts rather than the sciences become religion's natural allies. If this is indeed how we must now think of religion, it marks a major philosophical shift. Despite the intellectualist tenancy to mistake religion for theology, at most times and places (and in many places still) religion has been regarded as *essentially* practical. That is to say, religion is not primarily concerned with knowledge and explanation, or with contemplation, but with guidance and instruction. Some religions, in fact, are exclusively concerned with how life is to be lived, and have almost nothing to say about how the cosmos is to be explained. Neo-Baconianism relegates religion to the margins of practical life, because it supposes (with Hume) that religious 'remedies' for the material problems that people confront are the result of ignorance. They

---

15 These 17 goals include some conceptually problematic absolutes such as 'No Poverty' and 'Zero Hunger' and some very vague prospects—'Sustainable Cities and Communities' and 'Responsible Consumption and Production', for instance. In order to realize them, the UN planners have now identified no fewer than 169 Targets, 3,196 Events, and 6,178 Actions.

are vain attempts to influence the spiritual forces that supposedly cause them. Traditional religion, on this view, comprises a set of mistaken techniques. Consequently, the residual role for religion (if it has one) is as a personal preference of the individual. So construed, of course, religion loses almost all the importance it was hitherto thought to have, an importance that it is still thought to have in many places.

This relegation of religion presupposes the cogency of the neo-Baconian conception of the human condition. What if that conception is deeply flawed in some way? More importantly for present purposes, what if the human condition, so conceived, cannot offer real hope to the poor since the progress it promises fails to address the reality of their lives? In this case, it seems, there would be reason to consider afresh the nature of practical reason and its relation to religion. If the hope of the poor is truly to reside in projects that aim to secure economic and social development inspired by the neo-Baconian vision, it is plainly essential to undertake some assessment of the success and failure of those projects. The first task of the next chapter is to do just that. This cannot avoid highly contentious areas of debate where, as a result of the complexity of the issues, definitive answers often prove elusive. What the exploration will also reveal, however, is that these issues are not purely empirical. The questions that need to be investigated cannot be detached from the philosophical and ethical issues that were the topics of previous chapters.

Chapter Four

Poverty versus Impoverishment

The Argument So Far

We began with this question: what kind of life should human beings hope to have? It seems obvious that a worthwhile life will include good experiences and significant accomplishments. Yet, as I argued, it is important to resist the temptation to think in terms of *exceptional* experiences and *outstanding* accomplishments. Framing hopes in these terms excludes the vast majority of people, whose lives are certain to be *unexceptional*. This is not just a consequence of the logical point that 'exceptional' necessarily contrasts with the norm. It also acknowledges the fact that most people's physical, intellectual, and practical talents are limited, as are the opportunities they have. So the real question is: what is the best hope for an *ordinary* life?

Faced with this question there is reason to rank relationships more highly than either experiences or accomplishments. People who have neither the talent nor the opportunity to do something exceptional may reasonably hope to have a biography — a life story — that is made meaningful chiefly through personal relationships. Nor do enriching personal relationships rely on economic prosperity or social prestige. Indeed, the families of the wealthy and celebrated can be highly dysfunctional. Prosperous people in search of love and friendship can be vulnerable, and susceptible, to manipulation. Conversely, lives lived in relative material poverty can be greatly enriched by profound and enduring relationships.

The life-enriching power of personal relationships, then, is a key dimension of human equality. It is easy to romanticize 'love in a cottage', of course, and there is little doubt that material hardship can impose burdens that have the effect of distorting, corrupting, and undermining relationships between people. Personal relationships, in other words, are neither isolated from nor impervious to the contingencies of existence. The kind of life most worth hoping for has to be pursued within the human condition, a world containing hazards and obstacles as well as resources and opportunities, with the power to frustrate as well as to satisfy human plans and projects. Wealth may to some degree diminish the impact of illness, unemployment, conflict, or natural catastrophe, but it affords no protection against bereavement, betrayal, or deception. Vulnerability is an inescapable dimension of the relationships we choose to form, as well as those in which we simply find ourselves.

All this is part of what we call 'the human condition', and makes it another key dimension of human equality. The rich, strong, and powerful can no more escape it than the poor, weak, and powerless. Yet, as every period of history has confirmed, the human condition does not bear on everyone equally. Its benefits, hazards, resources, and opportunities are never evenly distributed. Furthermore, its inequalities tend to cluster. Wealth is allied to power and longevity, while poverty is frequently accompanied by sickness and subjugation. This fact complicates the question of the hope of the poor because it is in virtue of their poverty, frequently, that they lack the power they need if they are to have any hope of leaving poverty behind. How are they to escape this poverty trap? To address this issue we need to resolve a preliminary issue. Just who are 'the poor'?

I. Identifying 'the Poor'

A common approach to answering this question begins by focusing on *income* poverty. It defines the poor as those whose annual income falls below a specifiable 'poverty line'. Inevitably, there is always something arbitrary about where we draw this line. Life just above it is unlikely to be much better than just below it. Still, though the arbitrariness of any 'poverty line' is undeniable, it is also unavoidable. In this respect, the 'poverty line' is not unique. The age at which 'children' are held to become 'adults' is also arbitrary. In different places and for different purposes, 16, 18, and 21 have all been used as the age of 'maturity'. Despite this variety, each of them reflects something broadly correct about stages of human development, and despite their arbitrariness, they have proved useful for many purposes. So too with 'the poverty line'. Since the ability to buy goods and services is clearly a function of income, this is enough to establish the relevance of the poverty line as a way of expressing minimum material needs.

Things are more problematic when it comes to international comparisons and global statistics because the poverty line has to be expressed in monetary terms and there is no single currency in which to do this. For many years, poverty was defined globally as income below $1 a day (it has now been raised to $2.15). The US dollar is not accepted currency everywhere, and, even where it is, what $2.15 will buy can vary considerably from place to place. That is why the figure is commonly qualified by the expression 'purchasing power parity', abbreviated to 'PPP'. The concept of 'purchasing power parity' has been developed as a way of making meaningful comparisons across radically different economic contexts. However, even this more sophisticated version of 'the poverty line' can be difficult to translate into real conditions. The cost of some basic needs may vary greatly from place to place according to local conditions. For instance, heating is inessential most of the year in warm countries, but essential most of the year in cold ones. Again, in some places and climates suitable building materials are widely available, in others they are scarce. In light of such variations, some economists argue that realistic comparisons with respect to poverty must use different figures in different contexts—$4 PPP a day in one country may be the more accurate equivalent of $2.15 PPP in another. In both cases, of course, 'dollar PPP' is not an actual amount of money that can be spent. It is an abstract and artificial measure by means of which, it is hoped, we can identify conditions of extreme poverty wherever they may be found. The most important question, then, is whether it enables us to do so.

The problem of poverty is usually stated and investigated on the assumption that a poverty line of $2.15 PPP per day enables us to make meaningful comparisons. On the basis of this assumption, it is estimated that in 2021 650 million people (8.5% of the global population) were living in extreme poverty.[1] This figure, it needs to be emphasized, is an estimate, not a head count, and there are serious problems surrounding its calculation. To begin with, gathering statistics is a complex operation. Even in wealthy, stable countries with large and qualified civil administrations, accurate numbers about something as basic as the size of the population

---

[1] The reaction of many governments to the COVID-19 pandemic in 2020 had the effect of increasing the number of people in extreme poverty, ending a decades-long decline. Just how greatly the number increased has proved hard to determine. The 2021 World Bank estimate is 70–90 million.

can be surprisingly hard to establish.[2] Impoverished countries inevitably lack public administrations on anything like the same scale or with equal sophistication. Consequently, on many different dimensions, they are generally unable to provide statistics that can safely be relied upon, leaving intelligent guessing a lot of work to do. The problem is exacerbated by the fact that governments nevertheless issue 'official' numbers. Not infrequently they do this because the continuation of international loans and grants depends upon them. In such circumstances, government 'statistics' are not only likely to be factually inaccurate, but actively manipulated in favour of vested interests. Statistics frequently have implications for politicians and political parties, both domestically and in the world of international aid and economic development. Failure to acknowledge this is simply naïvety.

The problems surrounding published statistics must be borne in mind in any serious investigation of poverty and deprivation. At best, the numbers provided by state agencies, charities, and foundations are approximations based on careful and honest estimates. At worst, they are fabrications designed to aid the states and institutions that issue them.[3] Short of positive fabrication, governments often have powerful incentives to present statistics that serve their purposes, and to amend statistics that don't.

Even the most reputable international agencies can have institutional interests that lead them to rest content with misleading statistics. For example, throughout the 2010s the World Bank published a series of reports announcing 'tremendous progress' in reducing extreme poverty, reports that were later subjected to scrutiny by Philip Alston, the UN special envoy on extreme poverty and human rights. In 2020, he issued a highly critical retrospective assessment. It concluded that the reports were largely designed to enable the World Bank to tick off the development goals it had set itself. By using the (then) standard of $1.90 a day, the Bank had not alleviated poverty; it had simply defined it out of existence.

---

[2] Scotland has an advanced level of public administration, yet the Scottish census of 2022, deferred by the Scottish Government from 2021 and conducted online for the first time, attracted a response rate far below that required for meaningful statistics.

[3] A notorious example of this in recent history is the 'information' Greece produced for its admission to the European single currency. In the great recession of 2007–8, these were rapidly shown to be fabricated to an astonishing extent.

Using a more defensible line generates a radically different understanding of progress against poverty... Rather than one billion people lifted out of poverty and a global decline from 36 percent to 10 percent, the number living under a $5.50 line held almost steady between 1990 and 2015, declining from 3.5 to 3.4 billion, while the rate dropped from 67 percent to 46 percent... Even under the Bank's line,... [b]etween 1990 and 2015, the number of people living under the line in Sub-Saharan Africa and the Middle East *rose* by some 140 million.[4]

With these considerations in mind, it is easy to be sceptical and conclude that numbers on poverty are more likely to serve the purposes of propaganda than depict reality. Yet, it is a mistake to be unduly sceptical. As Alston's scrutiny of the World Bank for the United Nations demonstrates, institutions rarely have a free hand with the statistics they issue. Nor does the fact that figures like these are for the most part estimates make them valueless. It is better to have a rough idea than no idea at all. Practical wisdom requires good information and the challenge is to strike the right balance between scepticism on the one hand and credulity on the other. If statistics on poverty are not broadly correct, actions and programmes based upon them will be inadequately grounded. Moreover, they will lack the moral significance they are widely held to have. However good our intentions, there is no merit in helping the wrong people in the wrong way, and only reasonably good information will provide a check against this. On the other hand, it is no less a maxim of practical reason that 'the perfect is the enemy of the good'. Suspending action until fully validated information is available is a recipe for complete inactivity. If we are to act at all, we have no choice but to act on the best information we have, while acknowledging that it falls considerably short of the ideal.

It is reasonable, then, to proceed on the assumption that statistics issued by institutions such as the United Nations and the World Bank

---

4   https://chrgj.org/wp-content/uploads/2020/07/Alston-Poverty-Report-FINAL.pdf. Alston's report was issued at the time of the COVID-19 pandemic, and included a preliminary indication of the disastrous consequences for the poor of government actions taken in the name of public health. 'The impact of COVID-19 will be long-lasting... [erasing] all poverty alleviation progress over the past three years, and will push 176 million people into poverty at the $3.20 poverty line... Far from being the "great leveler", COVID-19 is a pandemic of poverty, exposing the parlous state of social safety nets for those on lower incomes or in poverty around the world.' It needs to be observed, of course, that it was the response of governments to COVID-19, not the virus itself, that had this catastrophic effect.

provide valuable information about the extent and distribution of poverty in the world. A key issue, as Alston's report indicated, relates to determining a 'poverty line'. A no less important matter, however, relates to defining poverty in terms of income, wherever the line is drawn. 'PPP income' is a helpfully *quantitative* concept because it allows us make numerical comparison between different times and places. On the other hand, it is poor lives, not low incomes, with which we ought to be concerned.

On reflection, this means that defining poverty in terms of income has serious limitations. First, while monetary income has *instrumental* value, it has no *intrinsic* value. Despite the near universal practice of expressing wealth in monetary terms, money has no value except insofar as it is the means to improving the quality of life. Accordingly, in places where food, clothing, housing, schooling, and so on are either in short supply, or of very poor quality, having more money does not automatically translate into being better off. For example, more money leads to improved housing only if better housing is available. Monetary increases without increases in the supply of goods simply results in higher prices.

Second, level of income takes no account of how the income is generated. This can disguise very important differences from the point of view of poverty. For instance, suppose a family's income rises. This may be the result of excessively long hours of work, or because of child labour, which deprives children of education and play. In such circumstances, there is more money in the family budget, but it is far from obvious the family is better off. Similarly, $PPP cannot distinguish between income generated from individual effort and legitimate trade and income generated from drug trafficking and mercenary soldiering. Illicit activities can be as (minimally) profitable as licit ones.

Third, as the familiar expressions 'poor health' and 'poor education' indicate, poverty can be experienced with respect to different dimensions of human life. Some of these can be captured in terms of monetary income, but others may not. The website *Poverty Stats and Facts* says that 'nearly a billion people entered the 21st century unable to read or write.' If so, this number is considerably higher than the number of people estimated to be living below the $PPP poverty line. It follows that people who are not deemed extremely poor with respect to income may still be extremely poor with respect to education. This is the illusion of improvement that Alston has in mind when he refers to defining poverty out of existence. Nor can substantially increased income always be expected to remedy poor education. An increase sufficient to meet the cost of school fees, for instance, will not give real access to education, if the ratio of teachers to students is 1:100, which it is in some places. The children of parents who can afford to send them to school may not in fact emerge from school any better educated than they were before.

Fourth, while purchasing power expressed in monetary terms enables us to make quantitative comparisons, some important dimensions of wealth and poverty are not quantifiable. What would it mean to say that one person is a third less literate than another? We can of course invent numerical scales to contrast positions with respect to any given dimension of poverty, but this is ranking, not measurement. For instance, people who have attained an above average standard of education can suffer from a below average standard of health. We can meaningfully assign numbers to register these differences, but this does not make the two dimensions commensurable. That is to say, a higher number on one scale does not in any sense offset a lower number on the other. Nor can we compute a single figure that represents their overall deprivation. The same point arises when we try to compare people who are well fed but poorly housed, with people who, though they have decent housing, have a very poor diet. Numerical indicators may have their uses, but they are not quantities of anything.

II. Assessing the Quality of Life

Complexities of this kind can be multiplied almost indefinitely. Poverty is not one thing—as the focus on monetary income misleadingly inclines us to suppose. It is multi-dimensional, and its multi-dimensionality raises serious doubts about the meaningfulness of any conception of a 'poverty line' that is based primarily on monetary income. Furthermore, exclusive focus on monetary income has this additional defect. It necessarily overlooks forms of deprivation that purchasing power can never remedy. Recorded income takes no account of security of employment. And even a relatively large income may do little to offset the dangers of violent neighbourhoods or environmental pollution. At best, more money allows people to escape those dangers only by abandoning their homes and jobs.

Once again, though, it is important not to let these complications prompt a retreat into outright scepticism about our ability to identify 'the poor'. The difficulties just considered have been widely acknowledged, and imaginative efforts have been made to devise alternative indicators (and measures) that properly accommodate poverty's multi-dimensionality. In 1990, economists Amartya Sen and Mahbub ul Haq devised a *Human Development Index* (HDI). This incorporated three dimensions of poverty and development, namely, standard of living, health, and education. Using the HDI as a basis, the United Nations created a slightly different *Human Poverty Index* (HPI), which was first used in 1997 to make comparisons between countries. A little over a decade later, the HPI was replaced by the UN's more sophisticated *Multidimensional Poverty Index* (MPI). This reverted to the three dimensions used by Sen and ul Haq, but it also broke each of them down into specific indicators. The dimension of 'health', for example, is specified in terms of two indicators—'nutrition' and 'child mortality'. On the basis of some plausible assumptions—that access to safe drinking water is more important than extensive household possessions, for instance—these indicators are then weighted. The MPI assesses standard of living by reference to the availability of electricity, quality of sanitation, distance from drinking water, type of floor covering, type of cooking fuel, and material possessions such as a radio, a refrigerator, a mobile phone, or a bicycle. Each indicator is given a relative weight, and the MPI repeats this strategy for the other two dimensions, health and education. On the basis of this weighting, it classifies people as 'poor' if they are deprived in at least a third of the weighted indicators, with the proportion of indicators in which they are deprived determining the depth of their poverty. Populations are then assessed, and a formula used to determine the degree to which the country as a whole can be declared 'poor' or not.

Like the simple '$2.15 PPP a day' poverty line, this approach can be made to produce comparative numbers. Though it is obviously much subtler, its greater subtlety still does not tell us much about vulnerability. It does not capture the degree to which the conditions it measures are secure. Supplies of food and water, and employment opportunities, can be precarious. Security with respect to these, it is widely agreed, is no less important than quantity and quality. A secure income of $1 PPP a day may be preferable to an insecure income of $5 PPP, and exactly the same point applies to figures generated by the MPI.

Even if we leave this crucial limitation aside, it is important to observe that more subtle measures of poverty require more detailed statistics than many governments are in fact able to supply. Consequently, the number of countries that it has proved possible to assess and compare using this MPI is rather limited—about 100. Furthermore, since the MPI requires a much richer set of statistics, all the doubts about how far $PPP figures accurately represent real lives will evidently be compounded. Calculating *per capita* income requires information on annual GDP and size of population. These may be difficult to determine accurately, but once we have these figures, the calculation is relatively simple. It is a far more complex matter to assess such variables as distance from drinking water, type of cooking fuel, and household possessions. Even where there are tolerably good systems of public administration, it is questionable whether 'the facts' on these matters are (or could be) recorded accurately, especially in countries where a significant proportion of the population lives in relatively inaccessible places. It is not clear that even with respect to indicators for which the use of numbers is unproblematic — infant mortality and life expectancy rates for instance — it is possible for the governments of poor countries to record these accurately.

Answering the questions 'who are the poor?' and 'where are they to be found?' is an essential preliminary to doing anything to alleviate their poverty. We have seen that answering them satisfactorily is fraught with great difficulty. Still, we ought not to let this paralyse us. As many people engaged in relief and development insist, while the statistics produced by institutions such as the United Nations, the World Bank, and the International Monetary Fund are less accurate and reliable than we might hope, they are the best we have to go on, and better now than they ever have been. In any serious attempt to eradicate poverty, we must either use these, or do nothing.

Given the plight of the world's poorest people, many argue, doing nothing is not an option. Though so frequently repeated as to seem incontestable, there is, in fact, good reason to contest this claim. For the moment, however, let us agree that there is a moral imperative to help the poor and that inaction on this score is unacceptable.[5] All action, of course, is susceptible to imperfect information, but such a huge effort is put into assembling statistics on poverty and deprivation, it seems reasonable to assume that the picture they paint, even if flawed in important ways, does represent the reality of some people's lives more than it misrepresents them. If this is true, then we have reason to make them the basis of action, albeit set round with a suitably cautious attitude. For the moment, at any

---

[5]   This is not obvious. There are circumstances in which it is morally preferable to do nothing because 'aid' makes matters worse. *When Helping Hurts* is the title of an informative book on Christian-inspired aid programmes based on research undertaken by the Chalmers Center at Covenant College.

rate, let us assume that while statistics based upon a 'poverty line' tell us very little, more sophisticated indicators, such as those of the *Multi-dimensional Poverty Index*, have practical value. Even with this assumption in place, however, there is a further issue. Do they really inform us about what the lives of 'the poor' are *like*, and thus capture the realities with which concern for those lives must grapple?

For the purposes of exploring this question, the matter of PPP *versus* MPI can be suspended temporarily. The key issues to be addressed are more simply identified if we start with the cruder measure of *per capita* income. As was noted earlier, its computation is relatively simple. The Gross Domestic Product of a country is the total value added in the pro-duction of goods and the delivery of services over a specified period, usually a year. It includes government expenditure, investments, and the foreign balance of trade. GDP is widely used as a broad measurement of a nation's overall economic activity, but for certain purposes it can be highly misleading. The calculation includes goods produced in a country even when they are simply passing through and contribute little to the livelihood of people in that country. It includes government expenditure, which may increase because of highly adverse conditions—higher expenditure on police and prisons because of a rising crime rate, for instance, will result in a greater Gross Domestic Product.

Some of these difficulties can be avoided if Gross National Product (GNP) is used as an alternative to GDP, and the World Bank and the United Nations, using the Human Development Index, have replaced GNP with Gross National Income (GNI). GDP remains the most commonly used, however, and the basis of the figures that are most easily accessed. To arrive at *per capita* income, GDP is divided by the size of the population. As was also noted earlier, calculating the value of GDP (or GNP or GNI) and the size of the population present their own difficulties, but let us discount any doubts about the statistics on which *per capita* GDP is based. When the dollar figure is converted into purchasing power parity dollars, we have in principle a measure of the extent to which 'an individual' within the country is able to meet the costs of food, shelter, medicine, and so on. This is a simple 'mean', of course, and may disguise highly unequal patterns of distribution. A small number of people might account for a large proportion of GDP so that the mean (the average) significantly exceeds the mode (the most common level of income). However, this is another complication that must be set aside, chiefly because, for good or ill, *per capita* GDP is the measure most commonly used.[6]

When comparative calculations were made for the year 2016, Malawi, a small landlocked republic in sub-Saharan Africa, came out with a *per capita* GDP of just $226.50. The comparable figure for the United States was $54,629. On the basis of these figures, Malawi was listed as the poorest country in the world for that year, while the USA was the ninth richest. But what do these figures and rankings actually tell us about the comparative quality of people's lives in Malawi or the USA? The most honest answer is 'almost nothing'. This is partly because neither figure records what anyone actually earns. While it is the case that the annual earnings of significant numbers of people in the US will be around $54,629 per year, the number of $226.50 might be no Malawian's actual income, and not just because it is preceded by a dollar sign.[7] Secondly, since these are averages, they tell us nothing about actual differences of income. As far as the figures go, it is quite possible (and is indeed the case) that a very small number of people in Malawi are better off than quite a large number of people in the USA. Nor can we say on the strength of these figures that none of the poverty found in the US is as severe or burdensome as poverty in Malawi. Indeed, it is precisely this conclusion that economists such as Angus Deaton have challenged. The burden of poverty is context relative. Heating and transportation, for instance, are basic needs in some places, but not in others. In many parts of the USA, unlike Malawi, personal transportation is essential for employment.

Still, since the figure for Malawi is so far below that of the US, it seems plausible, at a minimum, to suppose that the proportion of Malawi's 16+ million people who live below the poverty line is very much larger than the comparable proportion in the US. For the sake of argument, let us suppose this is indeed true. Even so, it may not tell us as much about comparable quality of life as we imagine. As well as totalling traded goods and services, GDP tries to estimate the value of food, shelter, clothing, and so on that people produce for themselves. Self-subsistence,

---

[6] In *Doughnut Economics: Seven Ways to Think Like a 21st Century Economist*, Kate Raworth aims to undermine the dominance of GDP in economics and formulate a radical alternative. It is striking, however, that the poverty statistics she cites are nonetheless based on GDP.

[7] Malawi's currency is the kwacha.

however, may leave some Malawians better off than some Americans in ways that this estimate does not reveal. Malawians who grow their own food may be able to provide better food for their children (fresh fruit and vegetables, for example) than some of the poorest people in America can afford to purchase.[8] If this is the case, then poor Malawians have a means of mitigating their poverty that poor Americans lack. Yet the *per capita* GDP figure, even though it includes an estimate of the value of self-subsistence, will not capture this difference.

It would be surprising, of course, if additional benefits of this kind successfully mitigated poverty in Malawi to any very great extent. It also seems likely that even the poorest people in America have possessions that Malawi's poorest lack—showers, washing machines, and refrigerators, for example. Still, if we confine our attention to something as basic as the experience of hunger, it is not difficult to see that the circumstances in which Malawians live may significantly affect this experience in ways that are not available to the American urban poor. Let us suppose that the regular allowance of food a US parent can collect from a food bank is as limited in nutritional value as the amount of food a poor farmer in Malawi is able to grow. There is nevertheless the further matter of personal autonomy. Irrespective of nutritional value, there is more satisfaction to be taken in providing food for one's family by skilled activity, than by standing in line at a food bank. Since the monetary value of the food is the same (let us suppose), the significance of autonomy over dependence is not captured in comparative measures of income. Such measures, consequently, may tell us relatively little about the comparative quality of life. When it comes to *calculation*, the simplicity of *per capita* GDP is an advantage; when it comes to *information*, this very same feature is a major limitation. Numerical comparisons, in other words, rarely tell us what we really want to know. What life is *like* for the poor?

Can this deficiency be remedied if we use more sophisticated indicators such as the MPI? And if so, to what extent? This index, as we saw, takes many more dimensions into account, and assesses them on a broader range of indicators. In the case of Malawi, using MPI produces a significantly different result. Judged by the standard $2.15 PPP as the measure of poverty, the proportion of poor people comes out at 70%; if

---

8   In *$2.00 a Day: Living on Almost Nothing in America* (2016), Kathryn J. Edin and H. Luke Shaefer recount several households of which this is true.

we use the MPI instead, it falls to 56%.[9] This suggests that as the number of dimensions is extended, the picture of poverty changes.[10] The central question remains, however. How much more does this expanded picture tell us about what the lives of the poor are like?

One important consideration is this. Are the measures adequately correlated across countries? Some measures of wellbeing seem to correlate differently in different places. For instance, India by most measures is wealthier than sub-Saharan Africa, and yet anthropometric measures such as child height favour sub-Saharan Africa over India. A second important point is this. Regardless of the index with which we are working, a quantified picture of poverty is essentially static. That is to say, it gives us a snapshot of how things stand at a particular point in time, but it conveys nothing about the causes from which this state of affairs has resulted, or the context in terms of which it needs to be understood.

Often a dynamic element *appears* to be introduced by making year on year comparisons, and these comparisons may be illuminating for other purposes — though they are too easily *assumed* to indicate progress or decline.[11] They still leave out of the account factors that can make a lot of difference to quality of life. This is the key message in the alternative approach to poverty and development that Amartya Sen pioneered in *Development as Freedom* (1999). As the book's title implies, its aim was to bring about a critical shift in thinking with regard to development. Sen argues that while income, assets, and economic growth are undoubtedly significant, their importance is a function of the broader conditions under which people live, and in particular the range of opportunities open to them. This range can indeed be constrained by economic factors such as low income, and perhaps it often is, but it can also be constrained by social and political factors. A male-oriented culture, for instance, will limit

---

9   Available figures relate to 2013/14 rather than 2016.

10   Since the comparable MPI figure for Afghanistan (before the return of the Taliban in 2021) was 90%, then presumably this also changes Malawi's position as the poorest country in the world.

11   This is especially true of income since monetary income can change much more easily and rapidly than, say, health and education. The general point has much wider application. In his study of conflict in the Congo — *The War That Doesn't Say Its Name* (2021) — Jason K. Stearns argues persuasively that 'process explanation' focused on events and actors provides a far better understanding of endemic social problems than statistical analysis in search of causal regularities.

the opportunities available to women irrespective of their disposable income or material assets. Moreover, each dimension of freedom tends to support and enhance the others.

A simple thought experiment illustrates the importance of Sen's point. Imagine an accurate set of statistics on income and assets that ranks Location A considerably higher than Location B. What these statistics do not reveal, however, is that Location A is a refugee camp, while location B is a peaceful rural village. In B, monetary income is low because the village relies to a large extent on self-subsistence. As a result, relatively little is produced, traded, or exchanged for money. The refugee camp, on the other hand, has no productive capacity of its own, but is generously provided with money and goods by relief agencies and external donors. Every transaction relating to food, shelter, and so on involves money. In these circumstances, A will inevitably have a higher *per diem PPP* than B. Still, it is rational for people in the camp to discount this difference. Their personal and productive lives have been disrupted by civil conflict, and despite a significant drop in income, life in a peaceful rural village would be much preferred. What the thought experiment shows is that comparative statistics on income and expenditure, no matter how accurate they are, will not capture the crucial difference that context can make to quality of life.

Essentially the same point can be made by a real case. In 2015 the Gulf state of Qatar recorded the highest *per capita* GDP in the world. At an astonishing $146,011.85, this is more than 500 times the figure for Malawi in 2016.[12] Furthermore, and again in sharp contrast to Malawi, Qatar's citizens have access to an exceptionally high level of healthcare, and a very well financed educational system. By these measures, then, quality of life in Qatar ranks best in the world. On the other hand, an Amnesty International report on Qatar for the same year says that: 'The authorities arbitrarily restricted the rights to freedom of expression, association and peaceful assembly. A prisoner of conscience was serving a lengthy sentence for writing and reciting poems. Migrant workers, including domestic workers and those employed in high-profile construction projects, continued to face exploitation and abuse. Discrimination against women remained entrenched in both law and practice.' The corres-

---

[12]   The figures are probably distorted by the existence of migrant workers and the production of oil which makes Qatar's GDP much higher than its GNP.

ponding report for Malawi records many fewer matters for concern, and in particular lists no restrictions on freedom of expression, association, or assembly. If our focus is exclusively economic, we can safely declare that Qatar is 500 times richer than Malawi. But we are not thereby automatically enabled to decide whether life is better in Qatar or in Malawi. It is the facts behind the numbers, not the numbers themselves, that determine this.[13]

Numbers permit straightforward comparison. That is their attraction. At the same time, even if they are multi-factorial and accurate (in itself a demanding requirement), the information they convey is necessarily limited in ways that leave important questions unanswered. Is the value of a good healthcare system substantially offset by the risk of arbitrary arrest? Does a low crime rate compensate citizens for the relatively repressive state institutions that have brought it about? Are well-fed children in poorly equipped schools better or worse off than hungrier children in good schools? Does secure employment in factories compensate for the air pollution in which the workers live? Such questions are not easy to answer from any perspective, but the use of numbers misleads us into thinking that with sufficient ingenuity we can devise an algorithm that will produce an answer. The point applies to all numerical indicators — *per capita* GDP, or HDI, or MPI. Some measures are an advance on others, but it is only to a very limited degree that the aspects of existence that make for a good or less good quality of life can be captured in quantifiable assessment and economic measures.

III. Living a Good Life

That is why Sen, Martha Nussbaum, and others try to work with a richer conception of what counts as 'development'. Their alternative conception aims to base quality of life on human 'capabilities'. In an Aristotelian spirit, it approaches the question of poverty from the other end, so to speak. Instead of trying to identify or characterize poor lives, it sets out the dimensions that are essential to good human lives. These do include some of the things that measures of poverty generally focus on — longevity, health, and nutrition, for instance — but adds more — personal

---

[13] For an illuminating study of the reality behind the statistics see John McManus, *Inside Qatar: Hidden Stories from One of the Richest Nations on Earth* (2022).

liberty, security, education, leisure, productive employment, creative activity, social standing, and political engagement. Some of these, it is true, are likely to be seriously hindered by low income, and conversely, advanced by a higher level of income. Consequently, all plausible indicators of wellbeing are likely to be *correlated* with income. Nevertheless, social and economic structures, along with cultural attitudes, limit and enhance the prospects of individuals in ways that measures of income cannot capture. The lives of human beings are enriched or impoverished by the context that surrounds them. The availability of schooling, vitality of local markets, employment opportunities, and working conditions, for instance, all bear directly on the quality of life. Broader social conditions are scarcely less important — political stability, the robustness of the legal institutions, the status of women, attitudes to physical and mental disabilities, the time and resources available for creativity and leisure, the preservation of cultural inheritance, and the quality of the natural environment. There are many acclaimed instances of 'developing' countries where *per capita* GPD, daily PPP income, or even MPI is growing at a rapid rate, but where the quality of life, on several of these dimensions, has remained poor, or even declined. Dirty, crowded, heavily polluted urban areas, unsafe workplaces, and a degradation of the landscape often accompany the rising wages and higher employment generated by commercial and industrial development.

The conclusion to be drawn is that as incomes rise 'the poor' generally become less 'poor', but only in this sense: they have better food, more possessions, live longer, and may have healthier children. These are undoubtedly welcome improvements. On the other hand, these improvements often come at significant cost — more hazardous working conditions, slum housing, violent neighbourhoods, and environmental degradation. Where such conditions do prevail, although rising income has improved the lives of the people in certain respects, in others the quality of their lives is unenviable. Conversely, there are rural communities where incomes are low, harvests irregular, and material possessions few, but where, nonetheless, ordinary people can lead lives that are good in many important respects. Low incomes and modest possessions are considerably offset in societies where political life is stable, violence is rare, freedom of expression is unfettered, the care and education of children is held to be important, and the landscape largely unspoiled. Societies that could not possibly fund art museums, theatres, and concert halls can still be rich in cultural activities and opportunities, and where funds for educational technology are lacking, schools may still offer effective teaching.

These reminders do more than warrant caution about the advantages of economic development and the figures in which it may be recorded. They invite us to explore a radically different way of thinking about poverty and, by implication, a different way of approaching the problems addressed in this chapter. A helpful first step lies in relinquishing the language of 'poverty' and 'wealth' and replacing it with the concepts of 'impoverishment' and 'enrichment'. This is more than a terminological recommendation. It serves to shift attention from the quantitative to the qualitative. Thinking in terms of 'impoverishment' and 'enrichment' does not require any problematic 'poverty line'. If we cease to employ a numerically calculated 'poverty line', we avoid the risk of mistaking instrumental *means* to enrichment (money and income) for enrichment *itself* (better lives). With the best of intentions, slogans such as 'Make Poverty History' reinforce the mistaken supposition that there is one key thing—poverty—whose elimination will then secure all basic goods. The concepts of 'impoverishment' and 'enrichment' naturally accommodate the wide range of dimensions on which lives can be deficient or improved. They direct our attention to a variety of important tasks, inviting us to investigate and reflect on social and cultural conditions, and not on purely economic parameters.

There is a further advantage to making this change. As Sen points out, it is easy to collapse ends into means quite inadvertently, and taking measures of income as the primary indicators of improvement strongly inclines us to do this. Actions and policies come to be framed around the erroneous belief that, for instance, better education and health are valuable chiefly for the contribution they make to economic growth, thus relegating them from primary values to instruments of wealth creation. The error is a common one, and yet it is obvious that this is thinking the wrong way round. It is only the degree to which economic growth enables such things as healthier and better educated lives that makes it valuable. To think that the value of education lies in the impact it has on income (personal or national) is like supposing that the writing and reading of books is to be encouraged primarily because it results in more jobs in printing and paper production. It is manifestly mistaken to think that this is the point of literary imagination. At most it is a welcome by-product.

Shifting attention from poverty to impoverishment has this further advantage. Poverty, conceived of as limited income and minimal possessions, is widely assumed to be a curse. This assumption, however, is an aspect of modern consumerism. In almost all cultures, there have been people for whom poverty *in precisely this sense* has been an ideal. The iconic figure of this way of thinking is St Francis of Assisi (1181/1182–1226). Famously, Francis was born into a wealthy family, and until his late twenties relished the lifestyle that went with great wealth. Then he relinquished it all, and, as tradition expresses it, 'married' Lady Poverty. From that point on, his dress, food, and accommodation were all of the simplest kind, and his aim was to lead what he regarded as a much better life. This embrace of poverty attracted many followers, and the emergence of a new religious order—the Franciscans. In more recent times, the Protestant Shakers present us with a similar phenomenon—a style of life that positively rejects many of the 'benefits' that economic growth and larger incomes bring.[14]

With the Franciscans and the Shakers in mind, what are we to make of the campaigning slogan 'Make Poverty History'? It is commonly remarked that voluntary poverty is quite different from involuntary poverty. Most poor people do not choose to be poor. This is true, but we need to ask whether the voluntary/involuntary distinction is germane to the issue with which we are concerned. If poverty is bad *per se*, why would anyone choose it? Did Francis make a mistake of some kind? The answer is 'No'. After his conversion, Francis lived a life *in poverty*, but he did not live *an impoverished life*. On the contrary, it was his wealth that he had found impoverishing. That is why he abandoned it. This sounds paradoxical, but there is no paradox here because material poverty is not bad in itself. It is bad only insofar as it leads to impoverished lives. This alerts us to the possibility that there are aspects of life which *wealth* can impoverish.

The distinction between material poverty and human impoverishment, then, is crucial. The two are not the same. It is impossible to deny that in many places and contexts, material poverty does lead to impoverished lives, though where this is the case, material poverty is rarely the only contributing factor, and often not the major one. Conflict and insecurity frequently play a part. As Sen points out, disadvantages tend to cluster,

---

[14] See Flo Morse, *The Story of the Shakers.*

with the result that the relation of cause to effect is highly uncertain. For instance, low quality education confines people to low paid jobs; industrial accidents leave people unable to earn; armed conflict disrupts commerce and production; housing shortages negatively impact disposable income. In all these cases, material poverty is the *consequence* and not the *cause*. It can be *relieved* by food aid or funds for projects, and hence by higher incomes. But the underlying problems are not thereby *remedied*. The impoverishment of human lives continues.

Distinguishing between poverty and impoverishment is critically important for the issues at the heart of this book, not least because it offers a better grounding for the moral motivation that underlies a concern for the lives of poor people. Material poverty in itself does not generate an obligation to assist. The Franciscan, after all, neither needs nor looks for more money, better housing, and so on. By contrast, impoverishment always generates reasons to assist because impoverished lives are less good than they should be. It is not poverty but impoverishment that we should strive to remedy. What difference does this conceptual shift make to the practical programmes that relief and development organizations undertake? It requires us to rethink the kinds of projects and strategies that national governments, international organizations, and charitable agencies have generally adopted. If the goal is that of enriching impoverished lives rather than increasing the purchasing power of 'the bottom billion', statistics will not be an adequate mark of success and failure. Rather, projects and strategies will have to be assessed qualitatively.

Chapter Five

Giving, Receiving, and Benefitting

Chapter 3 explored 'the Baconian vision' of the human condition. Nature, this vision tells us, is governed by laws. Science gives us knowledge of these laws, and as result we can exercise power over the forces of nature. The proper use of this power enables us to engineer radical improvements in the human condition. Originally, the theology of creation supplied the metaphysical background for this Baconian vision. As the law-governed creation of a beneficent God, the world is by its nature a fit habitation for human beings. Over time, neo-Baconianism, separated from theology, was thought to come into its own precisely because the separation was complete. The resulting, purely naturalistic, conception of the world, it was thought, put an end to religious superstition and theological dogma. Neo-Baconianism unleashes the power of science to give us the knowledge we need to improve the human condition, and brings into clearer focus the moral obligation to do so. The steady growth of knowledge in the natural and social sciences enables us to devise ever more effective means to securing human welfare creation. Possessed of this knowledge, we have both the power and the duty to eradicate poverty. It follows, on this neo-Baconian way of thinking, that science and technology are the best hope of the poor.

Chapter 4 took up this claim, but soon discovered the very considerable difficulties confronting the preliminary task of identifying 'the poor', and the subsequent task of determining what can be said to make them 'better off'. It concluded that a quantitative measure such as 'the poverty line' is misleadingly simplistic. Good lives are multi-faceted and context relative. Consequently, any monetary measure relates only partially, and tangentially, to what really matters. It is not 'the poor' economically defined that we should be thinking about, but people living impoverished lives.

I. Combatting Impoverishment

A key claim of this book, then, is that replacing the concept of poverty with the concept of impoverishment is an important step forward in addressing issues surrounding the inadequate conditions in which a great many human beings live. Nevertheless, some allowance must be made for the fact that most of the major agencies concerned with mitigating impoverished lives employ the concept of 'poverty line' and talk almost exclusively in terms of putting an end to 'poverty'. The World Bank's website, for instance, says that it has set itself 'two goals for the world to achieve by 2030: 1. End extreme poverty by decreasing the percentage of people living on less than $2.15 a day to no more than 3%. 2. Promote shared prosperity by fostering the income growth of the bottom 40% for every country.'[1] The Bill and Melinda Gates Foundation website says that '[i]n developing countries, we focus on improving people's health and wellbeing, helping individuals lift themselves out of hunger and extreme poverty.' Oxfam International's slogan is 'the power of people against poverty' and its declared mission is 'To create lasting solutions to poverty, hunger, and social injustice.'

All these declarations rest on important assumptions that we have found reason to question. They assume that we know who 'the poor' are, and that we know what it means to make their lives better. For present purposes, however, there is a further assumption requiring closer examination. This is the supposition that, while emergencies warrant food aid and the like, the best hope of improving the lives of the poor in the longer term lies with development projects focused on political, medical, educational, and economic infrastructure. Over many decades this assumption informed and guided major international organizations, governments, and politicians from across the political spectrum, as well as hundreds, if not thousands, of well-intentioned non-profits and charitable organizations. Yet there is no longer the universal consensus that there once was. Some prominent economists continue to advocate 'development' projects

---

[1] This second goal introduces an additional concern with inequality, and raises this question: why do people in the 40–50% bracket matter less?

as the path to greater prosperity. Others, no less prominent, have serious doubts about this approach.

A notable figure among the first group is Jeffrey Sachs. Sachs's best-known book is expressly entitled *The End of Poverty*, and on the strength of it he served as Special Adviser to the United Nations in the formulation of the original Millennium Development Goals (MDGs). These goals were endorsed at the United Nations Millennium Summit in 2000 by the leaders of 189 countries, and their principal aim was declared to be the 'eradication of extreme poverty'. In a similar spirit to Sachs, Paul Collier, author of *The Bottom Billion*, subtitled his book *Why the Poorest Countries are Failing and What Can Be Done About It*. Collier identifies 'the bottom billion' in terms of the world's poorest countries. He begins with Malawi as a prime example of the kind of country constrained by conditions he identifies as those that make poverty persistent. While Collier's analysis of the measures that have generally been taken to remedy this is highly critical, it is nonetheless conducted in terms of statistical data. The final part of the book is entitled 'An Agenda for Action', and while Collier departs to some degree from Sachs's belief in the efficacy of international aid, he does place considerable, if qualified, hope in a wider range of international policies.

Sachs and Collier are professional economists with knowledge and experience of the work of two major international organizations, but a second group of economists, no less well qualified, has expressly and emphatically rejected their approach. William Easterly, sometime research economist at the World Bank, makes his position clear by entitling his 2006 book *The White Man's Burden: Why the West's Efforts to Aid the Rest Have Done So Much Ill and So Little Good*. The title of Dambisa Moyo's book, published in 2009, is equally emphatic—*Dead Aid: Why Aid is Not Working and How there is Another Way for Africa*. Easterly and Moyo make a compelling case for thinking that the 'aid' poor countries have received from rich countries for decades, both directly and indirectly, has proved worse than useless. In reality, it has been a major obstacle to the enhancement of impoverished lives.[2] Easterly and Moyo's assessment is shared by Angus Deaton. Towards the end of *The Great Escape*, he writes:

---

2   In *Against Charity* (2018) Daniel Raventos and Julie Wark are even more
    scathing about the aid industry. Though their book is worth reading, it is not
    an academic study so much as a polemic, or even diatribe, against

Large-scale aid does not work because it cannot work, and attempts to reform it run aground on the same fundamental problems over and over again. Bridges get built, schools are opened, and drugs and vaccines save lives, but the pernicious effects are always there.

The most compelling case for reducing funding is seen in those (mostly African) countries in which foreign aid is a large share of national income and accounts for almost all of government expenditures... [T]he 'obvious' argument that giving money will reduce poverty is in fact obviously false... That dedicated and ethical people are doing harm to people who are already in such distress is not the least of the tragedies of aid. (*The Great Escape*, p.318)

Some of the pernicious effects to which Deaton alludes are powerfully documented in *The State of Africa: A History of Fifty Years of Independence*. This study by the journalist Martin Meredith, first published in 2005 and re-issued in a revised and expanded version in 2011, covers the whole of Africa, including the North African Arab countries that have not been such obvious recipients of Western aid.[3] Meredith's principal theme is that Africa, north and south, having been deeply scarred by its colonial history as a victim of nineteenth-century European power politics, had its problems greatly intensified by the sudden advent of political independence and the opportunistic leadership that independence spawned. In this context, the development aid that poured into sub-Saharan Africa, far from alleviating the problems of the countries to which it was given, exacerbated them, not least because a large part of it came from governments in France, the United States, the Soviet Union, and China, countries whose policies were deeply influenced by political and economic interests of their own.[4]

How is this profound disagreement among development experts to be adjudicated? Both sides of the debate can call upon economists with acknowledged authority. If we accept the view that, for more than sixty years, development projects intended to end poverty have proved wrong-headed, fruitless, and even damaging, then all such projects should stop. However, since it is impossible to deny that radical economic impoverish-

---

'philanthrocapitalism'. Jeffrey Sachs, Bill Gates, and Peter Singer all come in for intense criticism.

[3] A notable exception is Egypt which for some years has received an annual aid package from the USA worth about $1.5 billion.

[4] In *The War That Doesn't say Its Name* Jason K. Stearns observes that financial and military aid provided by the USA's anti-Islamist 'war on terror' has played its part in perpetuating armed conflict in the Congo.

ment persists in many places, it does not seem acceptable to do nothing, and wisest, therefore, to take the positive attitude that assisted development projects ought to continue, albeit with greater scrutiny. A sense of the overriding moral obligation to do *something* about persistent poverty explains why many people simply reject the negative conclusions of Easterly, Moyo, and Deaton.

Peter Singer's book, *The Life You Can Save*, defends traditional-style aid programmes, and has been widely acclaimed. Confronted with some of the circumstances he details, most readers very much *want* to be able to do something, and on this score, his book has a straightforward message. Do not spend money on things you don't need; give it to organizations that have a proven record of effective work in poor places.[5] Singer dismisses Easterly's doubts with just three brief references, yet his whole argument rests on the 'obvious' claim that Deaton declares to be 'obviously false', namely, that giving money will reduce poverty. In an enthusiastic endorsement, Bill and Melinda Gates describe it as a book that 'challenges every one of us to do more, to be smarter about the ways we go about giving, and shows us that, working together, we can make a profound difference in the lives of the world's poor'. In the abstract, it seems impossible not to respond to such a challenge. However, its moral appeal rests entirely on the contention that 'smarter giving' and 'working together' will 'make a profound difference to the lives of the poor'. This claim, though, is not an abstract moral principle to which we might, or might not, subscribe. It is a strictly empirical prediction, and a prediction whose plausibility Easterly and others dispute.

Do development projects work? Do they enrich or impoverish the lives of the people they are supposed to assist? The debate, clearly, is of the greatest importance, and both sides can call upon equally authoritative voices from the world of development economics. A question about means and methods lies at the heart of the deadlock, and there is deep division on the answer to this question. How, then, can the argument proceed? To make any headway, it seems that we need a different approach. I shall argue that the debate about means and methods should be suspended. Instead, we should consider the ends to which these means

---

5   As testimony to its conviction that giving money is doing good, the book includes a tear out pledge which readers are invited to return to Singer.

have been directed. Most importantly, we should think critically about the order of priority between those various ends.

II. Priorities

Neo-Baconianism, it will be recalled, holds that human beings are empowered by knowledge. Medical science, geology, psychology, sociology, economics, and so on all enable us to improve the human condition. Moreover, freed from religious presuppositions, human beings can determine for themselves what is to count as an improvement. The pervasive influence of neo-Baconianism is evident in the very many research centres and institutes devoted to 'development' that have been established by international bodies, national governments, leading universities, and major charitable foundations. The research work of these organizations, like that of research divisions in many commercial companies, is not undertaken for its own sake or motivated by purely academic interest. The results are expected to be of practical value. Of course, this vision's attractiveness and influence cannot guarantee that the work it stimulates actually proves valuable. Moreover, assessing the applicability, integrity, and effectiveness of the programmes and projects it has initiated is often difficult. Inevitably, some research will prove largely useless, or worse, successful inventions intended to serve good purposes will be turned to bad ones. Greater understanding of chemistry has produced nitrogen fertilizer; it has also produced mustard gas.

These are difficult matters to investigate, but for the purposes of examining the philosophical issues that underlie the choice of means and methods, let us assume that research inspired by neo-Baconianism has been productive in the promotion of health, education, business, and political governance. Still, even when we can identify means to ends with confidence, we need to set priorities. How is the choice to be made between the different ends to which research-based development strategies are directed? Secondly, who gets to make that choice?

Let us start with the second of these questions. In the context of development projects that aim to improve the lives of impoverished people, it evident that the choice is made by the aider, not the aided. This, it might be said, is predictable because of the familiar thought that those who pay the piper call the tune. On occasion, though, paying the piper gives donors a degree of power that can have widespread ramifications for the wellbeing of those to whom they donate. Here is one striking example. In 1988, the World Health Organization (WHO) adopted a landmark resolution to eradicate polio worldwide. This sounds highly commendable, comparable to the eradication of smallpox that finally put an end to one of the greatest scourges humankind has known. One notable difference between the two, though, is that in the late twentieth century polio, unlike smallpox, constituted a greater problem in richer industrialized countries than in developing agricultural countries. In compensation for this, the WHO expected the whole cost of eradication to be met by industrialized countries, something that proved more easily said than done. If the eradication was to be worldwide, then poor countries had to play their part in implementation, even if the *financial* cost were fully met by donor nations (rarely the case in fact). But cost is not only a matter of finance; there is also opportunity cost. Implementation places a substantial burden on the healthcare systems and public administrations of poor countries, not least because the time and effort that is given to polio eradication is, by the same token, time and effort denied to something else. In this case, opportunity cost proved a very significant matter. The eradication of polio certainly promised to benefit the lives of *some* people in poor countries, but, given those countries' very limited administrative resources, it would *not* have been the choice of their governments to make the eradication of polio a priority. Other health issues were far more pressing. The point of the example, of course, is not to debate this particular issue, but to illustrate the fact that in this case the recipients of aid could not do as they thought best. The question of priority was not left to them.

Despite the WHO resolution and the huge effort subsequently devoted to it, polio has not been eradicated. It still exists, and now constitutes a relatively minor threat to human wellbeing compared with many other diseases.[6] Nevertheless, eradicating it completely has retained its attraction, especially for some wealthy donors. In her investigation into the Gates Foundation, Lindsey McGoey records that in Nigeria, India, and Pakistan, polio vaccination was being administered when there was no similar protection against diphtheria or measles, even though these diseases constituted a greater risk for many more children.

> The emphasis on polio vaccination at the expense of other inoculations is not lost on local villagers. Time and again, they question the emphasis on a disease that places a less burdensome toll on them than other scourges. A

---

[6]   In 2012, only 223 cases of polio were reported worldwide.

number of villagers say "What is polio? We've never seen it—why are we worried about it?... our children are dying of measles.' (*No Such Thing As A Free Gift,* p.158)[7]

Because of Bill Gates's personal enthusiasm for the project of eradicating polio, these 'on the ground doubts' went unheeded, and the Gates Foundation continued to donate significant sums to polio eradication in preference to other programmes. This is not sheer dogma. A case can be made in support of this choice, but the important point is that, whatever the strength of the case for or against, the decision rests with the donor. It was Bill Gates and the Gates Foundation that decided to persist with polio vaccination, not the communities to whom it was provided.

This is the point at which to return to the first of the questions raised above—how is the choice to be made between the different ends to which research-based strategies could be directed? The problem is not simply a matter of ranking priorities. There is also the matter of the values on which ranking is based. Many aid programmes take it for granted that priority should be given to those things generally classed as 'basic needs'. These commonly include food, water, sanitation, and shelter, all of which may be said to be organic needs. However, the fact that something is a basic need of the human being *as an organism* does not automatically give it normative priority, because this does not guarantee that its satisfaction will make for a better life. Conversely, something that may be deemed to make life better may not be 'basic' in this sense.

In *Poor Economics*, Banerjee and Duflo uncover what they refer to as 'a puzzle'. Food is indisputably a basic need, and poor people often do not have sufficient income to purchase the calories physiology tells us they need. Yet, when people in these circumstances are given more money, they may well spend it on tastier food rather than more food, or even on beer and tobacco, things they evidently do not *need* physiologically speaking. Why is this? The answer is not that they are foolish or wasteful, but that even the very poor appreciate something more than the satis-faction of basic needs. Basic needs make life possible. Modest 'luxuries' make life more worth living. 'Generally,' Banerjee and Duflo conclude, 'it is clear that things that make life less boring are a priority for the poor' (*Poor Economics*, p.37). Matthew Desmond's masterly study of homeless-ness, *Evicted: Poverty and Profit in the American City*, notes the same

---

[7] McGoey is quoting Donald Henderson, a former WHO epidemiologist.

phenomenon. Chapter 18 is entitled 'Lobster on Food Stamps' and recounts the case of Larraine, who 'spent money or food stamps on inessentials' (including expensive lobster). This 'baffled and frustrated people around her', who thought that 'Larraine was poor because she threw money away.' But, Desmond says, 'the reverse was more true. Larraine threw money away because she was poor' (pp.218–9). This seemingly strange phenomenon — throwing away money because of poverty — is one we will find reason to consider again in a later chapter.

Inequality between donor and recipient is both inevitable and understandable. The funds belong to the donor, and neither individuals nor institutions are obligated or compelled to give anything to anyone. Consequently, and naturally, when donors give, they give to causes that move and inspire them, and an appeal to help with what donors perceive to be basic human needs is more likely to succeed than an appeal for what they think of as luxuries. If my resources are truly to be mine, this is how it must be. This element of choice is evidently desirable, yet it always raises the possibility that what moves and inspires the donor may differ significantly from what the beneficiaries of their generosity would identify as more desirable. The point can be made about any act of giving — a birthday present for instance. In giving you a gift, I choose what to give and how much to spend. Perhaps you are delighted and grateful. On the other hand, though reasonably pleased with the gift I have given you, with the same amount of money at your disposal, you would have chosen differently. That is why people often give cash as a gift. They think that it is better to let people choose for themselves.

This commendable principle — let the recipient choose — cannot easily be applied to aid programmes, however. Governments are constrained by the approved purposes of the aid budgets they have at their disposal. They cannot leave the recipient government free to spend financial aid in whatever way it chooses, lest it be spent in some way that conflicts with these approved purposes.[8] Similarly, charitable foundations are usually set up with specific aims, and must use their income to promote these aims, and not others. Individuals donate money to charitable organizations through such things as street collections and internet fundraising, and they do so in response to an advertised cause. If the money they have

---

8   I leave aside here the phenomenon of misspending, though it is a common occurrence in the world of 'aid'. The scale on which American dollars were misspent by recipients following the invasion of Iraq is literally inestimable.

donated is given to recipients to be spent in any way they choose, it has been taken on false pretenses. By the nature of the case, then, donors specify the purposes to which the aid they give may be directed, and recipients must direct it accordingly. This returns us to the problem. What if the intended beneficiaries have a different set of values and most want help for other things?

The worldwide eradication of polio is just one example of the phenomenon known as 'donor darlings'. These are good causes that states, foundations, and individuals favour very greatly. The reasons for favouring a 'donor darling' can vary. Some causes simply attract more support than others. An appeal on behalf of sick children, or endangered animals, may attract far more interest, and bring in substantially more money, than an appeal for refugees, for instance, irrespective of how pressing the need and how professional the fundraising has been. Additionally, where priorities are set by the founding purposes of the donor organization, causes and actions that seem to 'fit' these purposes better than others will become 'donor darlings'. Private foundations have greater flexibilty than government agencies or public charities, though, as with the Gates Foundation, their priorities are likely to be set by the causes their principal funders prefer. Furthermore, when billionaires, such as Gates, Buffet, and Zuckerberg, set aside vast sums of money for good causes, and describe at least some of the funds as 'unrestricted', this is somewhat misleading; they are always restricted by the purposes of the organization to which they are given. Furthermore, the institutional independence of the recipient organization may do little to protect its policy making from being shaped by a donor, if the donor is big enough. The World Health Organization is legally independent of the Gates Foundation, its second largest donor after the US Government. But, according to Laurie Garret, WHO policy decisions are 'casually, unofficially vetted by Gates Foundation staff', and the Director-General Margaret Chan has acknowledged that the WHO's budget is 'highly ear-marked, so it is driven by what I call donor interests' (quoted in *Against Charity*, pp.87–8).

Regardless of who has the final word in the establishment of priorities, there will always be 'mixed' motives. That is to say, inevitably self-interested motives will be found at work alongside a sincere intention to improve the lot of other people. Sometimes apparently altruistic motives are inseparable from less commendable self-promotion. There are wealthy benefactors, often, who sincerely want to give generously to good causes, but also want to be *seen* to have given. That is why fund raisers are open to having buildings, scholarships, or opportunities expressly named after those who gave the funds to create them. More strikingly, there has been a growth in 'celebrity' fund raising events, where the glamour and fame of the celebrities is used, but also promoted, in the name of good causes. There is reason to hold, as Raventos and Wark claim *(Against Charity,* Chapter 5), that when this happens good causes are being used to provide a morally respectable cloak for lives and livelihoods that do not bear scrutiny. Their scepticism may be excessive because good things do result from named benefactions and celebrity fund raisers. Yet the fact remains that these beneficial outcomes are importantly dependent on more than simple benevolence. Christ's injunction, "So when you give to the needy, do not announce it with trumpets" *(Matthew* 6:2), is very rarely followed by major donors, and the recommendation that celebrity support and attendance at fund raising events should be kept secret is contrary to the whole idea.

Even when the motives for charitable programmes are not self-promoting, and there are no hidden agendas, it is nonetheless an observable and publicly recognized fact that large organizations, and those who work for them, necessarily develop vested interests. The wider world in which they work is one where professional success and failure matter. This means that, to be successful, they have to be concerned with more than the good causes they are there to assist. They cannot be indifferent to career advancement or the sustainability of the organizations for which they work, for instance. The kind of neutrality that by implication the utilitarian philosophy of 'effective altruism' recommends is simply impossible. Relief and development organizations are not aid delivery *machines*. They are agencies run by human beings, who are very rarely, if ever, motivated by pure altruism. McGoey's study of the Gates Foundation reveals just how hard it has proved to separate the charitable interests of the Foundation from the business interests of Microsoft, on which the foundation is ultimately dependent for the resources it needs to support its benevolent activities. Good will is not enough to sustain the flow of significant resources and put them to effective use; it needs astute business practice as well.

This point about vested interests must be stated with care. It is not wrong in itself to promote or protect commercial interests that are vital to the income on which grants depend. In fact, those who run such organizations must acknowledge a dual responsibility. Their task is not only to advance the work of the foundation, but to safeguard its interests at the same time. The problem, of course, is that these two tasks may come into conflict. What is best for Oxfam as an organization may on occasions militate against the people whose lives it is there to improve. In short, its flourishing as an organization can come into conflict with its rationale. Once again, the point is not confined to the context of aid organizations. Pharmaceutical companies are in the business of inventing, manufacturing and selling effective drugs that will cure or alleviate sickness. Hospitals are there to make the sick better. Still, they are also commercial concerns whose continuation depends upon profitability. It is not difficult to imagine, or to identify, circumstances in which, if only for a time, the promotion of health by means of drugs takes second place to the profitability of the pharmaceutical company. The same conflict may arise in schools and colleges. The provision of teaching and the promotion of learning are inextricably interconnected with tuition fees, professorial salaries, and career prospects.

Allowing for these realities, however, there is a further possibility. When it comes to schools, universities, and hospitals, management, staff, and shareholders/trustees may be strongly tempted to pursue profit over health or education beyond the point necessary for commercial survival. This is unlikely to surprise anyone. However, it is less widely acknowledged that a similar temptation confronts charitable foundations, even when they are legally classified as 'not for profit'. While there are no shareholder interests to accommodate, many 'non–profits' pay salaries to CEOs that are much larger than would appear necessary for successful recruitment. More generally, concern for the terms and conditions of those who staff such organizations, whether 'for profit' or 'not for profit', can be given priority over the principal purpose for which they are employed. Working conditions for employees in relief and development organizations matter. That is not in question. What *is* in question is *how much* they matter, especially relative to the purposes for which those people have been employed.

A yet more complex case is that of 'government to government' aid. In the real world of politics, the motives behind decisions on foreign aid are multiple. China's assistance to African countries has been especially notable as an instrument of business investment and political influence. Even where (if anywhere) there is a sincere desire to help poor countries, electoral appeal, party alliances, defence agreements, and the international balance of power cannot fail to play a part in determining both the level of aid, and the kind of assistance that is given under this label. Peter Singer responds to Easterly's claim that most government to government aid programmes have failed, by observing that if we are to make a just assessment of their success in alleviating poverty and hardship, we need to separate out genuine aid from everything that governments choose to label in this way. Often 'aid' includes weapons and military assistance, for instance, and Singer is undoubtedly right that if we include the provision of weapons under the heading 'foreign aid', we are bound to find that it failed to alleviate poverty. Such inclusion, accordingly, is plainly a mistake.

On one level, this looks like a reasonable rejoinder to make. Discriminating between different kinds of 'aid' seems essential to assessing their effectiveness, though disentangling one form from another may not be straightforward, because military aid has often been part of a broader 'humanitarian' intervention. On another level, however, Singer's rejoinder misses the point of Easterly's and Moyo's central contention. The category of 'foreign aid' will always reflect the political interests of the governments who give it, as it will the political interests of the governments who receive it. All aid is, in effect, what is known as 'tied' aid. In principle, tied aid can serve the needs of those who are its ultimate recipients, while at the same time serving the political and commercial interests of the donor country. The problem is that when commercial and political interests are the levers that make a substantial amount of aid available, the conditions that the aid is supposed to alleviate can easily be neglected, and even subverted. The record of government to government aid, and aid by international organizations, as recounted by Easterly and Moyo shows that these are very far from being remote possibilities.

Even with the best of intentions, the pecularities of context, often imperfectly understood, play a significant role. Two important in-depth studies of development projects, one in Africa and one in India, reveal this in fascinating detail. In *The Anti-Politics Machine*, a study of the work of development agencies in Lesoto, James Ferguson observes that:

> The anthropologist knows well how easily structures can take on lives of their own that soon enough overtake intentional practices. Whatever interests may be at work, and whatever [development agencies] may think they are doing, they can only operate though a complex set of social and cultural practices so deeply embedded and so ill-perceived that the outcome may be only a baroque and unrecognizable transformation of the original intention. (*The Anti-Politics Machine*, p.17)

A key part of the problem is that the neo-Baconian conception of the development 'expert' brings with it abstraction from reality in the interests of theoretical simplicity.

> It is only natural that people who are entrusted with the task of producing acceptable 'development' discourse as a major part of their jobs should develop an ability to accumulate the kind of information that will be of use in constructing that discourse, while ignoring or even resisting the sort that would complicate that task. (*The Anti-Politics Machine*, p.245)

> By uncompromisingly reducing poverty to a technical problem, and by promising technical solutions to the sufferings of powerless and oppressed people, the hegemonic problematic of 'development' is the principal means by which the question of poverty is de-politicized. (p.256)

In *Cultivating Development*, David Mosse, who worked as a consultant with the Indo-British Rainfed Farming Project (IBRFP) with Bhil communities in north west India for most of the 1990s, reaches similar conclusions about the inevitable mismatch between development agencies and local contexts. 'It would be surprising if we did not find historically determined factors shaping the relationship between Bhil communities and their new development patron IBRFP and its discourse of improvement' (p.55). 'Of course we project makers were predisposed to view interactions with Bhil society in terms of our reading of donor priorities, tribal needs and project narratives of change' (*Cultivating Development*, p.74).

The accumulated experience of development projects in the second half of the twentieth century suggests that the combination of interest and ignorance on the part of donor countries and the well-intentioned but mistaken presuppositions of development agencies do not bode well for grandiose ambitions such as the UN's 2015 Sustainable Development Goals. However enthusiastically underwritten by economists, technologists, and politicians, they are a false hope for the poor. If we add the illicit diversion of aid by recipient governments away from the purposes for which it has been given, the probability that development projects will do good is diminished still further. Moyo notes that 'a World Bank study found that as much as 85 per cent of aid flows were used for purposes other than that for which they were intended, very often diverted to unproductive, if not grotesque ventures' (*Dead Aid*, p.39). The same problem can arise with respect to aid raised, for the best of reasons, by high profile charitable campaigns. One of the most striking examples of this is to be found in the Ethiopian famine of 1984. Meredith[9] recounts how food bought and transported with money raised through hugely successful public appeals, such as Bob Geldoff's 'Band Aid', was diverted by the Ethiopian government to feed the very army that was responsible for aggravating the famine.

III. Aid and Dependency

For the purposes of the present argument, however, it is enough to note these especially regrettable possibilities. The principal point to be made about donor–recipient relations also applies to cases in which government or non-government donors act (let us imagine) on only the purest of motives, and to maximum effect. Regardless of intentions, the donor-recipient relationship is never one between equals because dependence operates in one direction. The recipient is dependent on the donor; the donor is not dependent on the recipient. It is a desire to counter this relationship of dependency that has led to the widespread use of the term 'partnership'. Yet, as Mosse observes, '"partner" [is] an ambivalent concept that... in the context of aid relations, conveys the ideal of equality, while allowing the asymmetries of tutelage or clientship' (*Cultivating Development*, p.26). Indeed, later in the book he cites other studies that warrant an even stronger conclusion. 'Policy discourse generates mobilising metaphors ("participation", "partnership", "governance") whose vagueness, ambiguity and lack of conceptual precision is *required* to conceal ideological differences... But ideas that make for "good policy" —policy that legitimises and mobilises political and practical support— are not those that provide good guides to action' (p.230, emphasis original).

A similar rhetorical move is to be found when 'charity' is replaced by 'justice', which sounds better to modern ears. The change of terminology, however, is largely cosmetic. Justice properly so called implies the existence of enforceable rights. Since donors are not under any enforceable obligation to give, recipients have no enforceable right to receive. We can say, if we wish, that donors have a *moral* obligation to give, and that this obligation is grounded in principles of distributive justice. Raventos and Wark's *Against Charity*, as its title indicates, advocates this change. Part 2

---

9   In Chapter 19 of *The State of Africa*.

of the book is entitled 'a partial solution' and comes out in favour of 'justice' and 'rights', opting for the currently fashionable idea of 'basic income' as a right. Yet, as long as the circumstances are such that what is at issue is the transfer of resources to a good or needy cause, nothing is accomplished by this change of language. Despite its alleged radicalism, Raventos and Wark's 'partial solution' is subject to all the same objections as the 'charity' that their book deplores.

Let us suppose, though, that the change of terminology is more than this, and that principles of social justice do give the poor some sort of 'right' to share the resources of the rich. Even then, it remains the case that that they are wholly dependent on this 'right' being acknowledged and acted upon. That is to say, they are no less dependent on justice being recognized and done, than they are on aid offered in the name of charity. To appreciate the one-way nature of the donor–recipient relationship we can usefully contrast it with the relationship between buyer and seller. If I buy something from you, you are selling something to me, so that both of us are giving and getting. I get goods for money; you get money for goods. In this respect, whatever other differences there may be between us, we are equal parties in the transaction, and able, often, to bargain. By contrast, in the donor–recipient exchange, whether motivated by charity or a sense of justice, one side is *giving* while the other side is *getting*. And since the giving goes one way, it is inevitably givers who decide what, how much, and to whom they give. It is for the donor to decide how much the recipient receives, and under what conditions the donation is made. The recipient has no bargaining power in this.

The reality, and the dramatic effect, of this imbalance is perhaps most marked with respect to the work of international organizations such as the International Monetary Fund (IMF) and the World Bank. The principal purpose of the IMF is to ensure the stability of the international monetary system, an aim that often, but by no means always, necessitates involvement in the affairs of poor countries. As an international lender to both poor and not-so-poor countries, the IMF is in a powerful position to *require* the implementation of policies and programmes within the nations to which it lends. One consequence of this is that the recipient government is rendered correspondingly powerless. Perhaps this is only to be expected. The IMF is a regulatory institution, and the requirements it makes must apply to rich and poor countries alike. However, the same point can be made with respect to the World Bank, which is expressly concerned with the alleviation of poverty. Indeed, as was noted earlier, its published aims are to *end* extreme poverty, and to promote shared prosperity by fostering income growth among the bottom 40% in every country.[10] Leaving aside previous reservations, let us say that these are worthy aims. Once again, however, the historical record shows that the terms and conditions under which they are pursued have invariably been set by the World Bank's officials and policy makers, not by potential beneficiaries. In other words, the means of ending extreme poverty (if this ambition makes sense), and the way in which shared prosperity is to be promoted, are both determined from above. They are products of the economic theories, research outcomes, and policy decisions of these supra-national organizations. By itself, certainly, this does not mean that they must everywhere prove ineffective. Nevertheless, it constitutes an important imbalance of power that has often had deleterious consequences. 'It is impossible to have a real partnership', Angus Deaton observes, 'when one "partner" has all the money, and it is impossible to have recipient ownership when the accountability is owed to ill-informed (if well-meaning) foreigners' (*The Great Escape*, p.315).

Might a measure of equality be deliberately incorporated into the donor–recipient relationships? Could donors resolve to *treat* recipients as equals, not least by paying attention to *their* priorities? The World Bank describes its activities as those of 'a unique partnership to reduce poverty and support development', a partnership, that is to say, between the central organization and the governments with which it deals. But is this properly described as a partnership between 'donor' and 'recipient'? To answer this question positively, we have to determine who, exactly, should be taken to be 'the recipient'. In the case of aid to governments, a crucial gap opens up between the receiving 'partner' and the intended beneficiaries. Even in those relatively rare instances where the government of a poor country can truthfully be said to be representative of the people it governs, political decisions are always in the hands of a privileged group that could not possibly be classed as 'poor'. Consequently, the national government to which the World Bank, IMF, or similar institution grants aid is the recipient in name only. In reality, local government is the donor's agent, and in this way the donor continues to stand in an unequal relationship to the impoverished people who are the intended recipients. The actions of national governments are no less 'top down' than the

---

[10] See http://www.worldbank.org/en/about/what-we-do

actions of foreign governments or international organizations. In many cases, the fact that independence replaced European colonial rulers with an indigenous African ruling class made little difference to either the prospects or the wellbeing of the poor. This general truth emerges very clearly from Meredith's *The State of Africa*.

Some political leaders have been highly sceptical of the possibility of equality between donor and receiver in the world of relief and development. For this reason, occasionally, they have rejected aid, insisting that equality requires equal self-reliance. In this spirit, Julius Nyerere, leader of a newly independent Tanzania, wrote: 'Independence cannot be real if a nation depends upon gifts and loans from another for its development. How can we depend upon foreign governments and companies for the major part of our development without giving to those governments and countries a great part of our freedom to act as we please? The truth is we cannot' (quoted in *The State of Africa*, p.251). In the light of this assertion, Nyerere launched the *ujamaa* village campaign. Between 1973 and 1976, under his personal direction, a sustained attempt was made to gather small farmers into 'villages' where their individual efforts could be combined and organized into far more effective units, thereby producing a dramatic rise in productivity. The actual outcome was an almost total disaster that dislocated rural life to a hugely damaging degree. This was because Nyerere's approach to development also rested on a radically unequal relationship. The campaign was inaugurated and controlled by an educated political elite able to enforce its will without regard to the opinions and preferences of the people, in precisely the way that 'foreign' donors set priorities that the people they intend (ostensibly) to benefit must accept.[11]

Others, no less aware of the dangers than Nyerere, have hoped to affirm the equality and independence of the poor by the adoption of 'micro-finance' schemes in preference to aid from donors.[12] The most famous of these is the Grameen Bank, whose founder Mohammad Yunnus was awarded a Nobel Peace Prize for his work. Yunnus devised a

---

[11] The case of Tanzania is just one of several examples studied at length by James C. Scott in *Seeing Like a State: How Certain Schemes to Improve the Human Condition Have Failed*. The broader theme of Scott's book will be returned to in Chapter 6.

[12] Dambisa Moyo, who is intensely critical of foreign aid, is one of these enthusiasts. See *Dead Aid*, Chapter 9.

viable banking system that could lend very small sums to very poor people without collateral, and thereby enable them to finance small-scale money-making enterprises, get access to higher education, and undertake house building. A central feature of the scheme is the Grameen Bank's principled rejection of gifts and loans. By means of micro-finance, the poor sustainably invest in each other.

Since the establishment of the Grameen Bank in 1976, several other similar organizations have come into existence, amongst them Opportunity International and Women's World Banking. They are all dedicated to self-generated economic development that avoids the dependence that comes with the donations and large loans that are characteristic of 'aid'. This feature of what we might call ground-level independence has led many people to place great faith in micro-finance schemes, and there are impressive anecdotes of how micro-finance has transformed the lives of the poor. Still, as Banerjee and Duflo observe in *Poor Economics*, while 'microfinance, with its 150 to 200 million clients, has earned its place as one of the most visible anti-poverty policies... there is nevertheless this question:... does it work?' (p.108). This is a strictly empirical question, and as they note, anecdotal reports are not the same as critically scrutinized evidence. When such evidence is assembled, however, the advantages and effectiveness of MFIs become less clear than their proponents tend to believe.

To begin with, the independent self-sustainability that is the hallmark of micro-finance is something of an illusion. 'Most MFIs', Banerjee and Duflo found, 'are subsidized by the generosity of donors and the enthusiastic efforts of their staff, largely based on the belief that *microcredit is better than other ways to help the poor*. Sometimes they are subsidized by policy' (*Poor Economics*, p.169, emphasis original). Secondly, in the comparative study they made of the MFI Spandana's work in Hyderabad, they found that households who took loans were better off than they had been in a number of ways, but had not undergone anything that could plausibly be called an economic transformation. This was partly because, as they discovered, the take-up of micro-loans was relatively small, and also because 'there is a clear tension between the spirit of microcredit [in which repayment is rigidly policed by the members] and true entrepreneurship which is usually associated with taking risks and, no doubt, occasionally failing... By contrast, the MFI rules are set up not to tolerate any failure' (p.174). Thirdly, the more successful MFIs become, the more likely they are to encounter opposition from competing organizations—

unscrupulous lenders, political party leaders, and the like. This can pressure MFIs into changing their ways, and even end in their destruction. In short, MFIs, like all organizations, have their strengths and weaknesses, successes and failures. The mistake is to look to them as a panacea, the perfect remedy for the eradication of poverty without dependence, and to overlook the fact that they can also generate their own vested interests. Banerjee and Duflo found that, 'Trapped by decades of overpromising, many of the leading players in the microfinance world have apparently decided that they would rather rely on the power of denial than take stock, regroup and admit that microfinance is only one of the possible arrows in the fight against poverty' (p.172). People who are deeply committed to particular institutions, especially those that they have created or in which they have invested an immense amount of time and effort, do not easily accept their limitations. Why should this general truth not apply to MFIs?

Banerjee and Duflo are neo-Baconians *par excellence*. That is to say, at every turn they endorse empirical observation and experiment as the proper basis for devising and testing remedies for poverty. In their case the endorsement comes with commendable humility. They draw five key lessons about addressing the hardship of poverty, based on a large number of carefully constructed case studies. Yet their conclusion is tentative.

> Despite these five lessons, we are very far from knowing everything we can and need to know. This book is, in a sense, just an invitation to look more closely. If we resist the kind of lazy, formulaic thinking that reduces every problem to the same set of general principles. *If we listen to poor people themselves and force ourselves to understand the logic of their choices*; if we accept the possibility of error and subject every idea, including the most apparently commonsensical ones, to rigorous empirical testing, then *we will be able* not only to construct a toolbox of effective policies but also *to better understand why the poor live in the way they do.* (*Poor Economics*, p.274, emphasis added)

Poor Economics combines a deep humanity with both a close investigation of empirical realities and a refreshing modesty. These, no doubt, are among the features that won it both the *Financial Times'* 'Goldman Sachs Business Book of the Year' and the *Economist's* 'Best Book of the Year'. For present purposes, though, what matters is the close attention that Banerjee and Duflo give to the 'logic' of the lives of the people that aid is intended to help. This attention treats people not simply as recipients of aid, but as human beings who are very often striving to live in the best way they can, and whose practical knowledge of the circumstances in which they have to live far exceeds the knowledge any aid agency might derive from empirical research and statistical information. Their attitude thus displays a laudable respect for the rational agency of the poor, and this is highly important from the point of view of the efficacy of programmes intended to assist them. Banerjee and Duflo are under no illusion that aid programmes, of whatever kind, will ultimately result in the eradication of poverty. The causes of lasting prosperity, they think, lie elsewhere.

> Economists (and other experts) seem to have very little useful to say about why some countries grow and others do not. Basket cases, such as Bangladesh or Cambodia turn into small miracles. Poster children, such as Cote d'Ivoire fall into the 'bottom billion'. In retrospect, it is always possible to construct a rationale for what happened in each place. But the truth is, we are largely incapable of predicting where growth will happen, and we don't understand very well why things suddenly fire up.
>
> Given that economic growth requires manpower and brain power, it seems plausible, however, that whenever that spark occurs, it is more likely to catch fire if women and men are properly educated, well fed, and healthy, and if citizens feel secure and confident enough to invest in their children, and to let them leave home to get the new jobs in the city.
>
> It is also probably true that until that happens, something needs to be done to make that wait for the spark more bearable. (*Poor Economics*, p.268)

This is a passage with special interest for the present argument. For all their caution, Banerjee and Duflo endorse an assumption that underlies almost all aid organizations and programmes. This is the idea that the people in countries defined as 'poor' in terms of economic data are to be regarded as 'waiting' for a spark to ignite the economic growth that will almost miraculously take them out of the 'basket cases' in which they currently live. Aid programmes are instrumentally valuable, and public policies are to be commended insofar as they succeed in laying the foundations in education, health, and security that will increase the probability of economic success when growth eventually begins. Their value meantime lies in making the lives of the poor more 'bearable'.

This way of thinking about poverty and development invites us to ask two philosophical questions that Banerjee and Duflo neither raise nor consider. First, what makes economic growth a proper object of hope? Second, what is to be said about hope with respect to those who live and die during the 'waiting' period, whose lives, it seems, are at best to be described as 'bearable'? The first question has a familiar answer, namely, that self-sustaining economic growth offers the poor more hope because it is a real route out of material poverty into material prosperity. This implies of course, that material prosperity is the ultimate thing to be hoped for. We have already seen reason to question this, and it is a topic to be taken up again in the next section. In the section after that, we will address the second question: is a 'bearable' life the best that can be hoped for by those who die before material prosperity arrives?

IV. Poverty, Prosperity, and Frugality

Is ever greater material prosperity, understood as increased purchasing power and the possession of more goods, the best thing that people in poor places can hope for? It is indisputable that it is something for which a great many impoverished people do actually hope, and it is in search of significant material improvement that many migrants set out on hazardous journeys. Demea, one of the characters in Hume's *Dialogues Concerning Natural Religion*, presents it as a fact that the 'labour and poverty' to which most lives are confined are 'abhorred by everyone' (*Dialogues* Part X). Hume's great contemporary, Adam Smith, widely regarded as the founder of modern economics, expresses a similar thought when he asserts in *The Wealth of Nations* that labour necessarily requires the labourer to 'lay down the same proportion of his ease, his liberty and his happiness' (*Wealth of Nations* Iv 7). Stated thus baldly, however, the claim seems to be false. It may be true that (almost) everyone abhors *hard* labour and *abject* poverty, but it is not hard to identify a long line of philosophers and moralists stretching back to Plato who are sceptical about the value of wealth and opulence. The Franciscan ideal of poverty, which was discussed earlier, is minimalistic and holds that the less you have by way of material possessions the better your life will be. Frugality by contrast, is not minimalistic. It simply disputes the alternative idea that the more you have, the better.

The word 'frugality', like the expression 'honest toil', has a somewhat archaic ring to it. This should not mislead us into thinking that the ideal has no modern exponents. Nowadays, probably, people are more likely to speak about the 'simple' than the 'frugal' life. But the thought is the same. We are better off if we relinquish many of the material possessions whose value consumerist society takes for granted, than if we seek still more of them. A famous articulation of this contention is to be found in David Henry Thoreau's *Walden; or, Life in the Woods* (1854). Thoreau's classic description (and advocacy) of the frugal, self-reliant life has received renewed attention with the rise of environmentalism. The merits of a simpler lifestyle that reduces materialistic consumption has been

endorsed quite widely, often on the grounds of countering the environmental impact of wealthy societies. But the idea that such a lifestyle is
better for the person who lives it has been promoted very effectively by
the influential writer Wendell Berry, among others.

Even if we leave aside the Franciscan ideal of poverty, then, the
recurrent appeal of a simple, frugal life shows that increased material
prosperity is not an uncontentious object of hope. Indeed, the weight of
philosophical opinion over the ages seems to favour frugality over
opulence as a better way for human beings to live. Opulence (along with
celebrity) frequently figures as the object of both aspiration and envy in
stories and newspaper articles. As we observed in the first chapter, it also
serves to motivate the appeal of national and international lotteries. Yet
very few philosophers and religious thinkers have expressly advocated
the opulent life as an ideal—Aristotle being a partial exception perhaps.
While this might be taken to show that philosophers are out of touch with
the motivations of ordinary people, if those motivations are to amount to
more than unreflective desires, if they are to be the conclusions of
practical wisdom, then the extended reflections of philosophers cannot be
completely ignored. The question, to repeat, is not whether human beings
do look longingly at great wealth; they often do. More fundamental to
their nature as practical agents is whether they have good reason to view
it in this light. Is opulence a plausible candidate for that 'one great End in
Life' that Reid invited his ethics students to think about? Should people
aim 'to reduce the whole of [their] Life to a connected System [in which]
every part [is] subservient to [this] main End'?

Emrys Westacott's book, *The Wisdom of Frugality,* is a sustained
examination of this question. He offers a comprehensive consideration of
the respective merits of opulence and frugality, and in the spirit of Reid
(of whom the book makes no mention) he skilfully connects both
empirical observation and philosophical reflection to this end. With many
important qualifications, he finally comes down on the side of frugality,
while acknowledging that the philosophy of frugality is a 'hard sell'. That
is precisely because most people in the modern world, whether rich or
poor, live out their lives on the assumption that becoming more
prosperous is always a good thing. Even those who proclaim the merits of
a more frugal existence usually mean to denounce *conspicuous* consumption, a level of spending that only great wealth makes possible—*lavish*
weddings, *exotic* vacations, *palatial* houses, and so on. They rarely intend
that we (or they) should forgo the *inconspicuous* (yet very substantial)

consumption that underlies the use of, for instance, hot showers, washing machines, refrigeration, cars, smart phones, the internet, air travel, modern medicine, vacations, and dining out. This is true, even, of those who join religious orders that are not enclosed. In the modern world, their life relies on the use of cars, telephones, domestic appliances, and the like to go about their religious business effectively. Anyone who rejects all (or most) everyday conveniences is more likely be regarded as a Luddite, an eccentric, or a recluse than an advocate of wise frugality.

It is easy for those who are not in any meaningful sense *poor* to preach the merits of (relative) frugality. This alerts us to another important consideration alluded to briefly at an earlier point. Denying oneself luxuries is a *choice*, and an even greater level of self-denial is something the thinkers Westacott calls the 'sages of frugality' have *decided* upon. The poverty St Francis embraced may have been extreme, but it was nevertheless *voluntary* poverty, and while many of those who first followed him were poor to start with, their *embrace* of poverty was still a choice. The previous chapter argued that it is not the voluntariness of poverty that makes it good. Choice and benefit are logically independent; a bad thing does not become good by being chosen. Still, very many people lead seriously impoverished lives because they have been born into very poor material circumstances. Material poverty, we might say, is not their *lifestyle*, but their *lot*, and there is every reason to suppose that they want to escape it. What they lack is the means to do so. A great many people find themselves in a world of low incomes and few possessions, and, leaving aside a lucky minority, come to the realization that they are unlikely to escape it. What then is *their* hope?

Preaching *acceptance* to this audience, as all the great religions have done in one form or another, aims to make a virtue out of a necessity. There may be good reason to do this. Why stir up discontentment in people, if that is the only lot they can ever expect to have? Is it not preferable for people to accept the life they have if this averts the disappointment, frustration, and resentment that would arise from a fruitless longing after better things? On the other hand, 'hope springs eternal', so that preaching acceptance on the part of the poor in the name of Franciscan poverty or Epicurean frugality denies their equality as rational agents able to pursue goals and aspirations of their own choosing.

Sooner or later, such preaching must play the role of 'the Platonic lie'. In Plato's *Republic*, superior philosopher-kings 'protect' inferiors from the truth, but for their own good. Let us suppose their intention is sincere. It nevertheless relies on a profound inequality between those who are permitted to know the truth, and those who must be kept in the dark. If there is even a measure of cogency in Aristotle's contention that, at a certain level, material poverty necessarily results in a diminished life, then the 'poor' are having frugality preached to them in order to prevent them from knowing what they intuitively sense; that their existence from the cradle to the grave can never constitute a worthwhile life. Any philosophy that serves to aid this deception qualifies for Marx's compelling description — a 'robe of speculative cobwebs, embroidered with flowers of rhetoric, steeped in the dew of sickly sentiment' (*Communist Manifesto* Section 3c). Furthermore, Marx thought, while the acceptance of poverty in the name of religion or frugality (or any other ideological doctrine) may make for a more orderly society, it is a self-fulfilling counsel of despair. A Platonic lie (as perhaps Plato intended) deflects those who are its victims from taking any of the steps that might actually improve their condition significantly. The ringing affirmation at the end of the *Communist Manifesto* — 'The proletarians have nothing to lose but their chains' — makes the point: if poverty is as bad as Aristotle thinks it is, there is nothing to be lost by trying to leave it behind.

Suppose after reading Westacott we conclude that the frugal way of life is an intelligible and surprisingly attractive ideal. Even so, such a well-informed and judicious discussion does not seem germane to the lives of those trapped in involuntary poverty. Part of the reason is this: to reflect on the question 'Which way of life should we choose?' we need security and freedom, and these depend upon a certain level of material prosperity that the involuntary poor often lack. Where the satisfaction of basic needs is all consuming, there is no time for leisure or reflection.

A more telling point, though, is that the concept of frugality is context relative. Westacott's argument addresses 'the philosophy of frugality in a modern economy', a topic to which he devotes a whole chapter. 'Frugality' in a modern developed society means foregoing a significant measure of material prosperity. What counts as a 'frugal' lifestyle in such a context nevertheless represents a level of material prosperity that could scarcely have been imagined — still less enjoyed — just a few centuries ago. Even people who in their own time were regarded as wealthy did not have available to them things the poorest of people in developed societies take for granted — running water, sewage systems, transportation, a variety of clothing, and so on. It follows that philosophical arguments in favour of frugality cannot get much purchase within societies and sectors where material prosperity is very low. Subsistence farmers in sub-Saharan Africa could be a lot wealthier than they are, and still describe their improved standard of living as 'frugal' compared to what they know of Europe and America.

The broader debate about 'frugality versus opulence', however, nonetheless retains its relevance to people in poverty. They can dream of an opulent life, and hope to attain it. Should they do so? This returns us to an earlier topic, the prospect of winning a lottery, and the observation that suddenly coming into great wealth often messes up a life more than it enhances it. What are we to think, though, about the far more common case in which relatively poor people aspire to the *gradual* accumulation of wealth? Unlike the gambler, they place their faith not in chance, but in hard work, enterprise, and an expanding economy. The result is the steady accumulation, not the sudden acquisition, of wealth. A gradual process of this kind has underlain the striking material improvements recorded by Deaton in *The Great Escape*. Commerce and industry, allied to education, made Europeans and Americans healthier and wealthier than any of their ancestors had been. The outcome was not calamity such as befalls one or two lottery winners, but a much higher standard of living for the large majority. Even those few who made fortunes sufficient to adopt opulent lifestyles coped with their riches perfectly well, and often directed them to valuable philanthropic purposes. Why should poor people not hope to follow them? Opulence may not come their way, of course, but is there is any reason, other than the prospect of disappointment, for them not to hope that it will?

V. Wealth versus Enrichment

While the obvious answer appears to be 'No', this does not settle the matter. As the 'sages of frugality' have correctly pointed out, great wealth brings its own dangers, however it may have been acquired. In the eyes of many poor people, no doubt, the idea that wealth is *dangerous* must seem preposterous. Yet is hard to deny, and easy to demonstrate, that wealth in the form of purchasing power and/or material possessions has *intrinsic* limitations with respect to human wellbeing. This is well-known to economists. The principle of diminishing marginal utility (DMU) tells us that the more of a good I have, the less valuable still more of it is to me. The point can be expressed in terms of income, or possessions. If I have an income of $20,000 per annum, an additional $10,000 is a real benefit. But if I have an income of $1 million per annum, the same increase of $10,000 would not improve my situation to any significant degree. This is because there is almost nothing the increase will enable me to buy that I could not buy without it. DMU is no less applicable to goods and services. I can do many things with a cell phone that I could not do without it, but a third or fourth cell phone brings no additional benefit. It thus represents no real increase in value. Similarly, employing a lawn service will save me labour, but employing a second lawn service, even if I can easily afford it, will not save me twice the labour. A third may not save me any additional labour at all. The general point relevant to our current discussion is this. Even if becoming wealthier than I am now is a reasonable hope, it does not follow that hoping to become even more wealthy is equally reasonable. Since the value of wealth has its limits, past a certain point still greater wealth is valueless.

Surprisingly, perhaps, it does not immediately follow that acquiring additional wealth is pointless. Frugality is a 'hard sell' to a modern audience chiefly because of a widespread assumption that greater wealth is somehow connected with a better life. What sustains this assumption? It is a truism that wealth is no guarantee of happiness, and examples of people who are very wealthy but have profoundly unhappy lives are easy to find. However, data that economists have gathered in their efforts to go beyond wealth and income as a measure of 'happiness' suggest a more complex relationship than is revealed by correlations between wealth and happiness, construed as subjectively experienced emotional wellbeing. Angus Deaton and Daniel Kahneman of the Center for Health and Wellbeing at Princeton University have analysed a large body of relevant data and come to an interesting conclusion.[13] While low income does tend to intensify unhappiness, it seems to be true that past a certain point (an annual income of $75,000), increases in income do not bring any increase in happiness. However, if we ask people not only how happy they feel, but how satisfactory they judge the quality of their life to be, an importantly different conclusion emerges. With respect to self-estimates of satisfaction, Kahneman and Deaton found a firmer correlation between rising income and increased satisfaction. Once I have a good enough income, a larger income won't make me feel any happier. But it can nevertheless make me more satisfied with life.[14]

---

[13] http://www.pnas.org/content/107/38/16489.full
[14] Large though the data set was that Kaneman and Deaton used—450,000 responses to the Gallup-Healthways Well-Being Index—there is a major

In assessing the significance of this result, there is a very important observation to be made about satisfaction with one's life. Judging how satisfied I am is not just a matter of introspectively describing my state of mind. Comparative evaluation with the lives of others is essential, because people determine whether or not they are leading satisfactory lives by comparing the lives of those around them. I will think myself well off if I have possessions and opportunities equal to or better than most of the other people I know or know of. If at a later point in life I have fewer opportunities and less good possessions than people in the same comparison class, I will think myself badly off, despite the fact that there may be little material difference in what I have now and what I had then. Three weeks' annual vacation seems good if most people are getting two. When most people are getting six and I am still getting three, the circumstance I formerly found satisfactory is one I am now likely to find less satisfactory. My subjective emotional states are not relative to yours. So when asked about my emotional state, I can report directly. When asked about my life satisfaction, however, I inevitably look around at other lives and compare them with my own.

The difference between happiness interpreted as feeling or mood, and satisfaction interpreted as a comparative judgement is highly significant with respect to the argument between frugality and prosperity. If I live in a reasonably prosperous world, and simply take the standard of living that most people enjoy to be a norm by which to compare my life with theirs, then I shall probably be dissatisfied if my own standard of living falls below that norm. If, however, I have been persuaded of the merits of a much more simple (or 'frugal') way of life, I will not be dissatisfied by the fact that I have a lower income and fewer possessions than others. St Francis did not envy the wealth he had left behind. Indeed the contrary is more likely. When I look at the lives of those around me, it may make me more satisfied with my own. That is because I have had the strength of mind to reject conventional standards and pursue an ideal of my own. People who choose a simple lifestyle—the Amish of Pennsylvania, say— will not be envious or resentful of those who have large incomes that sustain a far more opulent life.

---

question about whether responses elicited from human beings at one time and place tell us much, or even anything, about the mentality of human beings at other times and in very different places. I leave that issue aside here.

The key point is this. When we ask people to evaluate their life-satisfaction, we are presupposing that, implicitly or explicitly, they have an answer to the philosophical question about what kind of life is most worth living. The answer they give, or assume, to this question determines their level of satisfaction/dissatisfaction. It follows that no data we obtain, by however sophisticated a method, can determine whether they are right or wrong to be satisfied with the life they have. As Socrates points out in one of the Platonic dialogues, pederasts may be quite satisfied with the lives they lead. That does not make those lives any less shameful. Similarly, if the Franciscans and the Epicureans are right, those who are thoroughly satisfied with the opulent life are also mistaken, and those who are envious of them no less so.

This returns us to Kahneman and Deaton's other result—that prosperity is correlated with emotional happiness, up to a point. Such a conclusion is not without its philosophical difficulties. To begin with, there is the issue of whether happiness is a subjective state or an objective condition. The inclination to regard it in the first way has a long history and continuing appeal, but philosophical arguments against subjective conceptions of happiness date as far back as Aristotle's *Nicomachean Ethics*.[15] For present purposes, however, let us leave this issue aside and assume that happiness is indeed a subjective state. If so, there are good reasons to deny that it can be measured. If it cannot, this matters, because correlations require comparative measurement. We cannot say to what extent X is correlated with Y unless we can give numbers to both sides of the correlation. What we can do is correlate wealth and income with responses to *questions about* subjective feeling, and that is what economic studies are based upon. However, the evidence they use is therefore necessarily *indirect*. Such correlations are not based on the happiness economists *observe*, but on the happiness *reported* to them. Notoriously, the two may diverge. People are not always honest in their responses to surveys, and sometimes they do not know their own minds. Consequently, any correlation we arrive at may tell us about how people *say* they feel, but not how they *actually* feel.

Once again we should leave these complications aside. If it is true, as Kahneman and Deaton's interpretation of the data suggests, that an

---

[15] I discuss the arguments at length in *Theories of Ethics* (Routledge NY, 2011) Chapter 4.

increase in prosperity has only a limited ability to increase happiness, we may wonder why this should be the case. What is it that limits the power of wealth in this respect? Whatever explanation we finally settle on, it seems obvious that the following interrelated facts are relevant. A great many (perhaps most) valuable things in life cannot be bought, and others come free. 'Money can't buy me love' is a line that a Beatles song made famous. The song is about romantic love, but the point could be made just as well about love between any two human beings, including especially parent and child. Love, very obviously, is not the only thing that money cannot buy. It cannot buy beauty, intelligence, artistic or sporting talent, wit and humour, or virtues of character—open-mindedness, courage, generosity, and so on. Money can buy loyalty, to a degree, but not friendship or collegiality; it can buy sycophancy, but not genuine admiration. These observations are all platitudes, not discoveries, but that is their strength.

Love, friendship, collegiality, and admiration are important components of a satisfying life. Plainly they cannot be bought, yet it would be wrong to conclude from this that income and purchasing power are wholly irrelevant to them. Deaton and Kahneman's study reveals a link between low income and dissatisfaction with life and that is because relative material poverty can seriously limit the chances of leading a happy and rewarding life. Love and friendship are not constituted by material prosperity, but they are often dependent upon it to a significant degree. Personal relationships benefit from leisure, for example, and this is possible only if the time spent working produces sufficient income to permit it. Family life benefits greatly (as Deaton elsewhere observes) from cameras, telephones, and other electronic devices. These cost money, but they serve to sustain and enhance relationships that might otherwise wither. To possess (and give) beautiful objects, interesting books, musical instruments, and many of the other things that enrich our lives, we have to be able to purchase them. Education feeds intelligence, and though 'education' is much broader than formal 'schooling', material resources obviously play an important part in the quality of education that we are able to access, and to offer. Similarly, training facilities with proper equipment can greatly enhance sporting accomplishment. All these examples are items of common knowledge that it would be foolish to discount. It is true, let us agree, that money can't buy me love. But without some of the things money *can* buy, the prospect of securing and sustaining love may be seriously diminished. Still, the contribution that level of income makes in all these cases remains instrumental, and thus secondary. As Sen repeatedly observes, its value is not intrinsic, but derived. Income's contribution to a good life has value in virtue of intrinsic values for which no amount of money can adequately substitute.

The title for another, less well-known song—*The Best Things in Life Are Free*, by Lew Brown and Ray Henderson—though it overstates the case, captures a further important idea. There are valuable and important things that we do not need money to buy because they are freely available to all. Good food, comfortable housing, and nice clothes are rarely free. What the song means to highlight is that many of the things that make life worth living come at no cost. The list includes conversation, storytelling, folk songs and nursery rhymes, simple games, physical embrace, natural beauty, sunshine. A life bereft of any of these is impoverished, and it is a recordable fact that children deprived of the first five are psychologically mutilated.[16] The critical importance of these free 'gifts' to human well-being is also dramatically illustrated by the effects of solitary confinement. This form of punishment is tantamount to torture because, if it is maintained long enough, it is guaranteed to derange those who are subjected to it. Like the children housed in the notorious orphanages of Nicolae Ceausescu's Romania, it is possible to wreak frightful destruction on human beings while providing them with (barely) sufficient food, clothing, and shelter. In normal life the human goods these children were denied—company, physical comfort, speech, amusement, recreation—come free.

Goods that cannot be purchased, and goods that it is not necessary to purchase, enrich our lives. Lack of them impoverishes us. This simple observation is enough to show that 'purchasing power', however accurately estimated, is of limited interest for the wider argument in which we are engaged. It also enables us to construe more plausibly the seemingly preposterous claim that material wealth can be dangerous. Once we see that non-monetary goods enrich lives, we can also see that monetary goods can impoverish them. For instance, we cannot buy friendship, but it is a familiar trope of literature, reflecting a general truth of life, that very wealthy people run the risk of attracting false friends,

---

16 This recorded fact was discounted in 2020–22 by governments which responded to the COVID-19 pandemic with lockdowns and school closures, although the consequent negative impact of this unprecedented policy on the lives of children and young people was predictable.

and may find it almost impossible to tell them from true ones. Similarly, while sexual attraction has no direct connection with income level, a very wealthy person may find it easy to 'attract' a sexual partner. The danger is that he or she is easily deceived (or self-deceived) into thinking that it is personal charm rather than wealth that lies at the heart of the attraction. Under this misapprehension, the wealthy person rests content with a relationship that is false, shallow, and manipulative, and of course, while the manipulator may reap material rewards, he or she misses out on true love and friendship also.

The seeming paradox that 'riches' can impoverish us is revealed to be no paradox at all if we are careful to distinguish poverty and impoverishment. It is important to see, however, that the phenomenon is not confined to a small class of very wealthy people. The same sort of impoverishment can result from levels of prosperity that many would regard as 'modest', and that are shared by the parties involved. For instance, the 'penetration' of computers, smart phones, and access to the internet is often used as an indicator of a society's prosperity. Their manufacture and sale have hugely increased GDP, and it is evident that all these things have made a valuable contribution to the quality of many people's lives. At the same time, there is good evidence that computer games and social media can lead to social isolation, with a resulting increase in the incidence of depression and suicide, especially among teenagers. Notoriously, smart phones often have the effect of killing conversation, and reducing 'companionship' to mere co-existence. Couples are at the same restaurant table, groups are in the same room, but their contiguity is a matter of physical location only. Each person's attention is in some other world of its own. The impact of the exceptionally rapid rise and spread of smart phones has yet to be properly understood. A strong case can be made already, however, for thinking that they may in some contexts result in relationships being importantly de-humanized.[17]

These few examples show the negative impact of wealth to be a familiar part of everyday experience. The pursuit of wealth comes at a cost, and this cost, though not itself monetary, may nonetheless outweigh the benefit. Once again, examples are not hard to find. In *How Much is Enough? Money and the Good Life*, Robert Skidelsky (an economist) and

---

[17] I offer a more detailed exploration of one way in which smart phones can impoverish relationships in 'To Swipe or Not to Swipe: Love, Technology and Tinder', *The Critique*, Feb 2017.

Edward Skidelsky (a philosopher) investigate, as their subtitle suggests, some of the questions that concern us here. They begin with an intriguing puzzle. In 1930, the economist John Maynard Keynes predicted that the rapidly increasing rate of economic growth would have a radical effect on the workplace. Within a hundred years, he thought, thanks to machines and automation, on average people would be far wealthier than human beings had ever been before. Since they would *need* to work less and less, they *would* work less and less. Keynes' reasoning is clear. If we work to earn money to buy things, then steadily rising incomes will allow us to buy more without working as much. The puzzle to which the Skidelskys draw attention, however, is this. While Keynes was right about auto-mation and economic growth—modern production is highly automated and the majority of people in many countries are indeed wealthier than ever before—he was wrong about work. Eighty years on, average incomes are far higher, yet people in employment are not working less. On the contrary, many working people—especially in the commercial sector— have longer hours and more stressful occupations than their counterparts had in times past. Why should this be?

Part of the explanation the Skidelskys offer points us to a kind of greed.

> [Keynes] believed that [material wants] would one day be fully satisfied, leaving us free for 'higher things'. We now know better. Experience has taught us that material wants know no natural bounds, that they will expand without end unless we consciously restrain them. Capitalism rests precisely on the endless expansion of wants... It has given us wealth beyond measure, but has taken away the chief benefit of wealth: the con-sciousness of having enough. (*How Much is Enough?* p.69)

People never settle the question of how much is enough, because they are locked into a system of wealth production that always drives them to seek more. The Skidelskys see this as a modern version of 'the Faustian bargain'. We are drawn into accepting a great benefit despite knowing of its dangers, and because of a false optimism that the toll it promises to take can be averted.

A simple version of this Faustian bargain affecting the lives of ordi-nary people is to be found in the experience of many middle-class nuclear families. A couple with two or three children, a house that comfortably accommodates them all, ready access to good food and healthcare, and enough money for vacations, may seem to have secured the kind of life for which any poor family has reason to dream. The reality is less desirable, however. Characteristically, both parents need to work because two incomes are required to cover the expenses involved in house, cars, childcare, schooling, summer camps, and vacations. This has considerable impact on the family's lifestyle. Running a household, meeting work requirements, arranging childcare, maintaining a home, and so on generates a pattern of activity that is not only stressful and tiring, but significantly limits the time parents spend with their children and with each other. Yet once the pattern is established, it cannot easily be altered. If either parent were to give up paid work, or work much less, the level of consumption that underwrites it all would be unsustainable. The irony, of course, is that the *free* pursuit of material prosperity has *trapped* them in a vicious circle. This level of expenditure is essential to the viability of two paying jobs; two paying jobs are essential to sustaining this level of expenditure.

Contrary to Keynes' reasonable supposition that greater prosperity would bring people greater ease, data on psychological conditions, psychiatric disorders, addiction, and suicide provide strong evidence that many people in prosperous societies lead stressful lives. As material prosperity rises, the task of sustaining an enlarged pattern of consumption takes centre stage. The outcome is that there is little or no opportunity to enjoy the life that greater material prosperity is supposed to serve. In this way, the pursuit of even modest wealth can be impoverishing. That is to say, seeking *and sustaining* the level of material prosperity that we think we need may have this paradoxical effect. By drawing us into a world of frenetic lifestyle, it leaves us less well off than we would have been had we been content to be less prosperous.

Consumption is essential to modern commerce. The 'health' of many modern economies is officially assessed in terms of consumer spending, and the goal of 'prosperity for all' is interpreted in terms of economic growth and increased purchasing power. For this reason, frugality is no friend of capitalism. Yet it may nonetheless have something important to say about the realities of life in a modern commercial society. Proponents of the simpler and more frugal life are often thought to base their appeal on otherworldly, 'spiritual' values. In the case of the Franciscan, this may be correct, at least to some extent, and the religious dimension will be considered in due course. But Epicurean frugality as I have elaborated it here is strictly humanistic. The sorts of examples on which the argument has focused are presented with the purpose of showing that *from a human point of view* the successful pursuit of material prosperity can turn out to be impoverishing. It is this observation that enables us to return to the topic of the hope of the poor. The people referred to as 'the poor' frequently do have impoverished lives, and it is rational for them to hope for a way out of their impoverishment. The key, though, is not to confuse impoverishment with poverty, or enrichment with wealth.

Summary of the Argument
Up to this Point

What hope do the poor have of living good lives? A familiar answer, and one that has motivated a great many 'development' projects, contends that economic development holds the key. The relatively recent history of the prosperous nations of the West reveals 'a great escape' from high rates of infant mortality, susceptibility to fatal diseases, food insecurity, poor housing, and very limited material resources. Such an escape from poverty has unquestionably brought about a dramatic and valuable change in quality and length of life for vast numbers of people. From this it seems we may conclude that they live far better lives than their ancestors ever did. If that inference is legitimate, then it seems obvious that the best hope of 'the bottom billion' lies with a plan of action that will enable them to make this 'great escape' as well.

What the arguments of this chapter have shown, however, is that the means by which such an escape might be engineered are very uncertain. The record of international aid and development schemes such as the United Nations Development Goals, and national programmes of assistance like the US 'war on poverty', is at best patchy, and in some cases disastrous. To the lives of ordinary people, the modern State proves more often hostile than beneficial, an instrument of repression, war, and even famine. Nor is improving this record simply a matter of better economic theories based on better economic data, or more generous and better targeted 'aid' by individuals, foundations, and governments. Quite what it is that 'sparks' economic growth, and quite what may be done to sustain it, are questions that by and large continue to allude us. Besides, even if we had a sure and certain path to economic development, the example of 'the great escape' tells us that this takes time. Europeans and Americans were not lifted from poverty to prosperity overnight, but over two centuries or more. Consequently, advancing to a condition of prosperity is not much of a hope for those who will not live to see it realized. This leaves us with the question: what hope is there for *them*? If our hopes are fastened on an indeterminate point in the future when what is taken to be a reasonable level of prosperity is universally enjoyed (i.e. the heralded 'end of poverty'), then the answer seems to be 'None'. Yet those who will live and die before economic development takes hold (if it does) have their own lives to lead, and children to raise. With what hopes can they reasonably pursue the adult lives that stretch out before them?

One way of approaching this question starts with two observations. First, innumerably many people who lived before 'the great escape' led admirable lives that they themselves cherished. Second, some people who enjoy all the benefits of 'the great escape' are so profoundly dissatisfied with their lives that they commit suicide. These facts must make us question a fundamental assumption behind the aspiration to economic growth — the supposition that greatly increased material prosperity is a rational aspiration for people to have. Is this true? The question is rarely asked, because people who live in developed commercial societies generally take the answer for granted, and the consumerist culture that surrounds them tends to confirm them in this. Clearly, the consumption of material goods stimulates business and generates employment. Consequently, in their various roles as farmers, manufacturers, workers, managers, investors, and politicians, human beings have reason to promote it. The key question, though, is whether those who do *not* live in developed commercial societies, or who live in the deep pockets of poverty that developed commercial societies often include, have equal reason to regard it in this light.

The supposition that wealth is something to aspire to has not gone uncontested. We may employ 'Franciscan' as a useful label for the many influential religious figures, and 'Epicurean' for the many moral philosophers, who have articulated and defended a sharply contrasting goal. These thinkers have argued for the superiority of a 'frugal' lifestyle that is largely free of commercial pressures, and unencumbered with the insatiable pursuit of possessions. Claims for the superiority of such a life, of course, are likely to ring a little hollow with those whose lot is involuntary poverty, and preaching the merits of frugality to those who have been born poor seems to commend a passive acquiescence that serves the interests of the powerful by forestalling the demand for social and political change. This, we must concede, is indeed a danger. Yet it does not close off the main question. What kind of life can the poor hope to have, if the prospects of economic advance and material prosperity are slim? More importantly, perhaps, what kind of life can the poor hope to have, if the price of economic advance is urbanization, industrialization, and environmental degradation? Is the promotion of consumerist compensation for all these losses any less objectionable than advocating passive acceptance?

We have identified the mistake in supposing that having a rich and rewarding life is the same as possessing material wealth, and the corresponding mistake that fails to see the way in which material possessions can impoverish us. In short, the contrast between wealth and poverty, however important in some contexts, it is not the same as the contrast between enrichment and impoverishment. Human lives can be enriched by goods that do not *need* to be bought, and they can be impoverished by a lack of goods that *cannot* be bought. While this observation may sound little better than homespun wisdom, it nevertheless enables us to set forth the hope for a life that is rich in ways that are to a significant degree independent of money and material possessions. Such a hope is one that even the poorest human beings can intelligibly entertain.

This possibility takes us back to the topics discussed in Chapter Two. How should we think of a good human life? Is it marked chiefly by high quality experiences, or major achievements, or good relationships? It is natural to hope that our lives will include all of these things to some extent, and the good news is that all of them are possible for people with very limited material resources. Of the three, human relationships are most fundamental because, while by the nature of the case exceptional experiences and exceptional achievements are confined to the lives of the few, exceptional relationships are not. In principle, every parent/child relationship, every adult friendship and partnership could embody love and trust to the greatest degree. For this reason, the value of relationships between human beings offers us the most satisfactory basis for a philosophy of ordinary life.

Why should this be the case? Why should relationships take pride of place in the scheme of human values? The evaluative priority of human relationships is not obvious. In fact, it is contrary to what is generally referred to as 'liberal individualism', a philosophical integration of morality, politics, and law that has proved so persuasive that it is widely thought to be incontestable. Underlying liberal individualism is a recurrent line of thought that locates the ultimate source of value in the individual. The most influential version of this way of thinking (prefigured in Locke) is the one we find in Immanuel Kant. The moral imperative of 'respect for persons' as ends in themselves, that Kant articulates, generates a corresponding political claim. Individuals have basic and inalienable human 'rights' that every free society ought to embody in law by means of democratic institutions.

What makes liberal individualism even harder to resist is the fact that the major alternatives to Kantian moral philosophy are no less individualistic. Jeremy Bentham, the founding father of utilitarianism, famously declared talk of natural rights to be 'Nonsense on Stilts'. Yet by making the balance of pleasure over pain the standard by which the quality of life should be assessed, he simply replaced the individual as a rights bearer with the individual as a subject of psychological experiences. In the rational egoism of Hobbes and Mandeville there is none of the 'high' moral tone that is to be found in Kant, and none of the egalitarianism characteristic of Bentham. Nevertheless, they too construe the ultimate aim of life to be the satisfaction of individual desires. This is also true of the Romantic individualism we find in Rousseau, Nietzsche, and the existentialists, a current of thought that has been scarcely less influential than Kantianism. Its highest goal is self-expression, or even more individualistically, self-realization. Of course, none of these thinkers supposes that human beings spring into existence as fully formed individuals, nor do they think that the solitary life is best. They acknowledge the necessity of family and society, but they think of family primarily as the preparatory context in which individual lives are formed, and society as the organization that allows individuals to relate to each other in accordance with mutually applicable rules. On this view, when children arrive at maturity, though they still have parents, they cease to be children, and effectively leave their families behind. The wider society into which they then emerge is a political and legal construct, a framework within which to lead their personal, commercial, and professional lives.

To question the individualism that underlies all these conceptions of the good life runs counter to a deeply ingrained way of thinking, one that not only influences, but invariably shapes the debates about aid and development. 'Modern philosophy', John Macmurray writes, 'is characteristically *egocentric...* it takes the Self as its starting point... [and] the Self... is conceived as the Subject; the correlate in experience of the object presented for cognition.' This quotation comes from Macmurray's Gifford Lectures, collectively entitled 'The Form of the Personal'. These largely neglected lectures raise philosophical issues of the greatest consequence to the topics with which this book has so far been concerned. To decide what kind of life it is rational to hope for requires an understanding of what the best kind of life is for *a person*. To be clear about this, we need to know what kind of thing a person *is*. Since this way of expressing the matter—'what a person is'—seems to make an implicit concession to individualism, it is preferable to phrase the question in the way in which Macmurray phrases it—what is the form of the personal? This is the topic of the next chapter.

Chapter Six

Economic Development and the Form of the Personal

I. The Crisis of the Personal

'The Crisis of the Personal' is the title of Macmurray's first Gifford lecture. Across the whole set of lectures, he tells us, he has set himself the ambitious task of rethinking the way philosophers since the early modern period have conceived of human beings.

> The traditional point of view is both theoretical and egocentric. It is theoretical in that it proceeds as though the Self were a pure subject for whom the world is object. This means that the point of view adopted by our philosophy is that of the Self in its moment of reflection, when its activity is directed towards the acquirement of knowledge. Since the Self in reflection is withdrawn from action, withdrawn into itself, withdrawn from participation in the life of the world into contemplation, this point of view is also egocentric. The Self in reflection is self isolated from the world which it knows. (*The Self as Agent*, p.11)

The conception that Macmurray seeks to counter is perfectly illustrated by a passage from David Hume's *Natural History of Religion*.

> We are placed in this world, as in a great theatre, where the true springs and causes of every event are entirely concealed from us, nor have we either sufficient wisdom to foresee, or power to prevent those ills, with which we are continually threatened. We hang in perpetual suspense between life and death, health and sickness, plenty and want; which are distributed amongst the human species by secret and unknown causes, whose operation is oft expected, and always unaccountable. These unknown causes, then, become the constant object of our hope and fear; and while the passions are kept in perpetual alarm by an anxious expectation of the events, the imagination is equally employed in forming ideas of those powers, on which we have so entire a dependence. Could men

anatomize nature, according to the most probable, at least the most intelligible philosophy, they would find that these causes are nothing but the
particular fabric and structure of the minute parts of their own bodies and
of external objects; and that, by a regular and constant machinery, all the
events are produced about which they are so much concerned. But this
philosophy exceeds the comprehension of the ignorant multitude...
(*Natural History*, Sect 3)

Macmurray does not cite this passage, but it illustrates his contention
exactly. Hume presents an image in which human beings are assumed to
be *perceiving* subjects, looking out onto an 'external' world of objects and
events. Their relation to this 'external' world is essentially passive. It has a
causal effect upon them both by 'impressing' perceptual images on their
minds, and by stimulating 'passions' such as hope and fear within them.
In accordance with the Baconian vision to which he subscribed, Hume
thinks that 'philosophy' (in modern parlance 'science') reveals that the
world of material objects can be analysed into mechanical relations that
explain its workings. This world of material objects includes our own
bodies. Genuine scientific understanding, however, surpasses most
people's intellectual capacity, and that explains why the imaginary
inventions of religion and superstition gain wide currency, especially in
more primitive societies. Given the ease and attractiveness of these
fanciful explanations, and the difficulty of securing genuine knowledge, it
is somewhat remarkable, Hume thinks, that anyone persists with the
search for 'mechanical' explanations. Scientific knowledge grows only
because in every generation a few human beings show a deep intellectual
love of 'system'.

Hume offers his picture of humanity and the human condition in the
tone of one simply stating a fact. This, perhaps, is precisely how it strikes
many readers. So what is wrong with the picture? Why should we *not*
think in this way? The answer is to be found in Hume's own analogy.
Theatres do house sets and audiences, but it is actors who are central to
their purpose, and actors, of course, are human beings too. This means
that while they are indeed 'externally' perceived by the audience, why
they do what they do on stage is not the outcome of 'secret and unknown
causes'. On the contrary, their motives are of the same kind as the
audience's. This question thus arises. Are they to be included in the class
of externally perceived Objects, like the backdrop on the stage, or among
the class of Subjects, like the audience? It is a question that cannot be
answered. Hume's division between 'internal' Subject and 'external'
Object leaves no place for agency, and so actors on stage fit *neither*

category. Human subjects, as Hume conceives them, can perceive, experience emotion, and engage in intellectual reflection, but they cannot act. This conclusion reveals the incoherence of the picture from which it is derived. Intellectual reflection is itself a kind of action. It is one of the things, alongside very many others, that human beings *do*. Perceiving and responding, when we consider them more carefully, are also things we do.

Hume's picture of our relation to 'the world' is incoherent because it combines the error in Rene Descartes' Rationalist conception of the Self as an isolated self-sufficient thinker, with John Locke's erroneous Empiricist conception of the mind as a *tabula rasa*, something like a photographic plate, on which 'external' stimuli cause mental 'impressions'. Cartesian dualism makes internal mind (or thought) so radically distinct from external (or extended) matter that there can be no relation between the two. Locke's empiricism, on the other hand, connects 'internal' and 'external' in the same causal relationship that prevails between external objects, thereby implicitly eliminating any difference between thought and its object. Macmurray's principal observation is that dualistic and monistic ways of thinking are *both* false to our experience. We do not merely see, hear, and feel the objects around us; we actively look at, listen to, and touch them. This active engagement immediately breaks down the distinction between 'internal' and 'external', not least because our own bodies are among the objects we can look at, listen to, and touch. A modern tendency to identify the mind with the brain inclines us to the idea that thinking takes place 'inside' the skull. But of course, surgeons can take a look inside the skull, and when they do, they find organic matter, not thoughts.

The need for a radical rethinking of the picture of the Self that Descartes, Locke, and Hume assume explains the significance of the title Macmurray chooses for his first volume of lectures – 'The Self as Agent'. 'A radical modification of our philosophical tradition is demanded... [that] requires us to substitute for the Self as subject, which is the starting point of modern philosophy, the Self as agent' (p.38). But why has 'the Self as subject', and the Humean picture of people that goes with it, proved so alluring? Macmurray identifies two important features underlying its success. First, it is the product of philosophical theorizing, and philosophers, being intellectuals *par excellence*, have a natural inclination to suppose that the intellectual activities of the mind are fundamental to everything else. This is a mistake; philosophical theories are in fact derivative—as the word 'reflection' itself suggests. This does not mean that action must replace reflection (as Marx famously suggests). Macmurray's point is more nuanced. 'Philosophy is necessarily theoretical, and must aim at a theoretical strictness. It does not follow that we must theorize *from the standpoint of theory*' (p.85, emphasis added). Secondly, the sense of sight is easily taken (not just by philosophers) to be the model for sense perception in general, and this supposition seriously misleads us.

> The influence of the visual model is very clear in this. In visual perception we do stand over against the object we see; it is set before us, and our seeing it has no causal effect upon it. Seeing it is prima facie a pure receptivity; to exercise it attentively, we withdraw from action altogether. We stop to look. In consequence, the visual model tends to instigate a strong contrast between knowing and acting, which in abstract theory passes easily into a conceptual dualism. (*Self as Agent*, p.106)

The things we see are 'external' in one sense, and this lends plausibility to Hume's and Locke's assertion that perceptions are internal 'copies' of the appearance of external objects. The same assertion made with respect to hearing or smell is much less plausible. What does the smell of cheese 'copy', and what is the 'object' when I hear someone play a chord? It is tempting to reply that sounds and smells give us indirect acquaintance with objects, whereas sight gives us direct acquaintance. But the immediacy of sight is an illusion. Time (albeit in most cases a very short time) must elapse before we receive the light rays that objects reflect, which means that connecting 'what we see' with 'our seeing it' requires more than visual apparatus. It requires memory. Touch, as Macmurray points out, is a much more obviously immediate mode of sense perception. When I touch something, I am directly in contact with it. Importantly, though, the internal/external dichotomy cannot be applied to tactile experience, because I am at *one and the same time* aware of its nature and of my own. Softness in an object is not the same as the feeling of softness I experience. Nevertheless, both are present, and inseparable, in the act of touching. This point about Self and Other may be extended. 'The Self does not first know itself and determine an objective; and then discover the other in carrying out its intention. The distinction of Self and Other is the awareness of both; the existence of both is the fact that their opposition is a practical, and not a theoretical opposition' (p.109).

The theoretical opposition of mind and world that Hume's analogy of the' audience in the theatre presents is, let us agree, alluring but misconceived. Why should this misconception occasion a 'crisis of the personal'? Once again Macmurray offers us a twofold explanation. First, since the division between subject and object leads to a false dichotomy — 'mind' *versus* 'matter' — it ultimately has the consequence of casting subjects, and hence people, into the category of object or 'entity', and entities are *impersonal*.

> The empirical genesis of 'mind' and 'matter' dualism lies in this, that having abstracted a 'material' object [the body] from the concept of a person... we then illegitimately form a concept, on the negative analogy of the 'material', by thinking a unity of what has been excluded. This is the concept of the 'non-material' or 'the mind', or of consciousness as an independently existing entity. (p.118)

Thus the 'mind' or 'soul' becomes a thing. This abstraction makes it a possible object of scientific investigation, and in this way a further dimension of depersonalization is ushered in. Hume effectively concedes the point when he holds that 'the particular fabric and structure of the minute parts of [our] own bodies and of external objects' are equally comprehended in the knowledge of the working of a 'regular and constant machinery'. People, in other words, are to be understood as objects (of a special kind) subject to natural laws. Famously, and in line with this contention, Hume's ambitious project in his *Treatise of Human Nature* was to 'put the science of man on a new footing'. This new footing should model the study of human beings on the success that the natural sciences as revolutionized by Newton and Bacon had attained. It should replicate their 'experiments in this science from a cautious observation of human life, and take them as they appear in the common course of the world'. 'Where experiments of this kind are judiciously collected and compared', Hume concludes, 'we may hope to establish on them a science...' (*Treatise*, Introduction). Initially, the concept of a 'non-material' mind or soul does not easily accommodate this emphasis on observation, which is why Hume has great difficulty in finding any place for 'the Self' in his philosophical system. Yet 'immateriality' did not prove to be a major obstacle in the development of the 'human' sciences of psychology and sociology. We observe the operations of the mind (it is easily assumed) via the behaviour of bodies (including 'brain states'), or more indirectly by means of questionnaires, surveys, and thought experiments.

All such sciences, in whatever way they are pursued, depersonalize by making persons functioning instances of general types. One major casualty of this way of thinking is the possibility of 'persons in relation' (the title of Macmurray's second set of lectures). If the concept of human being is exhausted by classification as a type of entity, whether material or non-material, then relations between human beings, though they may be more complex, are not in principle any different to relations between inanimate objects. Once again, Hume, whose great genius lay in eloquently articulating ideas that people recurrently find compelling, provides us with an illustration.

> Of all crimes that human creatures are capable of committing, the most horrid and unnatural is ingratitude, especially when it is committed against parents, and appears in the more flagrant instances of wounds and death… [But] let us chuse any inanimate object, such as an oak or elm; and let us suppose, that by the dropping of its seed, it produces a sapling below it, which springing up by degrees, at last overtops and destroys the parent tree: I ask, if in this instance there be wanting any relation, which is discoverable in parricide or in ingratitude? Is not the one tree the cause of the other's existence; and the latter the cause of the destruction of the former, in the same manner as when a child murders his parent? 'Tis not sufficient to reply that a choice or will is wanting. For in the case of parricide, a will does not give rise to any different relations, but is only the cause from which the action is derived… 'Tis a will or choice, that determines a man to kill his parent; and they are the same laws of matter and motion that determine a sapling to destroy the oak, from which it is sprung. Here then the same relations have different causes; but still the relations are the same. (*Treatise* III.1.1)

We could take this concluding sentence as a *reductio ad absurdum*, that is to say, a conclusion so absurd that it refutes the position from which it is derived. Such a refutation, however, only serves to confirm what we have already detected. Hume asks whether 'in this instance there be wanting any relation, which is discoverable in parricide or in ingratitude?' The obvious answer is 'a *personal* relationship'. The problem is that his 'science' excludes such an answer; it has reduced personal relations to impersonal relations in virtue of a mistaken conception of the Self and for this reason cannot mark any significant difference between trees and people.[1]

---

[1] Of course, Hume thinks that there is a psychological difference. We are greatly shocked by the murder of the human parent, while we are not shocked by the destruction of a parent tree. But what connection could there be between the event and the shock we feel except another, contingent, *causal* relation? We happen to be shocked by one case and not by the other. As far as the Humean system is concerned, it might have been the other way around.

A further implication to be drawn, and a point to be underlined, is that such a reduction of the personal to the impersonal eliminates the possibility of practical deliberation. Trees do not deliberate, and if relations between human beings can be encompassed within the same kind of 'science' as relations between trees, then human beings do not deliberate either; they simply impact each other causally. Such an implication runs directly counter to the claim that played a significant part in Chapter One; human equality is most adequately grounded in the nature of human beings as practical deliberators. At the heart of 'the Self' is agency — deliberating about action — and, consequently, relations between selves, or persons, are relationships between deliberating agents.

If we follow Macmurray, the false dualism of 'mind' and 'matter' is in large part a result of conceding to Descartes that the most fundamental and incontrovertible truth is *'cogito, ergo sum'* — 'I think, therefore I am.' The opposing affirmation of the Self as agent, however, is not to be found, as some have suggested, in Fichte's alternative dictum — *'Im Anfang war die Tat'* ('In the beginning was the Act'). Since the force of this dictum lies in its competition with the opening sentence of John's *Gospel* — 'In the beginning was the Word' — the implication is that thinking and acting are alternatives, a preference for 'practice' over 'theory'. Rather, the idea that Macmurray wants to urge upon his readers is that 'reason is primarily not cognitive but practical' (*Self as Agent*, p.63). It is essential to understand this contention properly. The point (*pace* Fichte perhaps) is not to prefer acting *over* thinking, or make action more foundational than thought, but to assert two propositions. First, thought is no less fully involved in practical deliberation over courses of action than it is in intellectual theorizing and the acquisition of knowledge. Second, practical deliberation underlies intellectual theorizing and the acquisition of knowledge as much as it does any other activity.

This emphasis on practical deliberation sustains a degree of resistance to what an earlier chapter characterized as 'intellectualism' — the contention that wise action arises from true belief. As Macmurray says: 'The Self that reflects and the Self that acts is the same Self; action and thought are contrasted modes of its activity. But it does not follow that they have an equal status in the being of the Self. In thinking the mind alone is active. In acting the body is indeed active, but also the mind' (p.86). 'Intellectualism' is the mistaken inclination to lend primacy to reflective thought. 'The question which underlies any philosophical inquiry into action is, "How can I do what is right?" It is not. "How can I know what it is right to do?".' What needs to be resisted is 'The belief that we can only do what is right by first knowing what it is right to do and then doing it' (p.140).

To conceive of the Self as agent, rather than a Cartesian thinker, is not to denigrate 'Reason', but to affirm that rational agency — deliberative action — is at the foundation of our lives. The things we believe, and the theories we advance, are as dependent on deliberative action as the clothes we make and the meals we prepare. The recurrent philosophical inclination to endorse the Cartesian dictum — 'I think, therefore I am' — abstracts the thinker from the person. Yet plainly persons must exist before they can think. Conceiving the Self as agent puts our existence as human beings first. It says, in effect, 'I am, that is why I think.' Human thinkers must be born into the world, but they do not think from the moment they are born; they must first learn how to do so, just as they must learn how to walk, feed themselves, speak, play games, make friends, and do all the other things that make them human. From this affirmation, we may draw a further critically important implication. Human experience is unitary. It cannot meaningfully be separated into the 'internal' apprehension of 'external' objects between which some correspondence relation must be sought. It is this dualist way of thinking that has led inescapably to the philosophical scepticism that Reid uncovered in Hume, and that Hume himself did not know how to escape.

> Where am I, or what? From what causes do I derive my existence, and to what condition shall I return?... What beings surround me?... I am confounded with all these questions, and begin to fancy myself in the most deplorable condition imaginable, inviron'd with the deepest darkness, and utterly deprived of the use of every member and faculty... [R]eason is incapable of dispelling these clouds.

Ironically, given his starting point, Hume finds a solution in activity, in agency.

> I dine, I play a game of back-gammon. I converse, and am merry with my friends; and when after three or four hours' amusement, I wou'd return to these speculations, they appear so cold and strained, and ridiculous, that I cannot find in my heart to enter into them any further. (*Treatise* 1.4.7)

What he does not seem to see is that the games and conversation in which he engages also involve an exercise of reason. It is reason *in the form of theorizing* that cannot dispel the clouds, not reasoning as such.

If human experience is unitary, the source of its unity must lie in the person whose experience it is. It is the acts of looking, touching, remembering, anticipating, counting, comparing, asking, conversing, explaining, and so on that unify our experience, and those acts, taken together, constitute Reality properly so called. Abstraction from this Reality often proves useful, as, for instance, when we isolate certain aspects of experience in order to understand them, or manipulate them more effectively. It remains an abstraction, nonetheless. Yet, there is a widespread tendency to treat abstractions as though they were the Reality on which experience depends. It is easily supposed, to use yet another Humean analogy, that the anatomist is to be contrasted with the portrait painter along these lines (*Enquiry Concerning Human Understanding* Sect 1). Anatomical drawings reveal the underlying reality of human beings; portraits give them an interesting appearance. The influence and effect of this inclination to identify the abstract with the real is the next theme to be explored.

II. The Form of the Personal, the Baconian Vision, and Economic Development

What does the Self as embodied agent, rather than perceiving subject, have to do with the topics of the previous chapter? The connection is to be found in Hume's favourable reference to Bacon. The 'new footing' from which he hopes to gain a more adequate science of human nature is one important manifestation of the Baconian vision of the human condition previously discussed. Bacon, it will be recalled, drew on biblical ideas of Creation and the Fall, to elaborate the thesis that human beings, despite their fallen nature, can ameliorate their condition by uncovering the divinely instituted laws that govern the workings of the created world in its entirety. Observation and experiment, properly conducted, will reveal to investigators (in Hume's words) the 'fabric and structure of the minute parts of their own bodies and of external objects' as well as the 'regular and constant machinery' by which 'all the events about which they are so much concerned' are produced. The value of this knowledge lies in the ability it gives us to manage and manipulate the world to our material advantage. The neo-Baconian vision promises greater 'power' over food production, medical remedies, disease control, and the like. Hume extends this ambition into the social world in, amongst other places, his essay 'That Politics may be reduced to a Science'. The aim embraced in this essay is replacing the personal with the impersonal, explaining political phenomena in terms of laws and systems rather than 'the character and conduct of governors'. Hume has this aim because, he says, he 'would be sorry to think that human affairs admit of no greater stability than what they receive from the casual humours and characters of particular men' (*Essays, Moral, Political, and Literary*, Vol 1, p.41).

What Hume called the 'pursuit of system' lies at the heart of the Baconian conception of science. The task of the scientist is to frame generalities and uncover systematic connections between phenomena within a given domain. Hume was not alone in extending this pursuit to the study of humanity and society. His near contemporary Enlightenment thinker, Condorcet, writes in a strikingly similar vein.

> Those sciences, created almost in our own days, the object of which is man himself, the direct goal of which is the happiness of man, will enjoy a progress no less sure than that of the physical sciences, and this idea so sweet, that our descendants will surpass us in wisdom and in enlightenment, is no longer an illusion. In meditating on the nature of the moral sciences, one cannot help seeing that, as they are based like physical sciences on the observation of fact, they must follow the same method, acquire a language equally exact and precise, attaining the same degree of certainty. (Quoted in *Seeing Like a State*, p.91)

It would be difficult to exaggerate the influence that this ambition has had in the study of societies, economies, and the human mind itself, and in the practical task of addressing the challenges, difficulties, and opportunities with which the human condition presents us. This passage from Condorcet is quoted by the anthropologist James C. Scott in *Seeing Like a State*, a detailed examination of several Baconian-style schemes for social and political improvement. Significantly subtitled *How Certain Schemes to Improve the Human Condition Have Failed*, Scott's case studies are drawn from a wide variety of times and places. These range from the introduction of 'scientific forestry' in eighteenth-century Germany to the twentieth-century projects of urban planning in Brazil and India, and from the collectivization of agriculture in the Soviet Union to the 'villagization' of life in Tanzania under Julius Nyerere. Scott's book is almost equally fascinating and depressing. It charts the impact of what he calls 'authoritarian high modernism'. In every case, regardless of context, authoritarian high modernism on the part of scientists, planners, and politicians led to disaster, with varying degrees of social dislocation and human suffering as a major side effect. Scott provides detailed empirical confirmation of what Macmurray identifies as a consequence of the philosophical conception he is seeking to undermine in his lectures. 'Totalitarianism is the result of determining the good as an object in the spatiotemporal world, and planning its achievement by the use of scientific techniques' (*Self as Agent*, p.89).

Scott's close study of Nyerere's compulsory 'villagization' of life in Tanzania is especially relevant to the issue of poverty and economic development. Although this programme was 'uncannily' like the collectivization of agriculture under in the Soviet Union, Nyerere was widely regarded as a hero of development in the 'Third World', a liberator who, quite unlike Stalin, set his people free from colonial servitude and inspired them to build better and more prosperous lives for themselves. This was not the reality.

> What a neutral observer might have taken as a new form of servitude, however benevolent, was largely unquestioned by the elites. For the policy sailed under the banner of 'development'... The same techno-economic vision was shared, until very late in the game, by the World Bank, the United States Agency of International Development (USAID), and other development agencies contributing to Tanzanian development. However enthusiastic they were in spearheading their campaign, the political leaders of Tanzania were more consumers of a high-modernist faith that had originated elsewhere much earlier than they were producers. (*Seeing Like a State*, pp.246-7)

This high-modernist faith is neo-Baconianism by another name.

Scott concludes his study with a section entitled 'The Missing Link'. He uses the French word *metis* to identify this missing link, though the Greek word *phronesis* has long been used by philosophers to indicate much the same kind of knowledge that Scott wants to highlight—the know-how, common-sense, experience, and knack that is embodied in the mastery of inherited practices. The principal aim of neo-Baconian high modernism is to replace *metis* with applied techniques derived from, and grounded in, scientific observation and experiment. David Mosse notes exactly the same phenomenon at work in the British funded development project among the Bhil farmers.

> [T]he analyses of consultants, scientists or government officers... matched programme priorities, but offered a simplified view of livelihoods and landscapes rationalized in terms of project models. It was knowledge *for* action not about livelihoods... In practice, what became prized as IBRFP's 'participatory planning process' was not a process of participatory learning based on local knowledge, but rather a process through which the Bhil farmers acquired a new kind of *planning knowledge* and learned how to manipulate it. (*Cultivating Development*, p.96, emphasis original)

The consequence of attempting to replace '*metis*' with 'science' is twofold. First, real knowledge is lost, with the wholly predictable result that practical failure ensues. Second, conflict between the skilled practitioners who possess this real knowledge and the theorists who believe that 'science' is superior is inevitable. Scott writes:

> The conflict between the officials and specialists actively planning the future on the one hand and the peasantry on the other has been billed by the first group as a struggle between progress and obscurantism, rationality and superstition, science and religion. Yet it is apparent from the high-modernist schemes that we have examined that the 'rational' plans they imposed were often spectacular failures. (p.253)

In the list of the errors that led to the social and economic disasters he recounts, Scott includes the *hubris* of 'visionary intellectuals and the planners behind them' who forgot that they were mortals and 'acted as if they were gods'. Yet, he thinks, their actions were not 'cynical grabs for power and wealth'. Often, they were 'animated by a genuine desire to improve the human condition'. Nevertheless, however good their intentions, their approach to the problems they identified was deeply mistaken, twice over. First, they made no allowance for contingency. Even where the Baconian methods of observation and experiment are restricted to the natural world – in 'scientific' agriculture for instance – the most rigorously conducted experiments on crop varieties and animal breeds still have to be *applied*. Application necessarily takes place in greatly varying conditions of climate, soil, plant life, terrain, weather, etcetera, and these contingent conditions seriously limit the significance of results obtained under controlled conditions.

> [T]he need to isolate a few variables while assuming everything else constant and the bracketing off interaction effects that lie outside the experimental method are very differently inscribed in scientific method. They are a condition of the formidable clarity it achieves within its field of vision. Taken together, the parts of the landscape occluded by actual scientific practice – the blind spots, the periphery, and the long view – also constitute a formidable portion of the real world. (*Seeing Like a State*, p.294)

In other words, the fields of ordinary farms are not at all like the plots specially constructed to be used as agricultural trial sites. In a similar spirit, Angus Deaton remarks that 'there is the irritating but frequently encountered problem that projects do much better as experiments than when they are rolled out for real' (*The Great Escape*, p.292).

Compared with the natural world, the number of contingencies with which attempts to control the human and social world must contend increases by a very large factor. No social science puts its practitioners in anything like the relationship that chemical engineers have to the materials with which they work. This is not just because of a hugely increased number of variables, but because the human beings that social sciences aim to study and assist have minds of their own. In *Poor Economics*, Duflo and Banarjee, speaking as development economists, make an observation relevant to precisely this point. 'The poor often resist the wonderful plans we think up for them because they do not share our faith that those plans work, or work as well as we claim.' Accordingly, listening to the recipients of aid is 'one of the running themes' of *Poor Economics* (p.35). Scott's point, though, is that science by its very nature encourages and sustains a certain sort of deafness. For instance:

> Modern agricultural research commonly proceeds as if yields, per unit of scarce inputs, were the central concern of the farmer. The assumption is enormously convenient... uniform commodities thus derived create the possibility both of quantitative comparisons between the yields of different cultivation techniques and of aggregate statistics. The familiar tabulations of acres planted, yields per acre, and total production from year to year are usually the decisive measure of success in a development program... But the premise that all rice, all corn, and all millet are 'equal', however useful, is simply not a plausible assumption about any crop... Each subspecies of grain has distinctive properties... [I]f we broaden our view to take in the rest of the plant... we see that there is a great deal more to be harvested from a plant than its seed... Its various parts from various stages of growth may come in handy for twine, vegetable dyes, medicinal poultices, greens to eat raw or cook, packaging material, bedding, or items for ritual or decorative purposes... Even from a commercial point of view, then, the plant is not simply its grain. Nor are all grains of all subspecies and hybrids... equal. The yield of seeds by weight or volume may therefore be only one of many ends—and perhaps not the most important one—for a cultivator. But once scientific agriculture or plant breeding begins to introduce this enormous range of value and uses into its own calculations, it is once again in the Newtonian dilemma of the ten heavenly bodies. (pp.294-6)

The second mistake of the high-modernist neo-Baconian visionaries, according to Scott, lies in a failure to understand the nature of practical knowledge. Scheme after scheme has discarded the practical wisdom embodied in the customary practices learned and mastered by the people whose lives are to be 'improved', aiming to replace it with abstract knowledge. This knowledge is expressed in quantifiable relations between isolated variables that are systematically acquired by laboratory experiments deliberately removed from all specific contexts.

Why should we be wary of knowledge of this kind being applied to plans and initiatives for development? Systematic techno-economic initiatives are not always a failure, at least within their own terms. The use of fertilizers does lead to greater crop yield; the administration of drugs does combat disease; the re-organization of schooling can enhance employment; the creation of infrastructure sometimes significantly assists commerce and government. Programmes of this kind are attractive for governments and aid agencies because they can be rationalized as something more than expenditure. They can be described as investments. Money, time, and effort are not merely spent, but 'invested', to bring about more food, better health, larger incomes, greater economic growth. If these outcomes can be quantified, then they can be set against the quantities 'invested', and a 'return' can be calculated.

A frequently cited example of a highly successful development programme of this type is the so-called 'Green Revolution' of the mid twentieth century, for which Norman Borlaug, the 'Father of the green revolution', was awarded the 1970 Nobel Peace Prize. Supported by USAID, the Ford Foundation, and the Rockefeller Foundation, this 'revolution' expressly aimed to supersede 'traditional' technology with a range of innovations made possible by agricultural science — new, high-yielding varieties of cereals, agro-chemicals, selective pesticides, controlled water-supply, and mechanized methods of cultivation. The wholesale adoption of these methods, someone has estimated, saved 1,000,000,000 lives from starvation. Setting aside doubts about the accuracy of this estimate, from a quantitative point of view the Green Revolution could be declared a resounding and incontestable success.

Of course, there is nothing in its success, estimated in these terms, that constitutes a general validation of the neo-Baconian vision, by which it may or may not have been inspired. The disasters that Scott recounts remain disasters. Still, let us concede for the sake of argument that the Green Revolution is a striking example of how proper investment by individuals and aid agencies in scientifically validated strategies can have hugely positive effects on the problem they seek to address — in this case shortage of food. At the same time, the impressive number of lives it is credited with saving disguises the partiality of its success. The Revolution's impact on food production was decidedly greater in India and Latin America than in Africa, where these new methods were often thwarted by complexities of climate and terrain.

Critics of the Green Revolution have tended to focus on its environmental impact — a significant reduction of biodiversity, for instance. This is evidently an important topic that is well worth investigation. And yet, the criticism itself is framed in a way that invites us to make consequences the key issue. Are the long-term consequences, for human welfare and for the natural environment, likely to outweigh more immediate gains? More important for present purposes, however, is a different kind of criticism, namely, the way in which quantitative measures can be seriously misleading in estimates of success. Suppose the number of lives saved truly is one billion. The arguments of previous chapters have shown that if we want to think properly about impoverished lives, it is a mistake to confine our attention to quantifiable dimensions like income, food production, and the incidence of disease. Alluring though numbers have regularly proved to be, they tell us very little, and sometimes nothing at all, about what matters, namely the *quality* of life for those who fall into a strictly economic category of 'poor'. The Green Revolution undoubtedly gave (some) people a lot more food, and it raised the income of some small farmers considerably. But did it enrich impoverished lives? It might seem that the answer is obvious. Where people are suffering from a shortage of food, surely more food means better lives? It is here that there is reason to return to the 'puzzle' uncovered by Banerjee and Duflo, whose consideration was suspended in a previous chapter.

The puzzle, to recap, is that 'people do not seem to want more food [when] more food and especially more judiciously purchased food would probably make them, and almost certainly their children, significantly more successful in life... households could easily get a lot more calories and nutriments by spending less on expensive grains (like rice and wheat), sugar and processed foods, and more on leafy vegetables and coarse grains' (*Poor Economics*, p.33). Scott makes a related point. 'In some cultures, certain varieties of rice are grown for use in certain distinctive dishes; other varieties of rice may be used only for specific ritual purposes or the settlement of local debts... [and sometimes importance attaches to] distinguishing one rice from another in terms of their cooking properties' (*Seeing Like a State*, p.295).

Banerjee and Duflo's way of stating the 'puzzle' supposes, of course, that we possess agreed criteria for what counts as being 'successful in life'. Scott's examples, on the other hand, show that there is more involved in choosing food stuffs than calorific value. Banerjee and Duflo acknowledge the importance of goods other than food, even in the value systems of people for whom food is scarce, sometimes to the point of hunger. In this connection they quote, not the results of their research, but the reflections of George Orwell in his 1937 autobiographical book, *The Road to Wigan*

Pier. In the first half of this book Orwell documents his experience of working-class life in the north of England at the time of the Depression. In a paragraph quoted by Banerjee and Duflo he writes:

> The basis of [the British workers'] diet... is white bread and Margarine, corned beef, sugared tea and potato—an appalling diet. Would it not be better if they spent more money on wholesome things like oranges and wholemeal bread, or if they, even,... saved on fuel and ate their carrots raw? Yes it would, but the point is, no human being would ever do such a thing. The ordinary human being would sooner starve than live on brown bread and raw carrots. And the peculiar evil is this, that the less money you have the less you are inclined to spend it on wholesome food... When you are unemployed, you don't *want* to eat dull wholesome food. You want to eat something a little *tasty*. (Quoted in *Poor Economics*, p.35, emphasis original)

In these impoverished circumstances, it is neither more, nor healthier, but *tastier* food, that makes life better. From the point of view that Friedrich Schleiermacher labelled 'extreme practicality', this may look like foolishness, just as growing a special type of rice for ritual purposes might seem like foolishness. But the key phrase in this paragraph from Orwell is 'no *human* being would ever do such a thing'. 'Practicality' of a certain kind, taken to the extreme, is *inhuman*. It de-humanizes the person who embraces it, and it de-humanizes the people towards whom it is directed. Extreme practicality is (in part) the theme of Charles Dickens' novel *Hard Times*. The name of Gradgrind, the school board chair who figures prominently in the story, has become a synonym for people who have concern with empirical facts, statistics, and quantitative measures so relentless that it blinds them to the humanity of others. At its farthest point 'extreme practicality' makes moral monsters.

The case of Franz Stangl, mentioned earlier, is one of a number of cases studied in detail by John Kekes in *The Roots of Evil*. When Stangl first encountered Treblinka, where he was appointed Kommandant, he was appalled by what he saw. 'The most awful thing I saw all during the Third Reich... Dante's Inferno come to life.' But what shocked him most was not the purpose of the concentration camp, but its haphazard disorder and dirtiness. 'Stangl put an end to this disorder. He organized the extermination and made sure it would proceed efficiently.' 'What he really cared about', an SS man recalled, 'was to have the place run like clockwork.' His 'success' in this regard involved him in 'a great deal of paperwork', but it led to the award of an Iron Cross as 'the best camp Kommandant in Poland' (*The Roots of Evil*, pp.48–51).

Stangl is far further down the road than Gradgrind, but it is the same road, one that leads us to see people as 'units' of supply and demand, or 'cases' to be provided for and dealt with. The lesson we should learn from this mistaken, and sometimes horrific, way of thinking is that our humanity is not to be found in our needs as organisms, however 'basic'. Consequently, our humanity is not automatically acknowledged by providing for them. Odd though it may sound, the combination of good intentions and scientifically well-informed systems to make widespread provision for adequate food, shelter, and disease control is compatible with the inhuman treatment of those who receive these benefits. What is missing? The answer is — 'the form of the personal'.

III. Persons, Objects, and Organisms

One valuable way of understanding our common humanity is to dwell upon the phenomenon of inhumanity, that is to say, de-humanizing ourselves and others. The example of Treblinka under Stangl's management is an egregious example, but the special horrors of genocide do not set it apart from other no less compelling examples — slavery in the United States, for instance. In his *Narrative Life of Frederick Douglass, an American Slave* (1845), Douglass describes what happened at mealtimes to him and other slave children on Colonel Lloyd's plantation.

> We were not regularly allowanced [given portions]. Our food was coarse corn boiled. This was called *mush*. It was put into a large wooden tray or trough, and set down upon the ground. The children were then called, like so many pigs, and like so many pigs they would come and devour the mush; some with oyster-shells, others with pieces of shingle, some with naked hands, and none with spoons. He that ate fastest got most. (*Narrative*, pp.37–8)

Douglass remarks, 'few left the trough satisfied'. But is this residual hunger the worst of it? Would the scene, and the treatment, be redeemed to any extent if there were sufficient 'mush' to leave the children satisfied? Would it be transformed if the food they were given was a lot better than mush? The answer is indisputably 'No'. So what exactly is horribly wrong here? Douglass compares the treatment of these slave children to the treatment of pigs, and it is easy to see the force of doing so. What needs to be emphasized, though, is not just that children are *not* pigs, but that their masters did not mistakenly think that they were pigs. They knew full well that they were human beings, and relied on this fact to call them to their miserable meal. The relationship, such as it was, was between human beings, but it was defective. It lacked the *form* of the personal.

The destruction of the personal, importantly, can be double-sided. Slavery de-humanized those sold or born into it. This is incontestable and easily acknowledged. But the institution of slavery also de-humanized slave-owners. At the age of seven or eight (the date of his birth was never recorded) Douglass was passed from one owner to another and was taken from Colonel Lloyd's plantation to the house of Mr and Mrs Auld in Baltimore. He writes:

> My new mistress proved to be all that she appeared when I first met her at the door—a woman of the kindest heart and finest feeling. She had never had a slave under her control previously to myself, and prior to her marriage she had been dependent upon her own industry for a living... But, alas, this kind heart had but a short time to remain such. The fatal poison of irresponsible power was already in her hands, and soon commenced its infernal work. That cheerful eye, under the influence of slavery, soon became red with rage; that voice, made all of sweet accord, changed to one of harsh and horrid discord; and that angelic face gave place to that of a demon. (*Narrative*, p.41)

This compelling reminiscence succinctly captures a dynamic in their relationship. Mrs Auld was stripped of her kind heart and fine feeling by irresponsible power. The flaw, however, is not lack of feeling. That is the result, not the cause, of this defective relationship. Benevolence is preferable to cruelty, and it is better that there be happy slaves (if there ever were such) than slaves who suffer greatly. But neither benevolent masters and mistresses nor contented slaves could remedy the essential defect, which lies in this fact: she had no obligations in her treatment of Douglass; Douglass had nothing but obligations to her. This inequality generates the frustration identified in Hegel's famous dialectic of 'Lordship and Bondage'. The 'lord', Hegel says (somewhat obscurely) 'achieves his recognition through another consciousness', but in dealing with his slaves, he encounters 'the servile consciousness of the bondsman' in part because 'what the bondsman does is really the action of the lord'. Yet 'recognition proper' is lacking, and so 'the outcome is a recognition that is one-sided and unequal' (*Phenomenology of Spirit*, pp.116–7). The point is this. The role of the slave is to be a pure instrument of the will of the master. Slaves are neither tools nor animals, however. To be effective, therefore, the will of the slave-owner relies on the slave's intelligence, will, desire, and intention. These are essential to the slave's recognition and acknowledgement of the slave-owner's intentions, desires, and instructions. These are the very same elements, however, in the slave's own, independent self-consciousness, which is precisely what the position as slave denies. The thing that is needed is the thing that is lacking—a relationship between persons. That is the contradiction that Hegel identifies.

Effectively the same point is illustrated by sexual relations on the plantations of the pre-bellum United States. Slave-owners and overseers were sometimes (maybe often) more sexually attracted to their women slaves than to their wives, and not infrequently fathered 'mulatto' children with them. Since they had no such relations with other forms of 'property', this signals an implicit recognition of the slave's humanity. But of course, a normal human relationship could rarely result. These sexual partners, however attractive, were mostly used and abused as slaves. The 'mulatto' children, despite being offspring as much as any other child, were often sold lest the father betray the kind of interest in them that would be natural and appropriate to offspring. Similarly, resentment at the physical attractiveness of female slaves revealed the wives' implicit acknowledgement that these slave women were their sexual rivals. This sense of rivalry could not be expressed by open competition for the favour of the menfolk. Sexual attractiveness had to be construed as a form of disobedience, and consequently, sexual jealousy showed itself in the deviant and destructive form of even greater cruelty. In other words, the slave-owners, overseers, and their wives were driven by one aspect of their consciousness to acknowledge the humanity of their slaves, while at the same time driven by another to deny it. The moral objection to slavery, then, does not ultimately rest on the cruelty and brutality that it licenses, or the immense amount of suffering that it causes. Slavery is intrinsically wrong because, while it cannot fail to acknowledge that slaves are human persons, it denies them respect as such, wilfully refusing to acknowledge that the master/slave relation is necessarily in the form of the personal.

Human beings are *both* organic creatures and subjective centres of consciousness and will. While their empirical nature is controlled by physical and biological laws, their rational nature means that they are able to act in accordance with principles of action that they themselves have framed. They are (in Kantian parlance) 'ends in themselves', and since this is true of every rational subject, the most fundamental law of practical reason implies an acknowledgement of the equality of rational subjects. To treat other people as 'ends in themselves' means not using them to our own ends (as the slave-owner uses the slave), but according them equal status with us. To repeat, we do this not out of kindness or benevolence (some slave-owners were kind to their slaves), but in full acknowledgement of a rational obligation to respect the autonomous self-consciousness of others. Hegel's account of 'lordship and bondage' aims to show that in the relationship of slave-owner to slave, the parties must, in one and the same thought, both acknowledge and deny their autonomous self-consciousness. To fail to treat another person as a person is to treat him or her as an object or an instrument. Slavery shows that human beings can treat each other in this way. Consequently, the moral principle of 'respect for persons' is something reason tells us we *ought* to exhibit. Failing to accord them equal status as deliberating agents is not just a moral failing; it is a rational error.

This idea that rational action requires us to acknowledge other human beings as ends in themselves is largely owing to Immanuel Kant, and has been hugely influential. It is widely endorsed, and underlies many legal rights and social policies as well as the everyday understanding of morality. As a result, it has spawned a very large literature, devoted to both elaborating and criticizing the concepts it employs. For present purposes, we need focus on only one central idea — the dual nature Kant attributes to human beings. This explains the difference between treating someone heteronomously, and treating them autonomously. Treating people heteronomously means regarding them as mere means to ends. Treating people autonomously means acknowledging their freedom and rationality to choose and pursue ends for themselves. Freedom, evidently, is central to this distinction, and the emphasis on deliberative choice has been interpreted as laying special emphasis on consent. This seems to explain the slavery case. Slaves may or may not do what they are ordered to do willingly, but this is a matter of indifference to their owners or overseers. There is, from their point of view, no more reason to seek the consent of slaves than of farm animals. Any measures are warranted that are necessary to ensure orders are carried out, and these include, of course, the use of severe physical chastisement.

Now it is not hard to see that, well short of the extreme of slavery, a problem arises about all sorts of human transactions. For instance, commanding officers are not expected to secure the consent of those they command, employers issue instructions which employees are simply expected to follow, customers make instrumental use of postal workers, restaurant waiters, cleaners, and so on. The waiter, like the table and the silverware, and the cleaner, like the brush and the mop, is just part of the service. In all these cases, it seems, the human beings involved are not slaves, but they are nonetheless treated simply as means to ends chosen by others. This is made evident whenever human beings are replaced by machines and robots. Does this mean that making use of other people in these contexts is morally wrong? It might be replied that, at some point or other, consent must be involved. The soldier signed up, the employee took the job, etc., and that this marks a fundamental difference with the slave who has never consented in any of these ways. The objection is not so easily overcome, in fact, but let us suppose that this response is effective. What it shows, if it works, is that consent is a *necessary* condition that our relationships to other people must satisfy. For present purposes it is more important to ask whether consent is *sufficient*.

Consider, for instance, sexual relationships. Kant says virtually nothing about these, but there is good reason to think that the dualism of the 'rational' and the 'empirical' cannot accommodate them very well. We experience both sexual desire and its satisfaction as part of our 'empirical' nature. They are biological, and accordingly must come under the governance of the natural laws that determine our behaviour as material objects. In this way, sexual relationships are a manifestation of our physical, not our rational, nature. At the same time, it seems plain that in sexual intercourse a human partner is *not* simply an object by means of which I satisfy the sexual desires that it stimulates within me. If that were so, a human corpse or an inflatable model would serve just as well. Rather, I *engage* in sexual intercourse with another human being, and he or she reciprocally *engages* in it with me. What is true is that sometimes this mutual engagement amounts to nothing more than the physical arousal and the satisfaction of sexual desires. Even in this case, however, there is a dimension of reciprocity that there would not be with an inflatable model or a corpse. What this shows is that mutual sexual engagement takes us beyond our existence as physical objects. Furthermore, sexual activity may be voluntary and consensual, but motivated by nothing more than the satisfaction of bodily needs and desires, in which case it does not take us beyond our existence as biological organisms. Two people may engage in voluntary, consenting sexual intercourse, while being motivated purely by lust. They are intensely interested in each other's *bodies*, but indifferent to each other as *persons*. In sexual engagements that are consensual and reciprocal, the people involved are not treating each other as objects. Yet, since it is confined to the organic, they are not treating each other as persons either. Something more is needed, it seems. How are we to include voluntary sexual activity within our lives, not merely as physical objects or even organic beings, but as *persons*?

It is only as long as we continue to think within the dualism of rationality and physicality that this question seems hard to answer. For all its merits, Kant's dictum of 'respect for persons' effectively espouses another version of the dualism that Macmurray thinks it essential to abandon.

> When we distinguish between persons and material objects, the character-istics we attribute to things are a selection from the characteristics we attribute to a person. All the characteristics of a material object are also characteristics of a person. He is a material object, though that is not a complete nor a sufficient characterization. When I say then that our knowl-edge of the physical world, however scientific, is anthropomorphic, I mean that unless I had fallen down stairs, or otherwise lost control of my move-ments, I could not understand what was meant by 'a body falling through space'. We can state this generally. The concept of 'a person' is inclusive of the concept of 'an organism', as the concept of 'an organism' is inclusive of that of 'a material body'. The included concepts can be derived from the concept of 'a person' by abstractions; by excluding from attention those characters which belong to the higher category alone. The empirical ground for these distinctions is found in practical experience. We cannot deal with organisms successfully in the same way that we can deal with material objects or with persons. The form of their resistance—in oppo-sition or support—necessitates a difference in our own behaviour. The empirical genesis of the 'mind' and 'matter' dualism lies in this, that having abstracted a 'material' object from the concept of a 'person' in this way, we illegitimately form a concept, on the negative analogy of the material by thinking a unity of what has been excluded. This is the concept of the 'non-material' or 'the mind' or of 'consciousness' as an independ-ently existing entity. (*The Self as Agent*, pp.117–8)

The form of the personal is not the mental or spiritual half of a dual nature, nor is it the monistic collapse of two into one such as mind/brain identity theories seek. Personhood is a unitary metaphysical status. We might say that human beings have a *tripartite* nature. Like sticks and stones, they are material objects and, as Macmurray's example illustrates, this means that they are 'bodies' that may fall down stairs. Like dogs and cats, they are also animals of a specific type, and are thus organisms needing distinctive kinds of treatment. For a wide variety of valuable purposes—designing stairwells or developing medicines, for example—we can concentrate on just one aspect of human nature. But only by abstraction. Treated as they *really* are—*compositely*—people are agents who make choices, plan their activities, and form personal relationships with other human beings.

This way of thinking enables us to say something more coherent about sexual relations than the dualistic picture will allow. When two people freely engage in sex, neither is treated by, nor treats, the other as an object. Their relationship is one between consenting adults, but to the extent that they abstract each other's character as an organism with sexual attractions and desires from the whole, the relationship is less than fully personal. The fact that the activity they engage in is mutual, consensual, and pleasurable does not alter that. Of course, the individuals concerned *are* persons, so their actions do not flow from biological instincts alone as, for instance, the sexual behaviour of other primates does. It follows that deliberately, even if not expressly, by confining their relationship to a mutual experience of lust and its satisfaction, they are *choosing* to be less than fully human and thus to some degree choosing to de-humanize each other.

A similar point is to be made about the much more lamentable case of slavery. Slave-owners (and overseers) may attempt to treat their slaves in the ways in which they treat the material and organic entities that they also own. They may beat them, push and pull them, as they do animals, machinery, items of furniture, and the like. Yet, since the slaves are persons, with thought, will, emotion, and imagination, they are invariably addressed by name, instructed, questioned, blamed, punished, and relied upon. In all these ways, slave-owners implicitly acknowledge that 'the servile consciousness' they attribute to their slaves is an abstraction, and they thus falsely ignore the understanding that slaves have of the instructions they receive and the motives and purposes behind them. A dog may be trained to sit when it hears the sound 'Sit', but it does not, as a slave would, understand this to be an instruction. If insufficiently well trained, it may 'disobey', but this is only in a manner of speaking. The dog cannot decide whether or not to obey the order, nor can it devise subtle ways of subverting it. A slave, to avert greater hardship, may decide to follow the slave-owner's instructions willingly, and even come to like his or her 'familiarity' with the slave-owner's family. To this degree, an element of consent and reciprocity may enter into the relationship. At bottom, however, the relationship rests upon abstraction from reality. And, as Hegel wants to insist, this abstraction goes in both directions. Slaves must abstract from the owner's whole person, treating him or her as merely the unmeaning source of tasks upon which they are compelled to work.

Such abstract relationships cannot be relied upon. Casual sexual partners have no reason to expect, and hence no reason to seek, friendship or advice. Notoriously, in the southern United States where 'familiarity' between slaves and their owners was not unknown, slave-holders nevertheless guarded against conspiratorial plans for escape. In so doing, of course, they acknowledged the status they sought to deny. Slaves can be regarded solely as a kind of property, valued primarily for their physical strength and economic productivity, to be housed, fed, and watered like the other farm animals. This is an abstraction, nonetheless, and as such a falsification of reality, whatever conceptions of 'servile consciousness' or theories of 'race' we may invent for ourselves. Organized conspiracies of escape are only a danger on the part of beings who can conspire and plan. Cattle and sheep cannot do this. Like it or not, slaves are people, and thus deliberative agents. It is possible not to accord them this status, of course, but insofar as this is supposed to have a rational basis, it rests upon a falsehood. Slaves *are* people, a reality that their enslavement expressly sets itself to deny. Slaves are denied the status of being fully human only by a deliberate act of abstraction. That is to say, they are *conceptually* de-humanized in order to be treated as less than human.

It is important to distinguish between de-humanization and brutalization. When I de-humanize another person there need be no element of aggression, domination, or violence, which is what the term 'brutalization' commonly means in English. Rather, I simply set aside any concern with their thoughts and feelings, hopes and fears, and treat my engagement with them as a mere transaction. In the world of the prostitute, as in the world of the slave, violence and aggression may never be very far away. The heart of sexual prostitution, even so, is not violence, but a de-humanized transaction — sexual satisfaction in return for money. When human conduct is described as 'brutish' this is usually interpreted the wrong way round. It is taken to imply that the offender acted like an animal. On the contrary, as has often been remarked, animals do not behave in 'brutish' ways. Rather, only human beings can be 'brutes' in this sense. Only people can treat others as animals on a par (at best) with pets.

IV. Humanity and 'Development'

How does a digression of this length into the nature of personhood relate to the principal topics of this book? It might seem that the protagonists of 'development' are in a quite different moral category to slave-owners, pimps, prostitutes, and callous brutes, and so indeed they are. Yet as the studies in *Seeing Like a State* demonstrate, there is an important sense in which their 'schemes of improvement' very easily de-humanize the people they are intended to benefit. This is chiefly because they operate with a conception of human beings abstracted from the concrete reality of the person. Any approach to development that lays emphasis on 'basic needs' for food, shelter, disease prevention, or medical assistance abstracts the organism from the person. Treating people as 'units' of calorific consumption, nutritional requirement, productive labour, purchasing power, health and illness, longevity, and so on sanctions their encapsulation in the sort of statistics that can be used for systematic financial expenditure and government planning. It enables us to construct correlations between 'input' and 'output', and thus determine the impact of 'investing' an amount of money by measuring the rise in incomes, or the number of lives 'saved', or the reduction in cases of illness, or the increased quantity of food produced. As we have seen time and again, however, all such statistics, regardless of their accuracy, and irrespective of the intentions with which they have been assembled, leave us ignorant of the quality of the lives that they purport to generalize over. Consequently, though they can provide us with striking correlations, they never provide the information we need to determine whether the 'aid', 'investment', or 'planning' they underwrite has successfully enriched impoverished lives, or whether it is likely to do so if repeated. Some schemes of 'development' will do this, no doubt, and some (arguably many more) will not. But even when planned development appears to succeed, it is generally more likely that this is the result of unanticipated effects than the 'plan' itself.

The result of this sort of abstraction is illustrated by the example of innovative food supply solutions considered in the previous section. The Green Revolution, let us suppose, put larger quantities of more nutritious food into the hands of many people who would otherwise have gone hungry, and in extreme cases would have starved to death. Here is a clear case, it seems, in which scientific knowledge, allied to finance from major funders and expert help from development agencies, was able to engineer a highly favourable outcome—no less than one billion lives saved, according to the estimate quoted earlier. What could be better than that? This is indeed a very impressive number, and the question most people want to ask is whether it is accurate. The more critical question, though, relates to its being a number. What does this number tell us about human lives? Almost nothing. This is a crucial issue for the case in point, because, when confronted (by environmental lobbyists) with the question about numbers, the architect of the 'Revolution', Norman Borlaug, did not in fact respond with numbers. Instead, he referred to its impact on human experience.

> Some of the environmental lobbyists of the Western nations [he wrote] are the salt of the earth, but... they've never experienced the physical sensation of hunger. They do their lobbying from comfortable office suites in Washington or Brussels... If they lived just one month amid the misery of the developing world, as I have for fifty years, they'd be crying out for tractors and fertilizer and irrigation canals and be outraged that fashionable elitists back home were trying to deny them these things. (See John Tierney, 'Greens and Hunger', *New York Times*, 19/05/2008)

This sounds unanswerable. Yet we should be careful not to assume that *hunger* was at the heart of the misery to which Borlaug rightly refers. Let us recall Banerjee and Duflo's discovery, that when given the opportunity by increased income, people living 'amid the misery of the developing world' do not always do what donors and development agencies expect. Instead of availing themselves of larger quantities of more nutritious food, they spend the extra money that they have on what, from some perspectives, are inessential luxuries — better rice, more tea, tobacco. It seems that even the very poorest people subscribe, unconsciously no doubt, to (one half of) the Mosaic maxim: 'Man does not live by bread alone.' As the passage from Orwell quoted earlier reminds us, 'When you are unemployed, you don't *want* to eat dull wholesome food. You want to eat something a little *tasty*.' Tasty food is usually more expensive, and not infrequently less nutritious, but it has this important advantage: it does not merely keep us alive, but makes life more worth living. As Banerjee and Duflo appreciate, this adds a new dimension to the ethics and economics of development. Let us agree that the *most basic* question we can ask about the hope of the poor relates to what will keep them living longer, since our lives can hardly be enriched if we are dead. Still, it is important to remember that naturalists and environmentalists can ask precisely the same question about endangered species of animals or varieties of plant. To address the condition of the poor *in their humanity*, we must not confine ourselves to their abstract character as organisms.

Rather, we should be thinking of them as persons, and asking about the conditions that are most likely to make their lives more worth living.

Biology will tell us what the 'basic' needs of a human organism are to ensure its survival. There is no corresponding science to tell us what makes a human being's life worth living. What people *find* satisfaction in is crucial. This does not imply, however, that 'aid' or 'development' should be directed to satisfying the desires and preferences that surveys and opinion polls reveal. When such devices are used to inform aid policies and development strategies, this kind of 'listening' to the recipient does not do much to counter paternalism on the part of donors. William Easterly finds paternalism at work in the vast majority of aid programmes, and this is why he thinks post-colonial aid has failed to throw off the colonialist attitude that addressing poverty and under-development is 'the white man's burden'.

> In his introduction to Sach's *The End of Poverty*, Bono [the singer/song-writer/philanthropist] said 'It's up to us'. Sachs writes of 'our generation's challenge.' Gordon Brown [former British Prime Minister], in announcing his Big Push aid plan [in 2005], saw himself telling Africans. 'We have to say. We will help you build the capacity you need to trade. Not just opening the door but helping you gain the strength to cross the threshold.' … The most infuriating thing about the Planners is how patronizing they are (usually unconsciously). Here's a secret: anytime you hear a Western politician or activist say 'we', they mean 'we whites' — today's version of the White Man's Burden. (*White Man's Burden*, p.26)

Mosse identifies the same hangover from times past. 'Even without the explicit missionary concept of "conversion", project workers could tacitly understand their role in terms of saving, rescuing or lifting a backward people "up to our level"' (*Cultivating Development*, p.49). Information that emerges from consultations, surveys, and opinion polls may modify the paternalistic character of aid a little, but it still preserves the 'top down' format that most large-scale aid and investment policies require.

Easterly's book is a protest against this whole approach.

> The world's poor do not have to wait passively for the West to save them (and they are not so waiting). The poor are their own best Searchers… It is a fantasy to think that the West can change very complex societies with very different histories and cultures into some image of itself.[2] The main

---

2   This 'fantasy' was destructively evident in US foreign policy with respect to both Iraq and Afghanistan.

hope for the poor is to be their own Searchers, borrowing ideas and
technology from the West when it suits them to do so. (pp.27–8)

The use of the term 'Searchers' here is significant. It marks a move away
from the conception of 'the poor' as recipients of benefits, albeit recipients
who have been 'consulted' or taken into 'partnership'. It attributes
autonomous agency to them. Since I have argued at length that practical
agency is at the heart of what it is to be a human being, this move
constitutes a step in the direction of acknowledging not only their
equality, but their humanity.

In order to appreciate the full implications of this shift in thinking, we
need to consider a rather more fundamental objection to basing aid on
preference satisfaction. In asking a group of potential recipients (usually
their politically appointed representatives, of course) what they most
want, surveys and polls aim to identify the most common shared subjective desires and preferences. The numbers they come up with may
differ significantly from the numbers that aim to measure levels of
nutrition, health, and life expectancy. Nevertheless, they are still *numbers*,
and hence impersonal abstractions. That is to say, they abstract
preferences from the reality of the people whose opinions and desires
they count.[3] The use of abstract quantitative measures is not objectionable
per se. It only becomes objectionable when it is mistakenly regarded as the
measure of reality itself. As Macmurray writes:

> We have to ask of any impersonal attitude under what conditions it is
> justifiable. The answer to this question which seems proper is that the
> impersonal attitude is justifiable when it is itself subordinated to the per-
> sonal attitude, and is itself included as a negative which is necessary to the
> positive... The other person may be treated rightly as a means to the
> realization of our intentions, and so conceived rightly as an object, only so
> far as this objective conception is recognized as a negative and subordinate
> aspect of his existence as a person, and so far as our treatment of him is
> regulated by this recognition. (*Persons in Relation*, pp.35–7)

In this lecture, entitled 'The Field of the Personal', Macmurray is primarily
interested in the attitude that scientifically minded psychologists and
psychiatrists should adopt towards their patients. His point about the personal and the impersonal, however, is directly applicable to the context

---

3   Not all consultations result in numbers, obviously. For present purposes this
     does not make much difference, but it is a point to be returned to at a later
     stage.

that concerns us here. When we survey a set of people with respect to their desires and priorities, and then combine their responses into an order of priorities for the group as a whole, we are treating those we survey as consumers or 'preference holders'. If the survey is well conducted, the results are accurate, and the computations correct, then we have genuine knowledge that we did not have before. Nevertheless, the knowledge we obtain is not a knowledge of reality, a knowledge of what real people think. It is an *abstraction from* reality.

Abstractions of this kind can properly inform conduct with respect to real people only insofar as we acknowledge that they are a 'subordinate aspect of their existence as persons'. There is a strong inclination to think otherwise, however, and to treat abstractions in a neo-Baconian fashion as though they were facts 'wrested' from reality by empirical observation. This inclination is partly a result of the speciously 'scientific' character that quantification lends to such results, but it also derives from an underlying picture of human beings that often, in Wittgenstein's phrase, 'holds us captive'. The 'picture' is an alluring one with a long history, a preconception that human beings are rational egoists, atomistically and instrumentally pursuing their felt desires. It construes us all as independent Selves, oriented within the human condition by the desires we seek to satisfy, and guided in our search for satisfaction by the calculation of means to ends and costs to benefits. It is this picture that shapes both the utilitarian's impartial promotion of the 'greatest happiness (i.e. optimal preference satisfaction) of the greatest number', and the political liberal's striving for a consensus based 'well-ordered society'[4] that impartially secures justice between individual rights holders.

A presupposition of this picture is that the beliefs and preferences of individual choosers are already formed. Obviously, I cannot act to satisfy my desires or express preferences unless I already *have* desires and preferences. This further assumes, of course, that the process of desire formation is complete, which is to say, that I am an adult. In line with this assumption, the thought experiments of political theorists from Hobbes to Rawls have supposed that political arrangements and social policies are answerable to mature deliberators.[5] And yet it is a simple fact of life that

---

4   See John Rawls, *Political Liberalism*, Lecture I §3 'The Idea of Society as a Fair System of Cooperation' (1993).

5   Before the nineteenth century, it was also assumed that they would be men, and, in Locke's *Treatise*, heads of household.

infancy and childhood constitute a significant part of all human lives, and the whole of life sometimes. Moreover, some of us are born with deficiencies that prevent our full physical and mental development, while some of us, at the end of life, slide into senile decay. How, on the rational egoist's conception, are these categories of human beings to be accommodated? It seems that infants, children, the disabled, and the senile can figure only as preference holders that some mature adult has the responsibility of guessing and representing. At most, of course, this too is an abstraction from reality. The real life of real children (and of parents and carers) is not like this.

While some point might be served by the rational egoist's picture of a human being, any value it has is greatly offset by its tendency to mislead and distort. In particular, it reveals a misunderstanding of human development. Importantly, this does not in fact take the form of gradually gaining the status of someone whose life is evermore shaped by self-directed rational action. On the contrary, human life is shaped by rational action from the very outset. While this may be hard to see, initially, it becomes apparent once we relinquish two common ideas. The first is that infants gradually 'develop' from biological organism to rational agent. The second is that the rational action shaping a person's life must be undertaken by that person. The rejection of these two false propositions is perhaps the most novel and important of all the interesting contentions in Macmurray's lectures. The relevant passages are worth quoting at length.

> [T]he start of human existence [is] where, if at all, we might expect to find a biological conception adequate. If it is not adequate to explain the behaviour of a new-born child, then *a fortiori* it must be completely inadequate as an account of human life in its maturity. The most obvious fact about the human infant is his total helplessness. He has no power of locomotion, nor even of co-ordinated movement. The random movements of limbs and trunk and head of which he is capable do not even suggest an unconscious purposiveness. The essential physiological rhythms are established, and perhaps a few automatic reflexes. Apart from these he has no power of behaviour; he cannot respond to any external stimulus by a reaction that would help to defend him from danger or maintain his own existence. In this total helplessness, and equally in the prolonged period of time before he can fend for himself at all, the baby differs from the young of all animals. Even the birds are not helpless in this sense. The chicks of those species which nest at a distance from their food supply must be fed by their parents till they are able to fly. But they peck their way out of the egg, and a lapwing chick engaged in breaking out of the shell will respond to its mother's danger call by stopping its activity and remaining quite still.

We may best express this negative difference, with reference to biological conceptions, by saying that the infant has no instincts… [defining] instinct as a specific adaptation to environment which does not require to be learned. If this is what we mean by 'instinct' then it becomes clear that we are born with none. All purposive human behavior has to be learned. To begin with, our responses to stimulus are, without exception, biologically random.

There must, however, be a positive side to this. The baby must be fitted by nature at birth to the condition into which he is born; for otherwise he could not survive. He is, in fact, 'adapted', to speak paradoxically, to being unadapted. He is made to be cared for. He is born into a love relationship which is inherently personal. Not merely his personal development, but his very survival depends upon the maintaining of this relation; he depends for his existence, that is to say, upon intelligent understanding, upon rational foresight. He cannot think for himself, yet he cannot do without thinking; so someone else must think for him. He cannot foresee his own needs and provide for them; so he must be provided for by another's foresight. He cannot do himself what is necessary to his own survival and development. It must be done for him by another who can, or he will die…

We can now realize why it is that the activities of an infant, taken as a whole, have a personal not an organic form. They are not merely motivated, but their motivation is governed by intention. The intention is the mother's necessarily; the motives, just as necessarily, are the baby's own. The infant is active; if his activities were unmotivated, he would be without any consciousness, and could not even develop a capacity to see or hear. But if he is hungry, he does not begin to feed, or go in search of food. His feeding occurs at regular intervals, as part of a planned routine, just as an adult's does. The satisfaction of his motives is governed by the mother's intention. It is part of the routine of family life… (*Persons in Relation*, pp.47-51)

Long before the child learns to speak he is able to communicate, meaningfully and intentionally, with his mother… It would, of course, be possible to find, in animal life, instances in plenty which seem to be, and perhaps actually are, cases of communication. To take these as objections to what has been urged here would be to miss the point. For these are not definitive. In the human infant—and this is the heart of the matter—the impulse to communication is his sole adaptation to the world into which he is born. Implicit and unconscious it may be, yet it is sufficient to constitute the mother–child relation as the basic form of human existence, as a personal mutuality, as a 'You and I' with a common life. For this reason the infant is born a person and not an animal. All his subsequent experience, all the habits he forms and the skills he acquires fall within this framework, and are fitted to it. (*Persons in Relation*, p.60)

VII. Returning to Practical Reason

To appreciate the import of Macmurray's observations for the topics of this book, it is useful to return once again to Thomas Reid and his guidance to students. In thinking about how to live, Reid observes that while some of the 'Roads we may take lead to Ruin... others are mean and below the dignity of our natures'. There is an unspoken implication here, namely that our sole concern cannot be with failure because courses of action that by certain measures are highly successful may nonetheless be 'mean and below the dignity of our nature'. With this reference to dignity, Reid identifies an aspect of practical reason that points us beyond the relatively simple consideration of consequences. While practical reason is certainly concerned with successfully securing desired outcomes, it cannot be exclusively concerned with this. A no less important issue is how we secure them. There are ways of getting (and being given) what we want, that are nevertheless 'below the dignity of our natures', and there is nothing in the nature of practical reason that requires us to ignore this in favour of efficacy. Accordingly, it is a mistake to think of practical reason as fundamentally, or even primarily, *instrumental*.

This conclusion is reinforced by Macmurray's observations. We think of practical reason as purely instrumental because we illegitimately confine it to discovering the means to the satisfaction of pre-existing desires (which is how Hume construes it). However, practical reason so conceived is in conflict with the reality of human experience. We have only to think about the new-born babies to whom Macmurray draws attention. If they are to survive, they 'cannot do without thinking'. Yet, it is evident that they cannot think for themselves. Consequently, since they do in fact survive, someone else must be thinking for them. And this is indeed the case. Parental care is rooted in thought, not *by* but *for* the child. When, at a later stage, children do come to think for themselves, their doing so is possible only because they have been inducted into an established rational practice — framing, giving, testing, accepting, and rejecting reasons. The practice of reasoning into which they are inducted, and which they come to master, is neither egoistic nor instrumental. It is not egoistic because the practical deliberations of the mother (or other carer) are addressed to securing the needs and comfort of someone other than the person doing the deliberating; it is not instrumental, because the actions that result are not performed as isolated acts of attention to the infant, but as part of the routine of family life. The same analysis applies at the other end of life, when senility returns a human being to total dependency.

For present purposes some important conclusions follow. First, we must reject the neo-Baconian approaches of 'high modernists' and

'Planners' whose deleterious effects Scott, Easterly, Mosse, and Ferguson have documented so fully. They are objectionable not because they lack the efficacy on which 'effective altruists' place such store, but because they are misconceived. All such ways of thinking mistakenly abstract from people as persons, to people as numbers, cases, or instances of organic beings with basic needs and/or basic desires. Secondly, while 'facts' and 'data' represented in statistics about income, nutrition, sickness, mortality, and so on can undoubtedly be useful, their practical relevance must be determined by the experienced judgement, or *metis*, of 'Searchers', whose rational deliberation about what course of action is best is thus informed, and shaped, by the particularities and contingencies of locality and context. Third, the practical wisdom that informs decisions about what goals are best for individuals, families, and their communities can be extricated from these particularities (and thus generalized over) only to a very limited degree. Practical wisdom, like competence in speaking a language, does indeed require us to obtain and possess information. Such information, however, is valuable only insofar as we have mastered the practices that enable us to make best use of it, and acquired the rational habits and skills that this implies. What we call 'information overload' is a case of being rationally confounded *by information*.

If we now return to the claim made in Chapter One—that the equality human beings share is a function of their capacity as agents who engage in practical deliberation—we can see why this is. Practical reason, properly understood, underlies our humanity. The truth of this may be illustrated by considering again Frederick Douglass's description of the slave children's meal time. Being fed with 'mush' like animals was instrumentally effective to a practical end that was highly consequential to the children—it kept them alive—and to their owners—it made them (just) fit enough to become valuable 'labour' in the future. Since this end could be served without assuaging their hunger, it was most 'practical' if 'few left the trough satisfied'. But if more or even all the children had left satisfied, it would still have fitted Reid's description as a way of living that is 'below the dignity of our nature'.

This description, it is to be noted, works in two directions. It is not only below the dignity of the slaves' nature to fed in this way; it is below the dignity of the slave-owners to offer a meal of this kind. Douglass remarks, interestingly, that city slaves were generally much better treated than those who lived on plantations. That was because of 'a vestige of decency, a sense of shame, that [did] much to curb and check those outbreaks of atrocious cruelty so commonly enacted upon the plantation. He is a desperate slaveholder, who will shock the humanity of his non-slaveholding neighbors with the cries of his lacerated slave... Every city slaveholder is anxious to have it known of him, that he feeds his slaves well' (*Narrative*, p.43). Even people who are quite capable of treating others inhumanely do not want those they regard as their equals to think of them as inhumane.

What features mark out mealtime for the slave children as 'inhumane'? The answer is not hard to find. A common trough rather than plates or bowls, shells and shingles rather than spoons, 'mush' rather than distinguishable foods, a premium on speedy consumption rather than conversable eating — all these features, which would be unobjectionable in the case of pigs, ignore (and thus deny) the humanity of the beings for whom the food is provided. The slave children, Douglass tells us elsewhere, were dressed in rags and housed in sheds that gave very limited protection against the weather, the minimal amount of shelter needed to prevent them freezing to death. In the same spirit, illness was an occasion for cost/benefit calculation. Was it worth 'investing' in a cure, or more economically rational to 'write off' the asset as exhausted? Protagonists of the instrumental conception of reason (like Hume) may deplore the sentiments of those who make such calculations, but they cannot point to any rational fault in them.[6] The richer conception of practical reason that Reid and Macmurray articulate allows us to think differently. Human beings cannot survive without thinking, but some of them — infants and children, the senile — cannot think for themselves. Consequently, someone else must do their thinking for them. Allowing children to scrabble for mush in a trough is not thinking *for them*. It is thinking *about them* — as assets and units of consumption — and thinking *for* someone else — the owners and overseers. Only a very narrow conception of practical reason as cost/benefit analysis could commend it. Practical reason properly understood as deliberative agency condemns it.

---

[6]   As Hume himself acknowledged: ''Tis not contrary to reason to prefer the destruction of the whole world to the scratching of my finger' (*Treatise* 2.3.3.6). Hume himself thought 'negroes' inferior, and was not an opponent of slavery. See his essay 'Of National Characters' (*Essays, Moral, Political and Literary*, pp.161–73).

To say that human beings are deliberating agents and that practical reason lies at the heart of their existence is not to deny, of course, that agents can deliberate badly. On the contrary, the concept of practical *wisdom* indicates a trajectory along which deliberating agents may be more or less advanced. The point to be emphasized in the present context is that advancing along the trajectory requires us to consider action as more than efficient causation. Though the Gradgrinds of this world pride themselves on their 'practicality', they are operating with a defective conception of practical reason that bids us confine our attention to a narrow range abstracted from the full range of attributes that apply to our actions. Consider the case of the slave children's 'trough' once more. What would be involved in providing them with a *good* meal? Nutrition and satisfaction are important requirements, certainly, but so too are flavour, taste, interest, temperature, and appearance. It is possible for 'mush' to meet the first two requirements, but not the rest. That is why it makes sense to say that, so long as the children have enough nutrition to survive, they are adequately *fed*; at the same time, they are denied *a good meal*. The distinction is identical to the one that is operative in the phenomenon observed by Banarjee and Duflo. For human beings, in contrast to non-human animals, there is more to food than providing nutrition and assuaging hunger. To disregard taste, appearance, and all the other requirements is not to focus on 'essentials' rather than inessentials; it is arbitrarily selecting just two of the attributes that go into eating well. And it is eating well, not providing adequate nutrition, that is the ultimate goal of practical wisdom in the kitchen.

How do we incorporate flavour, taste, and appearance as well as nutrition and satisfaction into the goal of eating well? The answer lies in a range of actions — growing and selecting ingredients, adding seasonings, following recipes, designing cooking devices — all of which are themselves the outcome of exercises in deliberation. Practical wisdom (as Aristotle long ago observed) is a matter of being able to act in the *right* way, in the *right* proportion, at the *right* time, and in the *right* context. This is what makes it wisdom. Practical ineptitude means acting in the *wrong* way, in the *wrong* proportions, at the *wrong* time, and in the *wrong* contexts. This is what makes it foolishness or stupidity.

Right and wrong here, it is important to observe, are not (in any interesting sense) moral discriminations. The meaningful exercise of deliberative judgement does not make us *moral*. Rather, taking thought is what makes us *human*. Conversely, it is the suppression of thought and judgement that dehumanizes us. 'I have found', Douglass writes, 'that to make a contented slave, it is necessary to make a thoughtless one. It is necessary to darken his moral and mental vision, and, as far as possible, to annihilate the power of reason. He must be able to detect no inconsistencies in slavery; he must be made to feel that slavery is right; and he can be brought to that only when he ceases to be a man' (*Narrative*, p.92). To cease to think is to become a creature of perception, instinct, and feeling only, which is to say, less than human. Slaves de-humanized to this degree invariably lose almost every scintilla of hope. Yet, as the case of Douglass himself demonstrates, this extreme is not the lot of every slave. More significantly, perhaps, even the most oppressed and degraded human beings can unconsciously reveal an awareness of their own humanity in the ways they respond to the wretchedness of their condition. Among his early memories as a slave, Douglass recounts how he heard slaves sing in chorus as they made their way through the dense plantation woods.

> I have sometimes thought that the mere hearing of those songs would do more to impress some minds with the horrible character of slavery, than the reading of whole volumes of philosophy on the subject could do. I did not, when a slave, understand the deep meaning of those rude and apparently incoherent songs. I was myself within the circle; so that I neither saw nor heard as those without might see or hear. They told a tale of woe which was then altogether beyond my feeble comprehension; they were tones, loud, long and deep; they breathed the prayer and complaint of souls boiling over with the bitterest anguish. Every tone was a testimony against slavery, and a prayer to God for deliverance from chains. The hearing of these wild notes always depressed my spirit, and filled me with ineffable sadness. The mere recurrence of those songs, even now, afflicts me;... [Yet] To those songs I trace my first glimmering conception of the dehumanizing character of slavery... If any one wishes to be impressed with the soul-killing effects of slavery, let him go to Colonel Lloyd's plantation, and, on allowance day, place himself in the deep pine woods, and there let him, in silence, analyze the sounds that shall pass through the chambers of his soul,—and if he is not thus impressed, it will only be because 'there is no flesh in his obdurate heart'. (*Narrative*, pp.27–8)[7]

'I have often been utterly astonished', he adds, 'to find persons who could speak of the singing, among slaves, as evidence of their happiness and contentment. It is impossible to conceive of a greater mistake.'

---

7   The quotation is from the English poet William Cowper (1731–1800).

De-humanization is not confined to slaves. Douglass's reflections make this plain. Often, the institution of slavery de-humanized the slave-holder no less than the slave. It destroyed the flesh in their obdurate hearts, but without generating any songs revealing that they knew this to be the case. Slave-holders were incomparably wealthier and more powerful than slaves, of course, but this simply serves to show that wealth and power are no guarantees of humanity. Still, if we cannot rely on economic prosperity to protect our humanity, we can hardly deny that what we call 'grinding poverty' may have effects upon our humanity not very much less destructive than those of slavery. This is a topic to be addressed further in the next chapter. For the moment, it is enough to observe as a fact that conditions other than slavery, and not only extreme material deprivation, can de-humanize the people who are subject to them. Social isolation, physical vulnerability, mass hysteria are all able to diminish and even kill the soul, sometimes by releasing the devil within. As the case of Douglass himself reveals, however, even people whose humanity is under the most severe attack may still entertain meaningful hope. De-humanization comes in degrees. It is possible for even the hardest pressed of human beings to dream of living a more fully human life, and yet more importantly, to rationally embrace the hope of doing so. What kind of life this is, is the topic of the next chapter, and the culmination of all the arguments that have brought us to this point.

Chapter Seven

Redeeming the Time

I. Life and Time

In the philosophical discussion of ethics, poverty, and development, Peter Singer's book *The Life You Can Save* (commended by Bill and Melinda Gates as 'inspiring'), has become one of the key texts of 'effective altruism'. The book expands on Singer's early and highly influential paper 'Famine, Affluence, and Morality'. The argument set out there undoubtedly has an alluring simplicity. It has proved persuasive to many people, while prompting vigorous criticism from others. Towards the end of *The Great Escape*, for example, Deaton remarks, 'Fixing poverty is nothing like... pulling a drowning child out of a shallow pond'(p.274), thereby wholly discounting the key analogy on which Singer's argument rests. But one question the book raises that has not received much attention is this: what is it to 'save' a life? Since all human lives must inevitably end in death, does it make sense (out of a strictly religious context) to speak of 'saving' lives at all? If it does, this can only be a way of referring to actions that extend lives beyond the period of time that they might otherwise have been expected to last.

'How long shall I live?' is a question of evident interest to any human being, so it is natural to make life expectancy and longevity the central criteria of human wellbeing.[1] Many of the measures of poverty previously discussed do this, and since longevity is causally related to food, health, and security, this is why these are so frequently identified as the 'basic needs' on which voluntary, governmental, and intergovernmental relief

---

[1] For present purposes I take life expectancy to be the predictable length of life at birth, and longevity to be the predictable length of life of those who survive early hazards.

and development organizations should focus. It is here we find the (putative) connection between saving lives and the Green Revolution that, as a previous chapter noted, is said to have 'saved' one billion lives. Plainly, this way of thinking strikes many people as obviously right, and yet the argument of previous chapters has shown that the question 'How long will I live?' is not the most fundamental one we ought to consider. A brutalized or unworthy life is worse, not better, for lasting longer, and the same observation applies, suicides statistics suggest, to the empty lives of healthy and wealthy people who have no difficulty in securing 'basic needs'. A longer life, sometimes, can be an object of dread. So a more fundamental issue is this. What will make my life one that is (and on reflection can be said to have been) worth living?

There are, of course, places and times in which 'basic needs' are so hard to satisfy that lives truly are at risk. Though this phenomenon exists, in the modern world it is rare. 'The world we live in today', Bannerjee and Duflo observe, 'is for the most part too rich for hunger to be a big part of the story of persistent poverty.' 'This is of course different during natural or manmade disasters', they add, 'or in famines that kill and weaken millions' (*Poor Economics*, p.280). Actually, the distinction between 'natural' and 'manmade' disasters is fluid. While armed conflicts are the most common source of human misery, many exceptional 'natural' events are turned into still greater 'disasters' by the inadequate or inappropriate response of governments.

Even in the context of adventitious famine, however, there is reason to ask what counts as 'saving' life. How long does a life need to be extended before it can plausibly be said to be 'saved'? Five hours, everyone would agree, is insufficient, as is five days or five months. Even giving someone five years of extra life could hardly be claimed as a life 'saved'. A decade sounds better, and it would be quite intelligible to take this as a criterion for statistical purposes. Yet the truth is that this time period too would be an arbitrary choice. There is, in fact, *no* measurable period of time that we could use to answer the question satisfactorily. One reason for this is that the age of the person 'saved' is relevant to assessing the value and significance of the extra time that he or she is given to live. Suppose, thanks to relief aid of some sort, a sixty-five-year-old victim of famine gains an additional ten years of life. When he dies at seventy-five, his friends and relatives may still grieve deeply, but the cause of their grief can hardly be described as 'a tragic loss of life'. Yet this same phrase is properly applicable to the death of a ten-year-old whose life was 'saved' at birth by the same sort of aid. In the first case, ten years of life is a welcome bonus; in the second, an identical period of time, it is too little. But surely a life is a life? Why does the age of the beneficiary matter? The obvious thing to say is that, without an extra decade, the sixty-five-year-old would still have had a life, but despite an extra decade, the ten-year-old did not. Both lives were 'saved', for the same number of years before death ended both of them. But death also *denied* the child a life.

The important point, that every death is not equally a source of ethical concern, can easily be overlooked. The 2020–22 COVID-19 pandemic death statistics, for instance, did not distinguish between death on the basis of age. Yet this matters greatly in assessing the seriousness of the pandemic. When the aim of 'saving lives' is expressed in purely numerical terms, morally pertinent differences are hidden. A large proportion of those who died in the pandemic were very elderly people in hospitals and care homes. Many of them were at the end of a good life, sometimes beyond life expectancy. Placing such deaths in the same category as deaths among active people below the age of 50 (say) is very misleading. It disguises the fact that 'saving lives' can come at great long-term costs for those who are not in need of saving. This was indeed the case for children and young adults. Minimizing mortality regardless of age came at the expense of the developmental needs of those setting out on life.

Having a life (like 'having no life'), is a normative, not a temporal concept. It is both evaluative and aspirational—something worth having and something to be hoped for. This should alert us to two issues of special importance. First, however tempting it may be, we cannot congratulate ourselves or others on 'saving lives' if this claim is simply based on numbers, because numbers tell us nothing about the quality of the 'lives' we have saved. Prison authorities who try to thwart the suicide attempts of prisoners on death row may have good reasons to do so. But while they undoubtedly extend the lives of those they thwart, it would be highly misleading to say that they were engaged in 'saving lives'. Secondly, the value recorded by measures of longevity, health, income, nutrition, and so on is *derived*. That is to say, it is a function of the quality of the 'lives' that these instrumental goods enable people to lead. It follows—contrary to Singer and the effective altruists—that we cannot tell from the provision of 'basic needs' alone whether any 'good' has been done at all. It would be statistically odd, certainly, if there were not a significant number of 'good' lives among a billion that the Green Revolution is said to have 'saved'. So we can plausibly surmise, cautiously, that the agricultural innovations to which this expression refers did indeed do a lot of good. Yet the number, however large, is strictly irrelevant to that judgement. It is of course an estimate, but even if it were an actual head count, it would tell us almost nothing. How much good was actually done is a qualitative, not a quantitative, question, and its answer rests to a large extent on the judgement of the people whose lives were 'saved'.

What statistics cannot show, moral philosophy might nevertheless illuminate. While counting accomplishes relatively little, a promising alternative is to reflect on what, in general, a good human life looks like. The 'capabilities approach' developed by Sen and Nussbaum aims to do this. In earlier chapters, I offered a similar but more abstract qualitative approach, and identified three principal sources of value in any human life—experiences, accomplishments, and relationships. Reflecting on any or all of the three tells us that a valuable human life cannot be confined to immediate feeling or perceiving, nor, by implication, to the pleasure/pain spectrum favoured by some versions of utilitarianism. Meaningful experience, accomplishments, and relationships are necessarily extended in time. Consequently, when it comes to a valuable life, past and future matter no less than the present, and the sophisticated faculties of memory and imagination that human beings possess facilitate a reach beyond the immediate. It is true that some of the experiences we value are relatively fleeting—laughter, tasty food, glimpsing a beautiful view—but even these cannot be entirely of the moment, and often their value derives from their place in a personal history—a *well-known* joke, a *favourite* dish, a *familiar* landscape. Similarly, the value of what we do in the present often depends upon an imagined and anticipated future. I study now for the examination that I plan to take in a few months' time with a view to preparing for an anticipated future career. Such examples serve to illustrate the importance of time within a human life.

The apprehension of time in the conduct of life takes place on at least three levels.[2] The first is what I shall call temporal *existence*. Insofar as our concern is solely with temporal existence, 'a life' is something whose length can be measured. It lasts from birth at a certain time on a certain date, to death at another time on a later date. All organisms have tempo-

---

[2] The first two that I identify here are tangentially related to the 'A-series' and 'B-series' that John McTaggart identified in his famous and influential paper 'The Philosophy of Time', but here I am interested in the relation of time to practical reason rather than time's metaphysical character.

ral existence, measured from the moment the plant is germinated or the animal conceived, to the moment that it dies. Measurable temporal existence, then, is not something that is unique to human beings, and it falls short of 'a life' as we customarily understand this expression. This is not only because it extends to all other organisms. Human beings in a persistent vegetative state are living organisms, but they no longer have a life. The missing element in this case is consciousness, and consciousness requires a different kind of temporality, which I shall call temporal *experience*.

As was noted a little earlier, the faculties of memory and imagination expand the reach of temporal experience far beyond the immediate. We identify things in our present experience as items remembered from the past, and we see in things present the promise (or threat) of things to come. With the faculties of memory and imagination, temporal experience takes on a personal character, and this lifts temporal existence—the measurable passage of time—to a new level of significance. We look back on the past with nostalgia, or regret, and sometimes have the experience of life going by 'too fast'. Conversely, we anticipate a future that is better in some way, and then we may find the passage of time 'too slow' in getting us there. In our more despondent moments, the future seems to hold little promise, and as a result, we experience time as something that 'drags'. Time 'flying' and time 'dragging' are very familiar descriptions of the passage of time, but they only make sense with respect to temporal *experience*. At the level of temporal *existence*, they make no sense. Measured time cannot pass at different speeds. Its 'pace' never varies, and one hour or one day is no longer or shorter than another.

Higher animals, thanks to their consciousness, share something of this temporal experience with human beings. Many have perception and emotion as well as sensation, and some have the capacity to remember people and places, and to anticipate harms and benefits. These capacities are exhibited in sophisticated behaviour—the dog greeting its owner, the cat watching the mouse before it pounces, or the donkey taking shelter as the rain clouds gather. Nevertheless, for human beings, temporal experience is substantially different to that of even the highest mammals, because the experience is *conceived* as temporal. This is revealed in the use of the temporal indexicals 'now' and 'then', which are temporal terms, but do not identify temporarily experienced events. Rather, they establish an experiential relation to temporal events. This is a highly significant difference between humans and animals. Animals have temporal experiences, but they cannot understand them as such. As the anthropologist Tim Ingold observes, 'while human and animals have histories of their mutual relations, only humans narrate such histories' (*Perception of the Environment*, p.70). This is true at the level of individual lives no less than cultures as a whole. The history of my pet ownership is a story about how certain animals have figured in my life. The narrative is importantly one-sided; while my pets have had temporal experience of my causal interactions with them, this falls far short of warranting the claim that I have figured in *their* lives.

The point is not just about articulation. Only I can *tell* the story of our relationship, certainly, but this is not because I can speak, while other animals cannot. Many have quite sophisticated means of communication, but these can be called 'language' only in the most attenuated sense. In any case, the one-sidedness of our relationship to animals springs from a deeper difference than linguistic facility. We have the ability not only to *experience*, but to *apprehend* the passage of time, to understand temporal events within a related sequence. The most basic sequence of this kind is purely chronological—this event came before or after that. Chronology, of course, falls short of history. We can do more than list events in chronological order, as we when we list the Kings and Queens of England according to their dates. We select some events and discount others in order to frame an intelligible narrative of what happened, why it happened, and what it signified.

The practice of history (by which we need mean nothing more than constructing true, as opposed to imaginary, narratives) alerts us to a third way in which the passage of time is apprehended. While the length of time taken by (many) events in our personal and communal lives can be measured, and the experience of those events can be described, recounting them is ordered not only by chronological sequence, but within a temporal *structure*. This temporal structure allows events to be both individual and repeatable, both novel and familiar. My birthday is an individual event, but so is my next birthday, and the same is true of the one after that.

Some temporal structures reflect natural patterns. The seasons are an obvious example. So is the pattern of birth, growth, maturity, aging, and death that is common to all organic life. Spring comes before summer, winter come after summer, infancy comes before maturity, old age comes after maturity. These are all temporal propositions, but it is obvious that they do not and cannot constitute a chronological sequence. Spring 2018 came after, not before, summer 2017, and the maturity of someone born in 1900 came many years before the childhood of someone born in 2000. Other structures in terms of which we arrange events are not the result of natural organic or meteorological patterns, but cultural accumulations — the days of the week for instance. Monday comes before Tuesday, but these are not dateable events because indefinitely many Mondays come before indefinitely many Tuesdays. Nor is there an experiential difference between them; the sun and the moon rise and set in just the same way, regardless of the day of the week. Nevertheless, distinguishing between Monday and Tuesday matters for all sorts of reasons, and in many cultures the days that comprise 'the weekend' differ markedly from the days that comprise 'the working week'. Importantly, though, this is true of *every* week.

So deeply ingrained is 'the week' in our consciousness, it takes a special effort to acknowledge it as a cultural construct. It is easier to recognize that the same is true of the political, religious, and sporting calendars that structure longer periods of time, and convey special significance on a range of actions — campaigning for the next election, preparing for Christmas, training for the Olympics, are obvious examples. In identifying all these as cultural constructs, it is tempting to suppose that they are importantly different in some way from temporal structures that reflect natural patterns. But this is a mistake. The cultural structures cannot be amended or abandoned at will, even collectively, any more than the course of the sun can be altered. Our deeply ingrained sense of the days of the week is evidence of this.[3]

The natural/cultural distinction has its uses, but is often redundant. Is a rose garden a natural or a cultural phenomenon? Is an athlete a product of nature or culture? There are no answers to such questions, and any attempt to extricate the 'natural' from the 'cultural' in this kind of case is certain to fail. Human events comprise the physical movements and psychological experiences of human beings within the structure lent to time by Mondays, spring, dawn, adolescence, Ramadan, the Olympics, the Presidential election, and so on. The narratives of indefinitely many personal and social histories are invariably cast within these structuring elements, and it could not be otherwise.

---

[3] The French revolutionaries' attempts to a impose a more 'rational' temporal structure — the decimally-based week and year — failed. For some purposes, seven and twelve, it appears, suits us better than ten.

It is important to see, moreover, that temporal structure is also invoked in the individuation of these narratives. The structure of events is what makes *this* story, *my* story. Dates and times and names identify and order events, but they do not thereby lend them meaning within the lives of either individuals or societies. Some event or experience (or more usually some set of events and experiences) is taken to be 'pivotal', and gives the narrative its shape—beginning, middle, end, build-up, climax, denouement, etc. From the point of view of temporal existence, one day is no different from another, and from the point of view of temporal experience, the same may be true. Day by day, for the most part we spend our time waking, eating, working, playing, talking, sleeping, and so on. Consequently, the idea of 'a day like no other' has to rely on temporal structure.

When people speak of historic 'turning points'—the French Revolution, say, or the American Civil War—they are employing a similar concept, one that identifies some of the events under consideration as key to the narrative structure that connects them all. The American Civil War began, let us say, with the attack on Fort Sumter in South Carolina in April 1861, and we may fasten upon Lee's surrender to Ulysses S. Grant, at the Battle of Appomattox Court House in April 1865, as the event with which it ended.[4] It is only with hindsight, and not in virtue of their dates, that these events can be described as the 'beginning' and 'end' of a war. Moreover, even those who were present at these events, and had personal experience of what happened, could not have identified them in this way. If we say (with some plausibility) that the Civil War was a 'turning point' in American history, this is a judgement that necessarily involves connecting it with what went before—the revolutionary creation of a federation of independent states—and what came after—the emancipation of slaves and Reconstruction of the South by the Federal Government. In short, the *meaning* of what participants experienced in the Civil War is not itself a matter of experience, or of the meaning they gave it, but of how the experience *is best understood*.

Similarly, the narrative of a personal life must pick on some events and experiences and make them the *terminus a quo* (starting point) and the *terminus ad quem* (point of completion) of the biography or autobiography, as well as the beginning and end of episodes within it. Laurence Sterne's

---

4   There were other later acts of surrender.

novel *The Life and Opinions of Tristram Shandy, Gentleman* demonstrates
brilliantly the insufficiency of a purely subjective sense of significance to
produce an intelligible narrative. The nine-volume novel is in large part a
satire on the philosophy of John Locke, the mind as a *tabula rasa* (blank
slate) upon which the experiences of seeing, hearing, and touching
impress traces. Common though this way of thinking is, it is in fact the
wrong way round. Without some ordering principle, sensuous experience
becomes what philosophers sometimes call an 'undifferentiated mani-
fold'. That is what Tristram's narration of his life-story reveals. His
resolve to capture the full character of immediate experience constantly
leads him into animadversions that prevent him from getting on with the
story. Tristram's own birth, for instance, is not even reached until the
third volume. An autobiography must be more than a simple sequence of
datable events, but the extra element cannot be supplied by 'a flow of
consciousness' from one point in time to another. That is what Sterne's
whimsical novel demonstrates. It is only once temporal *existence* and
temporal *experience* have been set within some temporal *structure* that they
have been cast into a narrative that amount to 'a life'.

This observation returns us to the end of Chapter Two, which used the
concept of biography to capture the sense in which a human life can
achieve an integrated unity. Biography holds out real 'hope for the poor'
because relative poverty and humble surroundings, despite being
involuntary, are not in themselves obstacles to biography, provided we
construe the concept in a way that does not imply a specially significant
or interesting life-story. Thus, leaving aside for the moment the condition
of 'grinding' poverty, the hope of the person born into poverty is the same
as that of the person born into wealth — to have a biography, which is to
say, a life with the sort of integrity that lends it meaning.

II. Vocation and Dwelling

How is this biography to be shaped? In *After Virtue*, MacIntyre advances
the claim that 'the unity of a human life is the unity of a narrative *quest*'
(*After Virtue*, p.203, emphasis added). This seems to make self-
consciousness in the pursuit of meaning a necessary condition of success.
If so, ordinary lives rarely have this degree of self-conscious reflection.
Most people live coherent and meaningful lives without expressly
thinking about coherence and meaning, still less self-consciously seeking
it. So if it is not the search for meaning that gives meaning, what is it? The
answer lies in what we might call an *intermediate* concept, an object self-

consciously pursued that lends a life integrity without the need for self-conscious reflection on how to integrate it. Such a concept, I shall argue, is a to be found in in the idea of a 'vocation'.

The term 'vocation' meaning 'calling' has theological roots and over-tones. I cannot be 'called', it seems, without someone to call me, and who could that be if not God? For this reason, the church and the monastery are the traditional places where those with a 'vocation' were thought to be found. Still, though the origins of 'vocation' may be religious, people make good use of a largely secularized version of the same concept. A vocation is more than a job or means of earning a living. Vocation shapes a life by conferring a social role that engages the multifarious activities, interests, and aptitudes of the individual. Across a striking variety of markedly different worlds—notably pre-industrial, industrial, and post-industrial—the pursuit of a vocation in this sense has served to integrate the experiences that human beings in general seek and value, the achieve-ments they admire and of which they are proud, and the personal relationships in which they stand. Vocations, however, are not invented, but chosen from a stock of roles that together comprise the culture into which we have been born. I cannot aspire to be a farmer, musician, priest, teacher, spouse, parent, or some combination of several of these, unless such roles exist. Vocations are dependent upon what Tim Ingold has called 'the taskscape'—the world of organized and meaningful activity into which all human beings are born. Heideggerian existentialism speaks of finding ourselves 'thrown' into this world. An alternative way of thinking, to be explored further in the remainder of this chapter, thinks of ourselves as being 'called' into the world. Hence the term 'vocation'.

One obstacle to employing the term vocation in the way suggested is the tendency to associate it with paid employment, as say, a surgeon, a nurse, a teacher, a soldier, or a chef. Underlying this tendency is a familiar way of thinking that divides human activity into two broad categories, namely 'work' and 'leisure', or 'work' and 'free time'. So familiar is the practice of differentiating activity in this way that commonly we find it hard to question its basis, and so challenge its validity. The topic is of central importance to the subject of this book, in fact. That is because societies in which poverty is held to be especially problematic are commonly called 'underdeveloped' and contrasted with 'developed' societies. This invites comparison with another contrast, the contrast between pre-industrial societies, and industrial (or post-industrial) societies. The contrast is not a uniquely historical one. The former category includes the hunter/gatherer and pastoral societies of the kind that anthropologists have studied in Africa and Asia as well as the societies of medieval and early modern Europe. The underdeveloped/ developed and pre-industrial/industrial contrasts both rest upon a wide-spread assumption that, while underdeveloped and/or pre-industrial societies characteristically make no distinction between 'work' and 'leisure', it is precisely this distinction that characterizes social organiza-tion in developed industrial and post-industrial societies. In medieval villages and tribal societies, the supposition is, 'work' was not, and is not, separated from 'non-work'. The activities that comprise the way of life fall within a single, seamless web. By contrast, in developed societies, activity is highly regulated by the working day and the working week, so that leisure and vacation are confined to special periods of time.

If this is the right way of thinking, and if economic development is the best hope for the poor, it would appear to follow that an important step lies in reconfiguring the activities of people in underdeveloped societies along these lines. Organization is a key element in economic development —a belief manifested time and again in the projects undertaken by the governments of 'developing' countries, often designed and funded by international agencies. With this cast of mind, development is the path to prosperity, and thus the escalator out of poverty. We (in the developed world) are already at a high point on that escalator. The natural aspira-tion, and the daunting task of 'poor' countries, is to get on to it.

This conception of development and wellbeing has proved a highly persuasive one. Peter Singer's argument in the paper 'Famine, Affluence, and Morality' relies upon it. Positioned well up the escalator of pros-perity, *we* have a moral responsibility to aid people in poor countries. This is because providing them with the essentials of life only requires us to forgo inessentials—expenditure on luxuries and so on. Not to engage in this transfer of resources is the moral equivalent of inflicting deprivation upon them. A life you fail to save is tantamount to a life you take away. The transfer of resources from rich to poor that Singer appears to recommend is sometimes criticized as mere short-term 'relief'. What is required, this criticism suggests, is more enduring 'development', and indeed the addition of 'development' to 'relief' has been a notable change in the mission statements of many international agencies. The rationale for this change is often expressed in the widely endorsed adage 'Give people fish and you feed them for a day; teach people to fish and you feed them for a lifetime.' This change of focus, however, relies no less significantly on the same conception. While the moral obligations of the rich call for agricultural projects rather than famine relief, and medical training in preference to medical missions, the road out of poverty still lies in helping poor countries to get on to the economic escalator.

From poverty to prosperity through economic development has proved a hugely persuasive ideal. W.W. Rostow's famous and influential book, *The Stages of Economic Growth: A Non-Communist Manifesto*, first published in 1960, is cast in precisely these terms, and its approach has suffused almost all the literature on 'development' ever since. Behind it lies a thought about production and consumption. Since producing goods is a necessary precondition to consuming them, in some sense work must come before leisure. Yet when we consider how human beings live in *any* society, it is easy to see that organizing a life, or even describing it, in accordance with this sharp demarcation between work and leisure (or free time) is very problematic. It is true that for a large proportion of people in a highly commercialized society (whether industrial manufacture or post-industrial service 'industries'), income is usually determined by fixed and measurable hours of work in a particular place where 'workers' engage in a particular task.[5] This fact misleads us into the false supposition that there are two kinds of activity here—primary income generation and secondary expenditure on consumption. Whenever we try to apply this supposition to real life, however, it quickly collapses. Even the briefest reflection reminds us that in a commercialized society *getting to* a place of employment—an activity for which I am *not* paid—is as vital to earning my wages or salary as the task I am paid to do when I get there. Similarly, a significant proportion of 'free time' when I am at not 'at work' will have to be spent on a range of tasks to which only a dogmatic insistence on the work/free time distinction would deny the label 'work'. Everyday life involves cooking, washing, cleaning, tidying, repairing, and so on, and indeed these are commonly, and unproblematically, referred to as house-*work*. Housework is not an income earning activity, but neither is it 'leisure' or 'free time'. It figures prominently in our lives, but simply does not fit this division. Precisely the same observation is to be made about

---

[5]   The proportion will not be so large, of course, in societies where children and/or the elderly outnumber the 'working' age population, and there are societies of which this is true. The position is also complicated, though not significantly altered, by a big increase in 'working from home' made possible by computers and the internet.

other important ranges of activity — raising children, nursing the sick, and caring for the elderly, for instance. Cooks, cleaners, nurses, nannies, and teachers can be paid to undertake these tasks, of course, but the nature of the task is not in any way altered. Whether paid or unpaid, the activities — cooking, cleaning, etc. — remain the same. In short, if we are to describe human life properly, the work/leisure distinction must be left aside as irrelevant. In an essay entitled 'Work, Time and Industry', Tim Ingold makes the point this way:

> Of all the manifold tasks that make up the total current of activity in a community, there are none that can be set aside as belonging to a separate category of 'work', nor is there any separate status of being a 'worker'. For work is life, and any distinctions one might make within the course of a life would be not between work and non-work, but between different fields of activity, such as farming, cooking, child-minding, weaving and so on. (*The Perception of the Environment*, p.324)

If 'work is life', why do we make so much use of the distinction? Ingold thinks the answer lies in this fact: the real difference between pre-industrial-agricultural and industrial-commercial societies is not the separation of work from non-work, but the commodification of time.

> With industrial capitalism, labour becomes a commodity measured out in units of time, goods become commodities measured out in units of money; since labour produces goods, so much time yields so much money, and time spent in idleness is equivalent to so much money lost. The result is not only a demarcation between work (time that yields money) and leisure (time that uses it up), but also a characteristic attitude to time as something to be *husbanded*... [T]he identification of the sphere of production with the ascendancy of clock time generates the expectation that the alternative sphere of consumption should be identified with a different kind of time, precisely opposed to clock time as individual freedom is opposed to mechanical constraint. This is what is colloquially called 'free time', and it is the time associated with what we call leisure when this is defined by its contrast to work. Free time is the time we experience (or rather think we experience) when we turn inwards on ourselves in the hedonistic pursuit of purely individual satisfactions. (*The Perception of the Environment*, pp.328–9)

Viewed in this light, we can see that the division of activity into work and leisure both reflects and distorts our understanding of social life in commercial societies. It reflects it, because it captures the way in which very many people in commercial societies do actually think about their lives. 'Work' brings status and meaning as well as income, and consequently being 'unemployed' is a serious blow, even though the vast majority of the tasks of ordinary life remain to be undertaken. And quite regardless of our 'work' status, they can be done well or badly. Conversely, free time in the form of consumption—shopping, entertainment, and vacationing, chiefly—comes to be understood as the principal validating reason for 'working'. The point of working is earning, the point of earning is spending, and the point of spending is consuming. This is highly paradoxical, of course, because it implies that even the most skilful, demanding and fulfilling work is of no value in itself. It is to be valued only for the income that it brings, and the *other* things this income 'frees' us to enjoy and to consume. It is a way of thinking made possible only by the false commodification of time.

A number of strands in the arguments we have been pursuing come together at this point. First, we can see where the deep error lies in the prospect with which we began—hoping to win a lottery. Such a hope rests on the supposition that winning would 'free' us from the need to secure the means of consumption. With a large enough pot of money, I can have whatever I want, without the need to earn the means to obtain it. This implies that the ideal world is one in which 'work' is unnecessary. But why should idleness be welcome? Since life is work in the only meaningful sense of the word, the complete cessation of work is the cessation of life. That can hardly be a proper object of hope.

Secondly, the commodification of activity over time reveals the destructive effect of neo-Baconianism. The industrialization of productive work flows from the drive to ameliorate the human condition 'scientifically', that is to say, by quantification, systemization, and technical expertise. The value of time invested in production is estimated in terms of increased returns for the purposes of consumption. This quantitative move necessarily abstracts from the particularity of activity, however, and by abstracting from its content, empties it of its intrinsic value. Thus, for instance, the value of education so construed does not lie in its content—what is learned—but in the return, in terms of higher wages and salaries on hours (or years) 'invested' in learning. The implication of such quantification is that people are reduced from being agents, to being producers and/or consumers.

Thirdly, the source of the impulse to construe the problem of impoverished lives in measurable terms—life expectancy, the poverty line, income, possessions—has now been revealed. Once we think of satisfying the desire to consume as the *terminus ad quem* of life, it is natural to construe poverty as lacking the means to purchase consumer goods. In this way we are led to ignore the value that meaningful activity has in itself. By the same token, the impoverishing effect of the pointless expenditure that wealth may permit is hidden. If consumption is the ultimate good, it seems to follow that more is better. Yet the phenomenon of diminishing marginal utility tells us this is not so, and even the most sophisticated measures of 'happiness' (if we take them seriously) show that past a certain point the possibility of increased consumption adds nothing.

Fourthly, the tendency to construe benefit as commodity acquisition, or the means to commodity acquisition, explains why the inequality of the donor–recipient relation discussed in a previous chapter distorts, and occasionally destroys, the lives that the donations are intended to aid. Aid in the form of distribution of consumer goods (mosquito nets, for instance) replaces activity with passivity. Nor does the move from 'relief' to 'development' change this. The adage quoted earlier in this connection —'Give people fish and you feed them for a day; teach people to fish and you feed them for a lifetime'—simply implies that instead of giving a commodity directly, it is better to give the means by which the recipient can acquire it. Either way, the underlying assumption is that what the recipient needs is a commodity. Moreover, it is further assumed that the activity of fishing is significant only for its productivity, and any other activity that was equally productive would do just as well. This ignores the fact that a recommendation to take up fishing as a preferred means of food production cannot be made in a vacuum, but only in a context where activities of various sorts are already going on. Consequently, promoting fishing on the grounds of its greater productivity (or the greater nutritional value of fish) displaces other activities, with the implication that those existing activities have no value in themselves. In other words, the promotion of fishing ignores the question of how, if at all, this new activity might integrate into, or even relate to, the 'taskscape' that already shapes the lives of those who are 'educated' into taking it up. The importance of existing 'taskscapes', and the error of ignoring them, is in effect the lesson to be learned from the detailed studies undertaken by Ferguson, Mosse, and Scott.

The distorting division of life into work and leisure may reflect modern ways of thinking, but behind it is an idea that has ancient pre-cursors—a vision of the good life as maximal desire satisfaction extended over time. This is a vision that Plato articulates and vigorously combats in the *Gorgias*, where he mocks his interlocutor Callicles with this question. 'Tell me whether one who suffers from the itch and longs to scratch

himself, if he can scratch himself to his heart's content and continue
scratching all his life, can be said to live happily' (*Gorgias* 49c). Callicles
dismisses the image as 'absurd', but of course this is just Plato's point. The
example is meant to function as a *reductio ad absurdum* of the general
contention that 'the good is the pleasant', which is to say, that the good
life consists in the continuous satisfaction of the desires we have.

Plato thinks the Calliclean ideal is defective chiefly on the grounds that
it makes no distinction between desires that are enlightened, noble, or
inspiring, and those that are trivial, nasty, and foolish. This is a compelling reason to reject it, but in the present context two further defects
are especially important. First, by making the life for which we ought to
hope one of maximal desire satisfaction, it conceives 'a life' in terms of
temporal existence and temporal experience, but allows no place for
temporal structure. The life of maximal desire satisfaction has no con-
tours, so to speak. It is simply an unstructured sequence of experiences
over time. It thus lacks a 'Great End' (of any kind) that could unify it into
a meaningful whole. Secondly, it implies a radical separation between the
desiring subject on the one hand, and the world within which he or she
hopes to satisfy those desires. An obvious analogy is with customers in
the cafeteria. They come to the cafeteria with their personal desires and
preference, and then choose what to eat from among a range of possibilities presented to them. The 'world as cafeteria', however, is not an
adequate image for the radical subjective freedom that the Calliclean
vision requires. The unspoken assumption is that the range choices presented to us is not random, but determined by natural and cultural
factors. All the dishes reflect judgements about what is nutritious, in
season, well cooked, authentic, and so on. Even the idea of a purely
desire-driven choice within this range is misleading. Our dietary likes and
dislikes do not spring direct from our psyches, but are a result of what we
have learned to like and dislike as a result of previous experience,
including previous visits to the cafeteria.

We should conclude from this that the ideal of maximal subjective
desire satisfaction falsely, and fruitlessly, tries to separate 'living' from
'dwelling'. We are living beings, but we do not spring into existence with
our desires and motivations in place, and then seek satisfaction in a
'world' that stands over against our subjectivity. Rather, we are born into
a dwelling place that is our home even before self-consciousness. To say
that we *dwell*, and do not merely *live* there, is to say that, though we are
organic beings, we are radically different from plants that spring up

wherever a seed happens to germinate. *How* we live is informed by *where* we live, in this sense. Just as the existence of a natural language is a necessary precondition for the ability of individuals to form and express their own opinions, so a purposeful human life requires antecedently existing 'taskscapes' and temporal structures within which rational agency can be exercised. Language is not a cultural construct waiting to be filled with organically or psychologically generated thoughts. Similarly, there is no value-neutral 'world' of objects waiting to be lent value by desiring subjects. We sometimes speak of choosing 'a way of life', but this is a rather unhelpful way of speaking. Human beings are invariably born into ways of life that they did not choose. At an early stage, individuals begin to make choices, certainly, but the way of life into which they have been born shapes and informs the individual's desires, choices, and projects, and thus the course of life. Heidegger's sometimes helpful term 'thrown' is misleading here.

Once we draw this distinction between 'living' and 'dwelling', it becomes possible to see how taking 'basic needs' (even if these are re-defined as 'basic rights') to be the motivating basis for philanthropy and development effectively construes people in poor places as deprived consumers. That is to say, it thinks of them as in need of the material means that will satisfy their most fundamental desires as organic beings. They are, so to speak, waiting for life to continue, standing in line as the victims of famine or drought are sometimes compelled to do. They are thus envisaged as *living*—i.e. having organic existence—but not as *dwelling*—i.e. agents deliberating about an ongoing life shaped by interests, aptitudes, tasks, and relationships. The tear-stained face of a child, the emaciated mother with arms outstretched, the lines of people waiting for a food truck, the neighbourhood squalor, these make the best visual images for arguments like Singer's. That is chiefly because they can so easily be used to awaken guilty consciences. Yet such pictures, effective though they may be in fund raising, exclude any aspect of the dwelling place in which such 'victims' live, and which they hope to restore. These pictures discount, because they do not show, the mix of enriching and the impoverishing aspects of a particular 'dwelling' place as a realization of human existence. By depicting the 'faces of hunger',[6] they rely on the

---

6   *Faces of Hunger* is the title of Onora O'Neill's pioneering, and well-regarded, book subtitled 'An Essay on Poverty, Justice and Development'. It has just such a picture on its front cover.

surface appearances of suffering. This has proven pulling power, but it keeps the reality hidden, ignoring both the most brutal destruction and the remarkable persistence of 'dwelling'.[7]

Singer's original essay on 'Famine, Affluence, and Morality' is a good example of 'need' abstracted from 'dwelling'. It chastises the morally lukewarm response of affluent Westerners in the hope of prompting them to donate money to assuage famine. Yet the essay makes only one fleeting reference to the civil war between East and West Bengal that was the cause of the famine that prompted him to write. In this war, in which Western governments played a part, it is estimated that hundreds of thousands, possibly millions, of civilians were killed by security forces, and thousands more compelled to flee their homes. The idea that 'saving' lives in such circumstances means contributing surplus spending money to famine relief naïvely fails to touch on the enormity. Lives were lost, and people went hungry, certainly, but these facts are just one aspect of the wholesale destruction of the patterns and practices of those who had been dwelling in East Bengal (now Bangladesh). Abating the risk of starvation was not the principal issue in the wretchedness experienced by thousands in makeshift Indian refugee camps. Deaton makes the same point more broadly. 'If poverty is not a result of the lack of resources or opportunities, but of poor institutions, poor government, and toxic politics, giving money to poor countries — particularly giving money to the *governments* of poor countries — is likely to perpetuate and prolong poverty, not eliminate it' (*The Great Escape*, pp.273–4, emphasis original). It is against the background of this remark that Deaton makes his oblique reference to the inappropriateness of Singer's analogy of the drowning child in the shallow pond.

In opposition to the mistaken simplifications of utilitarian morality and the 'effective altruism' that it promotes, the 'capabilities' approach offers a much more sophisticated understanding. Nussbaum identifies ten 'Central Capabilities' that every satisfactory human life should possess,

---

7   Kate Raworth, in *Doughnut Economics*, offers what she bills as a radical alternative to long-established ways of thinking about economics, one that aims to displace numbers and graphs by making greater use of pictures and diagrams. After a brief excursion in the neurophysiology of visual perception, she concludes: 'So the old adage turns out to be true: a picture really is worth a thousand words' (p.13). But she never acknowledges just how misleading a picture's 'thousand words' can be. Pictures used by fundraisers are a case in point.

capabilities that become 'functionings' as the conditions for their realization are put in place. Alongside such basic goods as 'bodily health' and
'bodily integrity', the list includes 'being able to form a conception of the
good', the ability to 'enjoy recreational activities', and 'control over one's
political and material environment' (*Creating Capabilities*, pp.33–4). This is
a far richer conception of development than the primitive utilitarian
model of maximizing pleasant experiences and minimizing painful ones.
Nevertheless, it too frames the goals it seeks to promote in terms of the
abstract individual. The 'functionings' that realize these capabilities are
abstractions in the same sense that 'basic needs' are — goods that anyone,
anywhere, would (or should) want. This perpetuates a way of thinking
that takes no account of the fact that goods are only given meaning and
substance once they are set within some specific form of 'dwelling'. What
counts as adequate bodily health, or a pursuable conception of 'the good',
or a recreational activity, is not determined by the individual's choice, but
by the mode of dwelling into which individuals have been inducted and
educated. Participating in a football match is a 'recreational activity', but
it is a possible activity for individuals only where football is played, and
some cultures do not have any collective equivalent of such 'recreational
activity'.

A related point can be made about Sen's conception of *Development as
Freedom*. While this is undoubtedly a significant advance on GDP and
PPP, it invokes the attractive ideals of liberal individualism and social
democracy, but does not sufficiently acknowledge that liberal individualism is itself an abstraction from historically specific modes of dwelling. As
Michael Oakeshott contended, 'freedom' cannot flow from following a set
of abstract principles, because such principles, if they are to have any
practical relevance, are not premeditated by political theorists in advance
of political society. They are, rather, an 'abridgement' of some historical
experience. Despite its many merits, liberal individualism is not an
articulation of fundamental principles most fitted for human life as such.
It is an abridgement, an abstract formulation, of concrete practices
embodied in actual ways of life. Oakeshott cites Locke's *Second Treatise of
Civil Government* as an especially striking example of 'abridgements of a
tradition, rationalizations purporting to be the "truth" of a tradition and
to exhibit it in a set of abstract principles, but from which, nevertheless,
the full significance of the tradition inevitably escapes' (*Rationalism in
Politics*, p.25). Freedom from arbitrary arrest, for example, is not realized
in laws. Even the most tyrannical regime can pass appropriately worded

laws and constitutional provisions, and, as the 'lockdowns' widely instituted during the 2020–22 pandemic showed, 'liberal democratic' governments can be quick to suspend such laws in the name of 'emergency'.[8] Real freedom rests on the actual practice of politicians, courts, law enforcement agencies, and individuals in a particular time and place.

It is incontestable, of course, that inherited and stable modes of dwelling can be importantly deficient. They often constrain very severely the lives of those who live within them. This has proved to be true especially of certain sectors — women, for instance. They can also be discriminatory and oppressive, dividing populations into castes, classes, and nationalities, or branding some groups as 'deviant', such as Jews, Romanies, or LGBTQ people. Patriarchal slave-holding societies of the kind that Frederick Douglass describes are a dramatic case in point. The slave-owning culture of the pre-bellum Southern states was a way of life, and one treasured by many. The question naturally arises as to why its being 'settled' and 'traditional' should generate any reason to preserve it. Proponents of 'development as freedom' might accept that this ideal is indeed an abstraction from historical, principally European, experience, but nonetheless a progressive ideal that the moral opponents of slave-holding societies are right to promote and pursue. Sometimes the fear of 'imposing Western values' on the 'traditions' or 'values' of tribal societies in Africa, or age-old cultures in Asia, has led people to endorse (or simply not to denounce) some truly vile practices — female circumcision is a notable example. Amongst anthropologists, even 'right-minded' feminists have not always expressly condemned it.

Accordingly, while it is important to be aware of the dangers of abstraction, and of the necessity for modes of dwelling to have concrete historical realization, it is no less important for traditional practices, along with the attitudes that constitute and sustain them, to be open to criticism. Often, established human practices need to be reformed, resisted and, on occasions, abandoned. In *The Honor Code: How Moral Revolutions Happen*, Kwame Anthony Appiah explores several important examples of how long-standing traditional practices, including slave trading and foot binding, were abandoned over a surprisingly short space of time as a

---

8   Contrary to what some have claimed, this was not 'unprecedented'. The British Government's response to the 'threat to health' it saw in the spread of COVID-19, in fact, was strikingly similar to its response to the 'threat to security' it saw in the French Revolution.

result of morally motivated reform movements occurring within changing historical circumstances. Does the ideal of 'development as freedom' go wrong in regarding such changes as 'advances', just because they reflect the goals and values of liberal individualism?

The answer is 'no', provided we bear in mind the necessity of also taking proper account of the concept of 'dwelling'. First, moral revolutions of this kind do not result from neo-Baconian schemes of improvement such as James C. Scott describes in *Seeing Like a State*. This is precisely what Michael Oakeshott meant by 'rationalism in politics', and rationalistic reform of this kind is often disastrous. For the most part, effective reform is motivated from within the cultures to which they relate. Appiah observes that the 'anti-footbinding associations' that sprang up in China in the early twentieth century, 'had roots among Christian missionaries and the Western business elite, but also among those members of the literati who saw some degree of Westernization as necessary if China was to find its place in the modern world. The focus of the literati was on the good of China, first' *(The Honor Code*, p.91). Moreover, Appiah argues, the success of these reforms is at best obliquely related to 'development'. The prime movers are honour and dignity rather than any desire for greater prosperity.

Secondly, while the cultures that we think of as free and democratic, and thus more hospitable to the aspirations of individuals, have strengths and merits that human beings rightly cherish, they are simply one form of dwelling, and not, as nineteenth-century progressivists tended to suppose, an especially *advanced* form. Progress or improvement in some respects is not progress or improvement in all. Indeed, the most economically advanced societies in the world have defects that are scarcely less evident than their merits. While 'modern' societies are markedly less hierarchical and more socially egalitarian than societies in the past, sociological study also shows that for many who live in them they are places of anomie, social isolation, radical economic inequality, deep political divisions, cultural superficiality, and environmental degradation. This perception of 'modernity' is one to which a great many twentieth-century dramatists, poets, novelists, and film-makers have given powerful artistic expression. Higher levels of material prosperity may in fact intensify, rather than offset, these deficiencies. This is an upshot that explains a renewed interest in simpler lifestyles (hence books such as *The Wisdom of Frugality*), as well as anxiety about the human cost of luxury and opulence. In short, while the 'human development approach', to which both Sen and Nussbaum have contributed, has much to commend it, it still runs the risk of misidentifying 'living' with 'dwelling'.

III. Development and Contingency

Even if this were not so, every conception of social and economic development as a source of hope for the poor encounters a further, intrinsic limitation. A question considered earlier, and to which there is now reason to return, is this. What can 'development' offer those who die before the anticipated improvement (or a significant part of it) is realized? All programmes of social and economic development take time, with the result that this limitation is of considerable consequence for large numbers of people. The 'great escape' that Deaton recounts took several centuries. Even if we regard the pace of change as having quickened considerably in the last half century, measurable advances may still require lifetimes to accomplish. One measure that Deaton employs, to considerable effect, is physical height. Though genetically determined to a large extent, the height to which adults grow is also a function of infant nutrition in preceding generations. As a result, average heights can serve as an indicator of wellbeing across populations. Comparing the height of adults around the world, Deaton tells us, reveals enormous inequality. 'For women born in 1980, the average adult Dane was 171cm, the average Guatemalan was 148 cm… If the shortest populations in the world were to grow at the European rate of 1cm every decade, it would take 230 years for the Guatemalan women to be as tall as Danish women are today' (*The Great Escape*, pp.160–1).

This calculation is just one possible measure of comparative material wellbeing, of course, but it provides a dramatic illustration of why we cannot regard social and economic development as a basis of hope for the lives of many people classed as 'poor'. We cannot even suppose that, confronted with the prospect of never having had a good life themselves, they can still take satisfaction in the thought that their children or grandchildren will. The distance in time is too great. This point applies whether we think of improved wellbeing in terms of income level, range of capabilities, or degree of freedom. For a very large number of people, the prospect of these improvements is too far in the future to be a source of hope for this life. Enthusiastic neo-Baconian progressivists like Stephen Pinker in *Enlightenment Now: The Case for Reason, Science, Humanism, and Progress* cite statistics which purport to show that human life has got progressively better and better since (and thanks to) the eighteenth-century Enlightenment. His book is more of a moral polemic than an academic investigation, so it is not hard to raise serious doubts about the case he tries to make. Even supposing it to be a good one, however, his story of 'human' progress can hardly provide hopeful motivation for (say) Guatemalan women. They are not obviously beneficiaries of that development, and can never expect to be so. It follows that they are not to be included within the 'humanity' that has progressed.

Temporal limitations on hope are not just a matter of the scope of economic and social development, or the 'speed' at which it can be expected to take place. Whatever the speed, it is obviously the case that some of the people such changes are intended to benefit could live to old age, and yet never enjoy the promised improvements. The same point, it has often been observed, applies to revolutionary movements. Why should a revolution that is very unlikely to happen in my lifetime inspire me to work for it now? Besides, there is this further limitation—contingency. All sorts of unexpected occurrences can alter—and end—the lives of those who are the intended beneficiaries of 'development'. Nussbaum begins her list of capabilities with the basic goal of 'being able to live to the end of a human life of normal length'. This sounds like a reasonable hope for anyone to have, both for themselves and for their family. On the other hand, we know that death is no respecter of persons. The knowledgeable, skilful, and serious are as mortal as the ignorant, idle, and frivolous. A great many people of all sorts will not, as a matter of fact, live to the end of a human life of normal length. While the cause in some cases is the absence of conditions required for rising income and/or increased capabilities, this need not be, and rarely is perhaps. Many lives are brought to a sudden end by accident, illness, violence, war, and natural catastrophe. Such contingent misfortunes can thwart the most rational of hopes. Consequently, no conception of increased material well-being, however cogent and persuasive, can offer well-grounded hope to someone who sees a significant chance that they (or their relatives) will *not* be able to live to the end of a human life of normal length.

It must be acknowledged immediately, of course, that precisely the same issue arises for the alternative claim—that the best hope for a human life lies in what I shall henceforth call 'vocational dwelling', that is to say, living purposefully and productively within a way of life that is firmly grounded in community. Vocational dwelling serves to unify the interests, desires, aptitudes, and experiences of the individual, while at the same time integrating them into the life of the community as a whole. Vocational dwelling means choosing and engaging in activities that are properly described as 'doing your own thing', but in a fashion that both serves and is sustained by communal life. Vocational dwelling is thus importantly different to having 'work' that pays for the cost of 'free time', not only because it transcends this distorting distinction, but because a job with a good income can be repetitive, exhausting, stressful, unfulfilling, or some combination of all of these. Similarly, people can be very wealthy, and yet lead lives bereft of vocational dwelling. In such cases, despite their wealth, the lives concerned are properly described as impoverished. Extremely wealthy recluses like Howard Hughes (1905–76), the film and aircraft magnate, are just the most striking examples.

The merits of vocational dwelling do not guarantee any particular level of material prosperity. If it is the life of a teacher within a well-established educational system, and in a culture where teaching and learning are highly regarded, then it is likely to bring success and security as well as personal fulfilment. If, on the other hand, it is the life of a peasant farmer in a country prone to droughts or floods, it will offer only limited protection against material hardship. Yet even in these more vulnerable circumstances, insofar as it sustains a purposeful and fulfilling life in community, it is far preferable to the isolated and alienated kind of life that can result from increased wealth, especially wealth suddenly acquired. The contrast is of great importance, because it illustrates how human *impoverishment* may diverge from *poverty* when this is construed as low income and/or material assets that are few and insecure. With respect to the topic of this book, then, the concept of vocational dwelling has this great advantage: as a hope for human beings, it is no less realistic for those classed as 'poor' in accordance with poverty line/GDP/PPP/and so on, as it is for people much further up the economic ladder. Furthermore, the pursuit of economic development can systematically destroy vocational dwelling, as Nyerere's misguided agricultural reforms in Tanzania illustrate.

Still, it has to be acknowledged that not every human life can take the form of vocational dwelling. There are children and adolescents who die before anything looking like a vocation is in place. Are they to be denied all hope of a meaningful life? There are people whose vocational dwelling is disrupted beyond repair by natural catastrophe, civil war, and disease. Are they to be regarded, in the end, as having lived without meaning? The same question arises, of course, with respect to prosperous and successful people in economically advanced societies. Their vocational dwelling may suddenly be ended by disaster – the gifted athlete who has a debilitating illness, for instance, or the scientist killed in a traffic accident at the height of his powers. In these cases, despite the success that marked their lives hitherto, it is hard to avoid the sense that catastrophe struck too soon. Yet this seems to imply that there was something better than vocational dwelling to hope for – not just a longer period of organic existence (which the athlete struck by illness may have), but a *completed* life. What, though, could be the mark of completion? It is at this point that religious ideas come into play, and in particular the idea of 'redeeming the time'.

'So teach us to number our days, that we may apply our hearts unto wisdom', the author of Psalm 90 writes. The idea is not that we keep count of the days we are alive, but that we acknowledge them to be confined to an unknown, but finite, number. We should, the Psalmist suggests, be constantly aware that our days may prove insufficient to accommodate even the best-laid life plans. If practical reason is the exercise of intelligence for the purposes of vocational dwelling, then practical wisdom is the ability to acknowledge the particularity of context in which the demands, satisfactions, and accomplishments of vocational dwelling must be pursued. Contingencies of many different sorts have the power to frustrate and undermine the very best that practical reason is able to accomplish. It seems, then, that the Psalmist's injunction requires us to distinguish between practical reason and human wisdom. What might this distinction be?

IV. Action, Purpose, and Style

The Aristotelian concept of practical reason – *phronesis* – has had an enormous influence on moral philosophy. 'From the time of Aristotle', J.L. Stocks observes, 'it has been more or less common form among philosophers to regard purposive action as the summit of human achievement on the practical side' (*Morality and Purpose*, p.15). Deleterious consequences result when we choose foolish ends, or insufficiently effective means to good ones. Shame and indignity, however, introduce importantly *non-purposive* considerations. They refer not to the goal of our actions, but to the *manner* in which the goal is pursued.

To grasp the importance of dignity, in contrast to effectiveness, we can return to an earlier example – a picture of famine victims crowding around a truck newly arrived with fresh supplies of food, while young aid workers toss life-saving portions into arms eager to receive them. Such a picture has great rhetorical power; it awakens horror and sympathy, and stimulates generosity. What better image could there be of 'doing good'? The ends it gestures at are good—the relief of suffering and the prevention of death—and the means to these ends that it depicts are commendable—nutrition speedily delivered. It is true, nevertheless, that the people depicted in these images are robbed of their dignity. On one side of the exchange, we see people reduced to hungry animals, and on the other side well-intentioned agents performing something like the role of zoo keepers at feeding time. To lament the loss of dignity in these scenes is not to deny that benefits are being given and received. It is to bring into play a moral dimension that makes it no longer sufficient to consider how good the ends are, or how efficient the means. Beyond good purposes effectively executed, there is always a relevant question about the manner in which they are being pursued. From a properly human point of view, style matters.

The same point arose earlier with respect to Frederick Douglass's description of mealtimes for slave children. Even if the food had been tastier, more nutritious, and more plentiful than it was, the manner in which it was served and eaten would have cancelled these merits. Meal times conducted in such a style de-humanized the children, which is to say, treated them as less than human. The value of the food for the purpose of sustaining biological organisms could have been far higher, excellent even, and yet its de-humanizing character would have remained. There are actions, in short, that *ought not* to be undertaken, even when they constitute effective means to beneficial ends. Conversely, there are actions that *ought to* be performed, even when they convey no benefit. Many simple actions fall into this category—saying 'thank you' for instance. This adds nothing to the value of the goods exchanged, but it humanizes the transaction.

It is possible, of course, that expressions of gratitude do have beneficial consequences. The person thanked is pleased, for instance, and sometimes the donor's gratification is a welcome additional benefit. It nevertheless seems a rather desperate move on the part of a consequentialist to suggest that that is why they are to be valued. More fundamentally, the assessment of consequences is plainly irrelevant where no beneficial consequences are possible. Consider, for instance, the treatment of the dead, who are beyond being benefitted.[9] The eponymous heroine of Sophocles' tragedy *Antigone* is the sister of Polynices, a prince killed in the course of his struggles against Creon, King of Thebes. Creon decrees that Polynices is not to be given a proper burial, and that his body is to be left exposed to the elements. Since he is dead, Polynices cannot suffer from this treatment, and so preventing it cannot benefit him. Creon does not think that Polynices will be harmed in some way. His actions give him a powerfully expressive way of humiliating his enemy, even when he is dead. Antigone appreciates this, and that is why she defies the order. Polynices does not deserve to be humiliated. Her rebellious act is intercepted, and despite a courageous self-defence, Creon orders her to be locked in a tomb. After a time, he changes his mind, but not before it is too late. She has hanged herself, a second death that in turn leads to a third—the suicide of Hæmon, Creon's son, to whom she was betrothed. It turns out, then, that Creon's determination to humiliate a dead person has catastrophic consequences for living people. The post-mortem humiliation's badness is not explained by this catastrophe, however. Rather, the badness of humiliating the dead is the cause of the catastrophe. What Sophocles' play illustrates is that, in some circumstances, the dignity of the dead matters more than the happiness of the living.

The same motif is at work in Toni Morrison's novel *Home*. At the beginning of the story, Frank and Cee, brother and sister, secretly witness the body of a 'negro' being thrown from a wheelbarrow into a pit, and watch as a recalcitrant leg is beaten down into the earth with a spade. It is only years later that Frank learns the full horror of the circumstances surrounding the man's death, and the inhumanity of the people who watched him die. He and Cee return to the spot so that he can rescue the bones, wrap them in a quilt that Cee has made, and reverently 'carry the gentleman in his arms'. Together they re-bury the remains in a perpendicular grave under a sweet bay tree. Frank then nails a roughly painted marker to the tree that reads 'Here stands a man'. These actions are profoundly human. In the context of the novel they not only restore humanity to the dead man, but express a redeeming humanity in Frank. None of this could be captured in terms of effective means to beneficial ends.

---

9   I leave aside here the interesting and almost universal practice of praying for the dead.

Humiliating the dead is more than treating their corpses badly as, in the *Home* example, by the casual use of the wheel barrow and spade. Disposing of human bodies in a safe and sanitary manner may also deny them the dignity they are owed. In *The Meaning of Belief*, Tim Crane quotes the historian Hugh Trevor-Roper expressing his dismay at a secular funeral.

> We stood silently around the coffin in the crematorium. No clergymen, no music, no articulate sound. Then suddenly the floor gaped and hey presto! The coffin sank out of sight. Whereupon we trooped silently away. I hope that my Doctorate of Divinity will at least save my corpse from such undignified disposal: like waste going down the sink. (*The Meaning of Belief*, p.114)

Why is a dead body not simply waste? Being equally incapable of suffering and satisfaction, it can neither be benefitted nor harmed. Nor can a corpse be regarded as a bearer of rights. Dead people cannot have their right to life violated, obviously, and since they no longer have wills of their own, it is impossible to coerce them improperly. This means that neither material interests nor moral rights can get conceptual purchase. Practical reason, narrowly construed, must turn its attention elsewhere and focus on the interests and rights of the living. It can generate a recommendation that funeral expenses should be minimized and costly ceremonies avoided, so that money can be spent on aiding and comforting the bereaved. Such a recommendation seems especially 'practical' in circumstances where resources are scarce.

Given this implication, it is curious that simple and less expensive 'disposal' of corpses is more common in wealthy societies than in poor ones. Indeed, in poor countries where incomes are low, 'unnecessary' expenditure of this kind is often remarkably high. In 'Paying the Piper: The High Cost of Funerals in South Africa', the economist Anne Case and others analysed funerals that took place in South Africa at the height of the AIDS epidemic. They found that many households spent the equivalent of *a year's income* on an adult's funeral, and that while in some cases insurance helped to defray part of the expense, where there was no insurance surviving relatives borrowed money to pay for funerals, that they would not borrow to meet living expenses.[10]

---

[10] https://www.ncbi.nlm.nih.gov/pmc/articles/PMC3824610/

Were they mistaken in some way? Did they contravene the principles of practical reason? Why spend money on the dead who are beyond benefitting instead of the living who continue to have pressing needs? To make expensive funerals in poor places intelligible we have to call upon the belief that dignity is owed to the dead, no less than to the living. The same belief is required to make sense of Creon's determination to heap indignities on the dead Polynices, and of Antigone's feeling a powerful family obligation to prevent this. A corpse is not merely a body; it is the body of a person. Metaphysical dualism separates 'body' and 'soul' in such a way that the person is the soul, and the body is merely the physical entity that it animates for a time.[11] The philosophical problems with metaphysical dualism are well known, but without entering into their discussion, we can see that in other contexts it is essential to acknowledge when a body is a body *of a person*. The physician who, with the best of intentions perhaps, abstracts from the patient to the patient's body, and focuses exclusively on physiological functions, is making the same mistake. People are sick or healthy; bodies merely function or mal-function. From a strictly medical point of view, pathology is as important as anatomy, and a cancerous body as interesting as a healthy one.

The pathologist, in this sense, de-humanizes the patient, just as the 'waste disposal' funeral de-humanizes the dead. There can be good reason to abstract from the humanity of the person and focus on the physicality of the body — the advancement of medical science and the containment of epidemics, for instance. These examples, however, alert us to one way of characterizing the distinction between practical reason and wisdom. Practical reason focuses on the selection of valuable ends and the choice of efficient means to them. Wisdom includes practical reason, but sets it within a broader sensibility to the proper and improper ways in which valuable ends are pursued. True wisdom, we might say, is the constant awareness that bodily integrity, material prosperity, individual freedom, political influence, and all the other valuable capabilities must *serve* humanity, and never be mistaken for it, either singly or collectively.

---

[11] It is a notable feature of an ever more secular society that sanitary disposal of the body without ceremony is now common, with a memorial event for 'the person' held at some point more convenient than the time of death. If this does imply subscription to metaphysical dualism, then it sits very uneasily with secular humanism.

This brings us back to a key theme, and the main contention of this book. The best hope of 'the poor' is no different to the best hope of 'the rich', whatever the basis on which we construct these categories. For people in either, the most rational hope is a life of 'vocational dwelling'. Previously, concepts such as 'the poverty line' have been criticized for their abstraction and indifference to the particularities of time, place, and context. Might it not now be said that pursuit of purposeful, self-directed activity within community is a no less abstract concept? The difference is this. Quantitative measures such as level of income, household assets, standards of health, average years of life, employment opportunities, and so on can be used to make comparative assessments between contexts. The purpose of doing this is to determine how far these contexts realize, or diverge from, acceptable norms — how far an 'underdeveloped' economy or nation falls short of a 'developed' one. By contrast, the concept of vocational dwelling neither permits nor invites such comparisons, any more than good cooking can be compared with good dog grooming. That is because it directs us to the necessity for particularity in the standards by which we assess things. Cooking and dog grooming can both be done well or badly, and for people who engage in either activity, the ideal is to do it excellently. To this extent they share an abstract ideal, but there is no common standard of excellence that can be applied to both activities.

Similarly, vocational dwelling is an abstract ideal, but its realization will differ in different contexts. Our common humanity lies in the possibility of living well by being at home in the world into which we have been born, and at the same time being personally fulfilled by the meaningful tasks and valuable social roles that we have learned to undertake and master. 'Vocational dwelling' is thus a common ideal, but it cannot be characterized in terms of a checklist of abstract features of worlds and tasks and roles. Rather, the ideal is made real (to varying degrees) by lives lived in historically generated social contexts. It follows that the ideal of vocational dwelling can be realized equally well in radically *different* contexts. Conversely, it may also prove exceedingly difficult to realize in radically different contexts. That is why the language of developed/underdeveloped is of such limited significance when we are concerned with the hope of the poor to have an enriching and rewarding life, and the danger that wealth brings its own forms of impoverishment.

Of course, it is true that material conditions can obstruct or enhance vocational dwelling. When people are able to do little more than survive, when they are disease ridden, perpetually hungry, and constantly at risk of accident and injury, the lives they lead are impoverished to a degree that threatens their humanity. That is why economics matters, and why better health, higher incomes, and more extensive assets are rightly valued. The historic 'great escape' that Deaton recounts saw succeeding generations lifted out of deprivation, and thus better able to live better. As Deaton says, 'Growth of income is good because it expands the opportunities for people to live a good life.' At the same time, he notes the limitations of quantitative measures of income. 'If people decide to work less, and take more time for things they value more than work, national income and consumers' expenditure will fall. One reason that French GDP is lower than American GDP *per capita* is because the French take longer holidays, but it is hard to argue that they are worse off as a result' (*The Great Escape*, p.175).

Nothing in the line of thought developed in this book should lead us to deny that higher income has played an important part in enhancing human life, and will continue to do so for many people in many ways. We should be on our guard, however, against the error of *identifying* the good life with prosperity. This error is compounded if it leads us to suppose (a) that economic prosperity guarantees a good life, and (b) that those who are (and remain) economically 'poor' cannot hope to lead a good life. Examples from both history and fiction serve to show how the pursuit of material prosperity can be destructive of humanity. The Franciscan ideal, on the other hand, while offering a way of life to which only a subsection will ever aspire, provides an important reminder that material poverty need not be an obstacle to vocational dwelling. In some circumstances, indeed, frugality increases the possibility of a more deeply human life.

The gap between economic prosperity and a good life is further revealed in the phenomenon of activity which, though purposeful, rationally pursued, and resulting in great wealth, is yet, as Reid says, 'below the dignity of our natures'. Ruthlessness is often profitable, and there is no certainty in this world that the wicked will ultimately come to a bad end. Neither fact makes the life of the gangster or the tyrant admirable. Nor does it make the wealth and status they enjoy (if they do) a proper object of hope. Our true nature lies in our humanity. Ruthless treatment of others jeopardizes our own humanity more than it threatens the humanity of the people it exploits. Though they suffer, and though their human dignity is violated and ignored, it is not the tyrannized, but the tyrant, whose course of action sinks beneath 'the dignity of our natures'. A common way of speaking brands concentration camp guards, not their prisoners, as 'animals'. This is an attempt to capture the loss of their humanity, though it mistakenly implies that other animals are capable of barbarity. Morrison's *Home* captures the same insight. Ultimately, it was not the unnamed 'negro' who was de-humanized; it was the men who made his death a sport. Could anyone with a clear conscience have pinned above *their* graves a sign that declared 'Here stands a man'?

It is undeniable, of course, that human beings are often and easily tempted by the prospect of great wealth and power. Historical attention tends to highlight religiously and ideologically motivated wars, but military and political campaigns in the pursuit of wealth and power — both within and between societies — are not any less evident as part of our past. In order to hold fast to the idea that such temptations should be resisted, we have to endorse some version of the ancient Stoic contention that it is better *to be murdered* than *to be a murderer*. But what about the person who has been murdered? Doesn't death destroy 'vocational dwelling'? And if death comes early, doesn't that remove any hope of it? These questions return us to the problem with which the previous section began. What about lives whose precariousness makes vocational dwelling an unlikely prospect?

V. Death and Meaning

An important supposition behind such questions is that the realization of our humanity requires us to reach the 'adult state'. At one level this is obviously correct, and accords with the common supposition that the death of a young person is more to lamented than the death of an old person, even though death always means the end of 'a life'. Yet, as we have seen, we do not have to reach the adult state in order for us to be incorporated into a common humanity and thus accorded human dignity. At birth and in infancy we are not little animals, upon whom the 'honorary' status of human being is bestowed until such time as we metamorphose from organisms into persons. Rather, as Macmurray contends, those who care for us in infancy act as human agents on our behalf, and not simply in our interest. Infants cannot deliberate, but their lives are shaped and formed by practical deliberation from the earliest stage. Accordingly, those who have the misfortune to die young have nonetheless been incorporated in a common humanity. Early death does not undo that incorporation any more than death in old age.

Interestingly, Macmurray's account of 'the form of the personal' applies to the dead no less than the newly born. Like neonates, dead human beings cannot deliberate for themselves, they no longer have needs that must be provided for, or sensibilities that require protection, and yet they are still to be accorded the dignity of human beings. Acknowledgement of this is most obvious in the familiar practices of wills, testaments, and deathbed promises. The dead do not suffer if their post-mortem wishes are ignored, nor are they offended. If solemn promises made to them as they die are broken, they will not know, and will not make any protest. Yet for all that, we recognize real obligations to the dead. In so doing we attribute a moral status to them, but not one, obviously, that requires them to be alive. Creon's treatment of the dead Polynices implicitly recognizes this. Denying his corpse the proper burial rites is a way of dishonouring him; the intelligibility of dishonouring the dead is parasitic upon the intelligibility of honouring them.

This throws important light on a strictly utilitarian point of view. When a life is past saving, there is neither suffering nor satisfaction, and so no further reason to consider the person whose life it was. The only obligation we can have, consequently, relates to 'saving' other lives, and thereby preventing pain. The underlying mentality is quite widely shared by people who are not self-conscious utilitarians, but who regard this attitude as commendably 'practical'. Yet it runs quite contrary to the age-old, almost universal, human practice of funeral rites. Funerals devote to the dead a lot of thought, time, and resources that could instead be given to improving the lives of the living. Moreover, as the example of funerals in AIDS stricken South Africa shows, even where resources are very scarce, people may still place a priority on honouring the dead.

Honouring the dead is an essentially public practice. Its most obvious instances are military, state, and royal occasions when those who have led armies and countries and nations are honoured as significant figures in political life, national culture, victory in battle, and so on. By their nature, events of this kind are inegalitarian in the sense that they mark the deaths of exceptional people. In some cases this is made especially clear by the monuments constructed afterwards. The Egyptian pyramids, the Taj Mahal, the Lincoln Memorial are on a scale that sets them far apart from gravestones and commemorative plaques which mark most people's passing. Behind this difference is a conceptual one that is captured by

Stephen Darwell's distinction between 'appraisal respect' and 'recognition respect'. Appraisal respect honours people for the social position they have occupied and/or what they have achieved. It cannot therefore be due to those who have attained no high office and achieved little of consequence. Recognition respect for someone, by contrast, rests on nothing other than their personhood, and thus calls into play once more the common humanity of rich and poor, successful and unsuccessful, gifted and ordinary. We do not 'appraise' the humanity of others; we simply recognize it.

The distinction between appraisal respect and recognition respect is reflected in two kinds of funeral rite which, though never wholly separated perhaps, we can usefully differentiate with the labels 'commemorations' and 'commendations'. Commemoration following a death is backward looking. It dwells on the life that is past, and it need anticipate no future existence for the dead, except insofar as they continue to be present in the memories of the living. A funeral commemoration can intelligibly be separated, in time, place, and style, from the disposal of the corpse, as it often is. Funeral rites that are commemorative are celebratory. They recount the accomplishments, experience, and character of the person who has died. The words, actions, and music that are used in a commemoration need not follow any liturgical form, and may further serve the commemoration by reflecting the tastes and preferences of the deceased.

By contrast, *commending* the dead is forward looking. That is to say, a commendatory funeral rite looks to what lies 'beyond' death. This is not necessarily to some new form of life, as in Christianity and Islam, but a new status to which the dead person has been admitted, or is journeying.[12] The mortal remains of the person are 'laid to rest' and God, or Heaven, or the divine, is called upon to receive the departed. The ceremonial form of commendatory funerals is almost always fixed by custom or a prescribed liturgy, and while it may include space for personal reminiscences and tributes, it need not. A funeral of this kind is not a celebration but a rite of passage, comparable to the rite of passage that marks the birth of a new person. Such rites are performed in accordance with prescribed or traditional words, actions, and music. A birth rite,

---

[12] In Greek mythology, Charon is the ferryman who carries the souls of the newly deceased across the rivers Styx and Acheron that separated the world of the living from the world of the dead.

obviously, cannot show the newborn a 'respect of appraisal' because there are no accomplishments to be celebrated, and the experience and character of the newly born is unknown. Similarly, from the perspective of a rite of passage, the accomplishments, experience, and character of the deceased are irrelevant to the proper acknowledgement of the end of a life.

There is a still deeper philosophical difference between commemoration and commendation as responses to death. In *The Meaning of Belief: Religion from an Atheist's Point of View*, Tim Crane draws a distinction between 'meaning *in* life' and the 'meaning *of* life'.

> Some people find meaning in their relationships with loved ones, their children and their families. Others find it in their experience of art, music and beautiful things; others in developing their life plans, or their ethical, moral or political, lives. But this does not touch the question of the meaning *of our lives as a whole*. James Tartaglia has pointed out that when philosophers answer that question by talking about the meaning *in* a person's life, they have in effect changed the subject, often without acknowledging it. Simon Blackburn, for example, briskly reminds those atheists who might find the world meaningless that 'there is plenty of meaning to be found during life. The smile of the baby means the world to the mother; successes mean a lot to those who have struggled to achieve them, and so on.' These things... are attempts to find meaning in life; religion as I understand it, attempts to find the meaning *of* life as a whole... (*The Meaning of Belief*, p.8, emphasis original)[13]

Commemorative rites are celebratory occasions for recounting the meaning found *in* life by the deceased—their relationships with children and families, their experience of art and music, their careers, their moral and political lives. Commendatory rites, on the other hand, are solemn, though not necessarily sombre, ceremonies reflecting an understanding of the meaning *of* a life in its relation to eternity—a dimension (however we conceive it) intimated by, but radically different to, the finite world in which a human life must be lived.

Secularized cultures tend to favour the commemorative rite. This does, however, raise a difficult question. How do we commemorate a life when there was little in it worthy of commemoration? It is no answer to this question to assert, dogmatically, that there *must* be something to

---

[13] The reference in this passage is to James Tartaglia, *Philosophy in a Meaningless Life* (2015) and the quotation is from Simon Blackburn's interview with Rick Lewis in *Philosophy Now* (Nov/Dec 2013).

commemorate. Take Blackburn's examples — a mother's delight in the smile of her baby, the success emerging from struggle. What of those who never gave birth, and those whose struggles never succeeded? The same observation can be made of all examples of how people can find meaning in life. Tartaglia's, and Crane's, point is that no account of meaning *in* life will ever add up to an explanation of the meaning *of* life.

We here return by a different route to an earlier topic. Just as any conception of the hope of the poor must be able to draw on a philosophy of ordinary life, so it must be able to draw on a philosophy of ordinary death. If all we have is commemoration, what are we to say when there is little or nothing to commemorate? The issue is more acute when the deceased is a child, an adolescent, or someone whose physical and mental disabilities make success, accomplishment, and a career impossible. It is notable that bereaved relatives often try to supply the deficiency with an affirmation that the deceased 'has not died in vain'. The baby who dies of a congenital defect or a rare disease, for instance, will stimulate research that prevents such cases in the future, or perhaps lead to highly publicized campaign that raises funds for it. The death of a student in the course of a school shooting will (at last!) initiate a reform of the laws on gun control. Sudden death as the result of an industrial accident will lead to better health and safety regulations. And so on. These are understandable psychological manoeuvres since they mitigate the dread sense that those we love have lived and died to no significant purpose. Yet every prediction of this kind could turn out to be false. To explain the meaningfulness of a life that has ended in terms of future consequences is to make it dependent on pure contingency. Perhaps the publicity campaign falters, insufficient funds are raised, and so no research is undertaken. Perhaps the anti-gun publicity campaign attracts widespread attention, but the gun laws remain unchanged. Perhaps as a result of the accident new industrial health and safety recommendations are indeed put in place, only to be widely ignored. If our hopes are pinned on the *consequences* of a death, and things do not turn out as we wish, then the person in question *has* died in vain.

Commemorative rites require something to commemorate, either with respect to the life itself or its post-mortem causal consequences, so that if there is nothing of this sort to commemorate, the rite is empty. A rite of commendation, contrastingly, rests upon the supposition that every human life, whether or not it is one in which anything of special significance has been accomplished, nevertheless warrants recognition. This is the concept of human dignity, which applies to the dead no less than the living. The claim that life is *sacred* is often made without any regard to its full import, but it correctly signals the idea that a religious attitude is in the end indispensable to the affirmation of our humanity. In his long and celebrated poem *In Memoriam*, written in the wake of a friend's unexpected early death, Tennyson gives memorable expression to this thought.

> Oh yet we trust that somehow good
> Will be the final goal of ill,
> To pangs of nature, sins of will,
> Defects of doubt, and taints of blood;
>
> That nothing walks with aimless feet;
> That not one life shall be destroy'd,
> Or cast as rubbish to the void,
> When God hath made the pile complete.

VI. Practical Wisdom and Religion

Peter Berger's book *The Desecularization of the World*, published in 1999, was something of a recantation. It brought important evidence against the 'secularization thesis' to which Berger, along with the majority of sociologists had hitherto subscribed. The idea of secularization as a steady and inevitable process in which religious belief and practice would continue to decline in proportion to rising economic prosperity, technological innovation, and medical advances was heralded quite widely as the inevitable outcome of Baconianism, though that term was not often used in this connection. In the last third of the twentieth century, however, renewal and rapid growth in almost all the world's religions seemed to present powerful empirical evidence against it. Far from fading away, religion appeared to be on the rise again. According to the Pew Research Center, of the world's 7.16 billion people, 6 billion are adherents of some religion or other, greatly exceeding the 1.1 billion who profess no such attachment.

For present purposes, an important point to notice is that a very large part of the growth in religious adherence has taken place in those regions of the world that have drawn the most attention from development agencies, namely Africa, Asia, and Latin America. It has been estimated, for instance, that in 1900 there were 8.7 million adherents of Christianity in Africa. By 2000 it had risen to 390 million, and is predicted to reach 600 million by 2025. The same body of research finds, in sharp contrast to the secularization thesis, that atheists, agnostics, and people who do not affiliate with any religion, while likely to increase in the highly developed countries of North America, Western Europe, and Australasia, will comprise a declining share of the world's total population. Why should there be this affinity between poverty and religion, and a corresponding affinity between atheism and prosperity?

The Marxist account of religion, touched upon in an earlier chapter, offers us one explanation. Marx held that religion is an opiate, a kind of painkiller. Religion persists among the poor because the hope of another world that it offers, eases the harshness of this one. However hard the struggle of the labouring class in this life, a second world awaits them, one where 'death shall be no more; neither shall there be mourning, nor crying, nor pain', as the *Book of Revelation* puts it.[14] While most development agencies expect their work to result in a gradual improvement in the lot of the poor, Marx expected a much more dramatic change, a crisis that would lead to the revolutionary overthrow of capitalistic industrialization. Capitalism's immense productive potential would suddenly fall into the ownership of the workers, thereby enabling a new, equitable distribution of plenty — 'To each according to his need; from each according to his ability.' As a result, religion would fade away because a painkiller is no longer needed when the cause of the pain has been taken away.

History has not followed the path Marx predicted. Britain and Germany, the most highly industrialized countries in his own day, witnessed no proletarian revolution, while the communist-led revolutions in Russia and China decades after his death took place in pre-industrialized countries. Despite this, Marx's view of religion has continued to exercise considerable sway. From the perspective of the people Schleiermacher called 'cultured despisers of religion',[15] religion is no more than superstition and thus most likely to thrive in places where people are ill-educated, oppressed, or insecure. When people are ignorant of the real causes of things, when their most basic needs go unsatisfied, and when their lives are constantly at risk, the myths and superstitions of religion naturally provide psychological comfort and a sense of security. By the same token, religion then becomes expendable when knowledge grows, deprivation is reduced, and resources are increased. With the assistance of

---

14 *Revelation* 21.4 ASV.
15 One of the most celebrated being Frederick the Great, King of Prussia.

science and technology, human beings gain far greater control of the human condition, and thereby make life easier and much less precarious.

Whatever its surface plausibility, there are important objections to the Marxist account of the relationship between religion and prosperity. To begin with, the United States has long been held a striking counter-example to its central causal claim. Though the wealthiest and most technologically advanced society in human history, the US has long been noted for its religiosity. There are signs of a change in the twenty-first century, but if religious observance in America does decline, it cannot plausibly be attributed to increased prosperity. Conversely, among urbanized industrial workers crammed into slums in nineteenth-century Europe—the proletariat with whom Marx was most concerned—religious practices were not in fact especially common. Victorian England witnessed a revival of religion, but it was principally a middle-class affair, and in many cities left the urban poor largely untouched.

Secondly, while it is true that the language of 'another world' can be used to convey consolatory hope of a better life after this one, many religions subscribe to the existence of hell as well as heaven. Consequently, belief in an afterlife holds out the prospect of punishment no less than reward. There may be consolation for the oppressed in the thought that their oppressors will go to hell, but this does not in itself guarantee that the privation they have experienced in this world will be made up for in the next. In any case, the other world to which religions bid us look is often of a radically different kind to the rather primitive conception of 'pie in the sky when you die' that fits the Marxist model. The Christian Beatific vision, for instance, does not hold out the prospect of finally getting all the good things that life on earth has denied us, but overcoming these deprivations with goodness of a quite different order—the bliss (not satisfaction) of enjoying God for ever. So too, the Buddhist's Nirvana is not a future condition in which the desires of the poor are finally fulfilled. Rather, since desire or 'craving' is the ultimate source of our suffering, Nirvana is the promise of complete freedom from desire.

Thirdly, and most importantly in the present context, the 'opiate' story relies on life conceived as temporal experience. It cannot accommodate the importance of temporal structure. Yet it is temporal structure that is relevant to the life 'cut short', as well as to the life marked by failure or inconsequentiality. Such lives matter, not because of what they contained or accomplished, but for no other reason than that they were human lives. They cannot sustain the respect of appraisal, but they nonetheless demand the respect of recognition. What is being recognized is not the *content*, but the *fact* of existence. There was a *person* who lived and died. Respect of recognition means resisting any way of thinking that carries the implication: it would have made no difference if they had never existed.

What should we make, then, of the role of religion in the lives of the poor? The Marxist 'opiate of the people' explanation may fail, but the phenomenon it is trying to explain still appears to be a reality. Religion, broadly speaking, is more vibrant among the poor, and tends to lose its appeal as people become more prosperous. Whether there is a causal relation, and, if so, just what it is, are complex sociological questions. The philosophical issues we have been exploring, however, may explain why we should not be especially surprised by the data. Following Macmurray, we may say that a distinguishing feature of every human life lies in its being constituted and shaped by deliberative agency. If we think of practical reason as deliberation in the service of purpose, we can then think of *wisdom* as deliberation at the limits of practical reason, delibera-tion about the value and meaning of the purposes we are pursuing. Thanks to deprivation, sickness, disability, and insecurity, poor and vulnerable people arrive at the limits of practical reason in this sense more often and more quickly than those with greater wealth and security. When the order of priorities is more pressing, people are more alive to wisdom, wisdom finds its completion in religion. If so, this goes some way to explaining the intriguing resonance between religion and poverty.

From such a perspective, funerals that confine themselves to honour-ing and commemorating the accomplishments of the dead are deficient. The causal impact that the vast majority of human beings have on the way the future goes—for good or ill—is negligible. Viewed from this stand-point, it would indeed have made no difference whether they had lived or not. The thought is one that is easy to accommodate when we think of plants and others animals, even pets. When a dog dies, a natural question is: 'Will you get another one?' When a child dies, the same question rankles in its inappropriateness. Confronted with the death of an infant, the suggestion that their brief life 'made no difference', insofar as it is true, is irrelevant. One indication of this is the speed with which new-borns are given names, and the bestowing of a name is the recognition of a person.

This example serves to remind us that rites of passage are not confined to the end of life. As well as funeral rites to mark a death, most cultures have rites for when people are born, rites when they 'come of age', and marriage rites that unite people in intimacy. Human beings are ceremonial animals, Wittgenstein remarks, and there are non-religious ceremonies. Graduation from college, retirement from work, inauguration in political office are familiar examples of non-religious ceremonies. Rites of passage, on the other hand, are inherently religious, which is why thoroughly secularized cultures sometimes discard them altogether. The distinctive role of religious rites, I shall say, is 'redeeming the time'. This expression comes from Paul's *Letter to the Ephesians* (5:16) where he tells his readers to 'walk circumspectly, not as fools, but as wise, redeeming the time'. Redeeming the time, as I understand it, means rescuing the passage of time from transience. There is of course a perspective from which this seems impossible since the 'flow' of time cannot be arrested and is unrepeatable, a version of the Heraclitean conception of reality in which everything changes, nothing remains still, and no one ever steps twice into the same stream. The recognition of persons as persons implies the rejection of this conception. It affirms, to the contrary, that in contrast to all other living things, no human being can be replaced by another. Each is unique, and accordingly each 'life' is unique. Since each life must occur in time, and time must pass, each life must end. Yet its ending is not its disappearance, and its ultimate value does not lie in its length or in what it contained. Tennyson's lines capture the thought brilliantly. However fleeting or inconsequential, 'not one life shall be destroy'd, or cast as rubbish to the void', to which he adds the theological supposition this requires, 'when God has made the pile complete'.

This conclusion is pertinent to the hope of the poor. A constant struggle to survive sets limits to hope, but these limits are not necessarily imposed by low income measured in terms of purchasing power parity. Civil strife, political oppression, discrimination, and natural disasters are also seriously limiting conditions. Consequently, economic development that raises purchasing power is no guarantee of brighter hopes. The important point to grasp, however, is that impoverishment and enrichment are to be distinguished from material poverty and material wealth. Low income need not be a barrier to a rewarding life of vocational dwelling, and opulence can in fact obstruct this. In other words, strange as it may sound, those who live in relative economic poverty may not lead impoverished lives, and those who are very wealthy may not lead enriching ones. The key issue is how, and to what extent, the desires, talents, and interests of the individual are fulfilled and sustained within the communal life that generates them. The role of community, however, is misunderstood if it is taken to be merely the necessary condition of individuals attaining the capabilities that abstractly characterize the sort of life 'development' is intended to assist. Rather, community makes possible the form of the personal that underlies vocational dwelling. It extends the form of the personal, importantly, even to those whose hopes are limited by the misfortunes of disability, illness, and accident. The form of the personal can embrace the humblest and the weakest, and thereby recognize their essential dignity, even past the point of death. Though the context and conditions of life may be different, the true hope of the poor, in the end, is simply the same as the hope of every human being—to live a valued and meaningful life.

Bibliography

Books

Adams, R.M. (1999) *Finite and Infinite Goods: A Framework for Ethics*, New York: Oxford University Press.

Anscombe, G.E.M. and von Wright, G.H. (eds.) (1974) *On Certainty: By Ludwig Wittgenstein*, Oxford: Basil Blackwell.

Bacon, F. (1996) *The Major Works: Including New Atlantis and the Essays*, New York: Oxford University Press.

Banerjee, A.V. and Duflo, E. (2011) *Poor Economics: A Radical Rethinking of the Way to Fight Global Poverty*, New York: Public Affairs.

Bottomore, T.B. (ed.) (1963) *Karl Marx: Early Writings*, London: C.A. Watts & Co Ltd.

Butterfield, H. (1950) *The Origins of Modern Science 1300–1800*, London: G. Bell and Sons Ltd.

Collier, P. (2007) *The Bottom Billion: Why the Poorest Countries Are Failing and What Can Be Done About It*, New York: Oxford University Press.

Collini, S. (ed.) (1989) *J.S. Mill: On Liberty and Other Writings*, New York: Cambridge University Press.

Corbett, S. and Fikkert, B. (2009/2012) *When Helping Hurts: How to Alleviate Poverty without Hurting the Poor and Yourself*, Chicago, IL: Moody Publishers.

Crane, T. (2017) *The Meaning of Belief: Religion from an Atheist's Point of View*, Cambridge, MA: Harvard University Press.

Crisp, R. (ed.) (1998) *J.S. Mill Utilitarianism*, New York: Oxford University Press.

Darwin, C.M.A. (1902) *The Origin of Species: By Means of Natural Selection of the Preservation of Favoured Races in the Struggle for Life*, London: Edinburgh Press.

Deaton, A. (2013) *The Great Escape: Health, Wealth, and the Origins of Inequality*, Princeton, NJ: Princeton University Press.

Desmond, M. (2016) *Evicted: Poverty and Profit in the American City,* New York: Crown.

Douglass, F. (2014) *Narrative of the Life of Frederick Douglass, and American Slave,* New York: Penguin Books.

Easterly, W. (2006) *The White Man's Burden: Why The West's Efforts to Aid the Rest Have Done So Much Ill and So Little Good,* New York: Penguin Books.

Edin, K.J. and Shaefer, H.L. (2015) *$2.00 a Day: Living On Almost Nothing in America,* New York: Houghton Mifflin Harcourt.

Fabian, A. (2000) *The Unvarnished Truth: Personal Narratives in Nineteenth-Century America,* Berkeley and Los Angeles, CA: University of California Press.

Ferguson, J. (1994) *The Anti-Politics Machine: 'Development,' Depoliticization, and Bureaucratic Power in Lesotho,* Minneapolis, MN: University of Minnesota Press.

Fraser, A.C. (1894–96) *Philosophy of Theism: The Gifford Lectures,* Edinburgh: William Blackwood and Sons.

Frazer, J.G. (1978) *The Golden Bough: A Study in Magic and Religion,* London: Richard Clay (The Chaucer Press) Ltd.

Gadamer, H.-G. (1986) *The Relevance of the Beautiful and Other Essays,* ed. Robert Bernasconi, transl. Nicholas Walker, Cambridge: Press Syndicate of the University of Cambridge.

Geertz, C. (2000) *Available Light: Anthropological Reflections on Philosophical Topics,* Princeton, NJ: Princeton University Press.

Graham, C. (2017) *Happiness for All? Unequal Hopes and Lives in Pursuit of the American Dream,* Princeton, NJ: Princeton University Press.

Graham, G. (2001) *Evil and Christian Ethics,* Cambridge: Cambridge University Press.

Graham, G. (2011) *Theories of Ethics: An Introduction to Moral Philosophy with a Selection of Classical Readings,* New York: Routledge.

Graham, G. (2014) *Wittgenstein & Natural Religion,* Oxford: Oxford University Press.

Haakonssen, K. (ed.) (2007) *Thomas Reid on Practical Ethics,* Edinburgh: Edinburgh University Press Ltd.

Harris, J.A. (2015) *Hume: An Intellectual Biography,* New York: Cambridge University Press.

Hegel, G.W.F. (1977) *Phenomenology of Spirit,* transl. A.V. Miller, New York: Oxford University Press.

Hume, D. (1739–40/1978) *A Treatise of Human Nature,* ed. L.A. Selby-Bigge, Oxford: Clarendon Press.

Hume, D. (1993) *Dialogues Concerning Natural History and The Natural History of Religion*, ed. with introduction and notes by J.C.A. Gaskin, Oxford: Oxford University Press.

Hume, D. (1999) *An Enquiry concerning Human Understanding*, ed. Tom L. Beauchamp, Oxford: Oxford University Press.

Hume, D. (2007) *A Treatise of Human Nature*, eds. David Fate Norton and Mary J. Norton, New York: Oxford University Press.

Hume, D. (2007) *A Dissertation on the Passions The Natural History of Religion*, ed. Tom L. Beauchamp, New York: Oxford University Press.

Hume, D. (2021) *Essays, Moral Political, and Literary*, ed. Tom L. Beauchamp and Mark A. Box, Oxford: Oxford University Press.

Ingold, T. (2000) *The Perception of The Environment: Essays in Livelihood, Dwelling and Skill*, New York: Routledge.

Kant, I. (1956) *Critique of Practical Reason*, transl. Lewis White Beck, New York: The Library of Liberal Arts, The Bobbs-Merrill Company, Inc.

Kant, I. (1991) *Political Writings*, transl. H.B. Nisbet, Cambridge: Cambridge University Press.

Kekes, J. (2005) *The Roots of Evil*, New York: Cornell University Press.

Luce, E. (2006) *In Spite of The Gods: The Strange Rise of Modern India*, London: Little, Brown Book Group.

Lupton, R.D. (2011) *Toxic Charity: How Churches and Charities Hurt Those They Help (And How to Reverse It)*, New York: HarperCollins Publishers.

Macintyre, A. (1981) *After Virtue: A Study in Moral Theory*, London: Gerald Duckworth & Co. Ltd.

MacMurray, J. (1957) *The Self As Agent: The Gifford Lectures for 1953*, London: Faber and Faber Limited.

MacMurray, J. (1961) *Persons in Relation*, London: Faber and Faber Limited.

Manson, N.A. (ed.) (2003) *God and Design: The Teleological Argument and Modern Science*, London and New York: Routledge Taylor & Francis Group.

Marx, K. and Engels, F. (1968) 'Manifesto of the Communist Party', in *Selected Works*, London: Lawrence and Wishart.

McGoey, L. (2015) *No Such Thing as a Free Gift: The Gates Foundation and the Price of Philanthropy*, New York: Verso.

McManus, J. (2022) *Inside Qatar*, London: Icon Books Ltd.

Meredith, M. (2005, 2006, 2011) *The State of Africa: A History of the Continent Since Independence*, London: Simon & Schuster.

Mosse, D. (2005) *Cultivating Development*, London: Pluto Press.

Morrison, T. (2012) *Home*, New York: Vintage International.

Morse, F. (1986) *The Story of the Shakers*, Woodstock, VT: The Countryman Press.

Moyo, D. (2009) *Dead Aid: Why Aid Makes Things Worse and How There is Another Way for Africa*, London: Penguin Books.

Muller, J.Z. (2018) *The Tyranny of Metrics*, Princeton, NJ: Princeton University Press.

Nietzche, F. (1990) *The Anti-Christ*, transl. R.J. Hollingdale, London: Penguin Books.

Nietzche, F. (2001) *The Gay Science*, transl. Josefine Nauckhoff, Cambridge: Cambridge University Press.

Nussbaum, M.C. (2000) *Women and Human Development: The Capabilities Approach*, New York: Cambridge University Press.

Nussbaum, M.C. (2011) *Creating Capabilities: The Human Development Approach*, Cambridge, MA, and London: The Belknap Press of Harvard University Press.

Oakeshott, M. (1962) *Rationalism in Politics and Other Essays*, London: Methuen & Co Ltd.

O'Neill, O. (1986) *Faces of Hunger: An Essay on Poverty, Justice and Development*, London: Allen & Unwin.

Plantinga, A. (2011) *Where the Conflict Really Lies: Science, Religion, & Naturalism*, New York: Oxford University Press.

Raventós, D. and Wark, J. (2018) *Against Charity*, Petrolia, CA: CounterPunch.

Rawls, J. (1993) *Political Liberalism*, New York: Columbia University Press.

Raworth, K. (2017) *Doughnut Economics: Seven Ways to Think Like a 21st-Century Economist*, London: Random House Business.

Reid, T. (1969) *Essays on the Active Powers of the Human Mind*, Cambridge, MA: MIT Press.

Risen, J. (2014) *Pay Any Price: Greed, Power, and Endless War*, New York: Houghton Mifflin Harcourt.

Roeser, S. (ed.) (2010) *Reid on Ethics*, London: Palgrave Macmillan.

Sachs, J.D. (2005) *The End of Poverty: Economic Possibilities For Our Time*, New York: Penguin Press.

Sandis, C. and Cain, M.J. (eds.) (2012) *Human Nature: Royal Institute of Philosophy Supplement: 70*, Cambridge: Cambridge University Press.

Schleiermacher, F. (1799/1996) *On Religion – Speeches to its Cultured Despisers*, ed. Richard Crouter, Cambridge: Cambridge University Press.

Scott, J.C. (1998) *Seeing Like a State: How Certain Schemes to Improve the Human Condition Have Failed*, New Haven, CT, and London: Yale University Press.

Sen, A. (1999) *Development as Freedom*, New York: Anchor Books.

Sider, R.J. (1999/2007) *Just Generosity: A New Vision for Overcoming Poverty in America,* Grand Rapids, MI: Baker Books.

Singer, P. (2009/2010) *The Life You Can Save,* New York: Random House Trade Paperback.

Skidelsky, R. and Skidelsky, E. (2012) *How Much is Enough? Money and the Good Life*, New York: Other Press.

Smith, A. (1976) *An Inquiry into the Nature and Causes of the Wealth of Nations,* New York: Oxford University Press.

Stearns, J.K. (2021) *The War That Doesn't Say Its Name: The Unending Conflict in the Congo*, Princeton, NJ: Princeton University Press.

Stocks, J.L. (1969) *Morality and Purpose,* New York: Schocken Books.

Westacott, E. (2016) *The Wisdom of Frugality: Why Less is More — More or Less,* Princeton, NJ: Princeton University Press.

Wilson, E.O. (1978) *On Human Nature,* London: Penguin Books.

Woolhouse, M. (2022) *The Year the World Went Mad*, Muir of Ord: Sandstone Press Ltd.

Index